PSYCHOTIC ORGANISATION OF THE PERSONALITY

PSYCHOANALYTIC IDEAS AND APPLICATIONS SERIES
IPA Publications Committee

Gennaro Saragnano (Rome), Chair and General Editor; Leticia Glocer Fiorini (Buenos Aires), Consultant; Samuel Arbiser (Buenos Aires); Paulo Cesar Sandler (São Paulo); Christian Seulin (Lyon); Mary Kay O'Neil (Montreal); Gail S. Reed (New York); Catalina Bronstein (London); Rhoda Bawdekar (London), Ex-officio as Publications Officer; Paul Crake (London): IPA Executive Director (ex-officio)

Recent titles in the Series include

Theory of Psychoanalytical Practice: A Relational Process Approach
  Juan Tubert-Oklander

Art in Psychoanalysis: A Contemporary Approach to Creativity and Analytic Practice
  edited by Gabriela Goldstein

The Female Body: Inside and Outside
  edited by Ingrid Moeslein-Teising and Frances Thomson-Salo

Death and Identity: Being and the Psycho-Sexual Drama
  Michel de M'Uzan

Unpresented States and the Construction of Meaning: Clinical and Theoretical Contributions
  edited by Howard B. Levine and Gail S. Reed

The Ethical Seduction of the Analytic Situation: The Feminine–Maternal Origins of Responsibility for the Other
  Viviane Chetrit-Vatine

Time for Change: Tracking Transformations in Psychoanalysis— The Three-Level Model
  edited by Marina Altmann de Litvan

Hostile and Malignant Prejudice: Psychoanalytic Approaches
  edited by Cyril Levitt

Freud and Culture
  Eric Smadja

Play, Gender, Therapy: Selected Papers of Eleanor Galenson
  edited by Nellie L. Thompson

Psychopathology of Work: Clinical Observations
  edited by Christophe Dejours

Finding the Body in the Mind: Embodied Memories, Trauma, and Depression
  Marianne Leuzinger-Bohleber

The Future of Psychoanalysis: The Debate about the Training Analyst System
  edited by Peter Zagermann

The Analytical Process: Journeys and Pathways
  Thierry Bokanowski

PSYCHOTIC ORGANISATION OF THE PERSONALITY

Psychoanalytic Keys

Antonio Pérez-Sánchez

LONDON AND NEW YORK

First published 2018
by Routledge
2 Park Square, Milton Park, Abingdon, Oxon OX14 4RN

and by Routledge
711 Third Avenue, New York, NY 10017

Routledge is an imprint of the Taylor & Francis Group, an informa business

© 2018 Antonio Pérez-Sánchez

The right of Antonio Pérez-Sánchez to be identified as the author has been asserted in accordance with sections 77 and 78 of the Copyright, Designs and Patents Act 1988.

All rights reserved. No part of this book may be reprinted or reproduced or utilised in any form or by any electronic, mechanical, or other means, now known or hereafter invented, including photocopying and recording, or in any information storage or retrieval system, without permission in writing from the publishers.

Trademark notice: Product or corporate names may be trademarks or registered trademarks, and are used only for identification and explanation without intent to infringe.

British Library Cataloguing-in-Publication Data
A catalogue record for this book is available from the British Library

Library of Congress Cataloging-in-Publication Data
A catalog record has been requested for this book

ISBN: 9781782205685 (pbk)

Typeset in Palatino
by The Studio Publishing Services Ltd
email: studio@publishingservicesuk.co.uk

CONTENTS

ACKNOWLEDGEMENTS　　　　　　　　　　　　　　　　vii

ABOUT THE AUTHOR　　　　　　　　　　　　　　　　ix

SERIES EDITOR'S FOREWORD　　　　　　　　　　　　xi

PREFACE by Dr Ronald Britton　　　　　　　　　　　xiii

INTRODUCTION　　　　　　　　　　　　　　　　　　xvii

PART I
THEORETICAL (AND CLINICAL) ASPECTS

CHAPTER ONE
Psychic pain, the psychotic part of the personality, 　　3
and pathological organisation

CHAPTER TWO
Communication and the psychotic part of the
personality　　　　　　　　　　　　　　　　　　　　　25

CHAPTER THREE
Psychotic organisation of the personality: 55
psychopathological dynamics and foundations

CHAPTER FOUR
Consequences of the dynamics of the psychotic   87
organisation of the personality

CHAPTER FIVE
Symbolisation in the psychotic organisation of   121
the personality

CHAPTER SIX
Delusional world, mental emptiness, and other   135
clinical manifestations

CHAPTER SEVEN
Technical aspects of psychoanalysis in patients with   159
psychotic organisation of the personality

PART II
CLINICAL (AND THEORY)

CHAPTER EIGHT
The psychoanalytic method in a schizophrenic patient: 183
indication and beginning of analytical process—
psychic pain and transferential vertex

CHAPTER NINE
Emerging from psychotic organisation   217

CHAPTER TEN
General discussion and conclusions   247

REFERENCES   261

INDEX   267

ACKNOWLEDGEMENTS

First of all, I would like to express my gratitude to Ms B for allowing me to share the unusual experience of being in intimate contact with madness within the framework of a psychoanalytic treatment. I learnt a lot about psychotic functioning, not only for her, but also for our non-psychotic patients and even for ourselves. This gratitude is increased if we consider the enormous psychic pain, concomitant to this adventure in this analytic work, that Ms B had to endure. This experience, on which the book is based, would not have been possible without the help and support of many professionals who collaborated with me in a kind of "container therapeutic structure" (Pérez-Sánchez, 1996b), which included my psychoanalysis with Ms B. I refer to the psychiatrists and psychiatric hospital professionals present when she was briefly hospitalized during her breakdowns, as well as those who attended her for the psychopharmacological prescription and control. My appreciation to all of them.

In a special way I must thank Dr Pere Bofill (Barcelona) and Dr Hanna Segal (London), for their help in understanding the clinical material and, above all, in avoiding my too often losing my analytical identity in dealing with such emotional turbulence.

Many other people accompanied me at different times during the preparation of the book. In the Spanish Psychoanalytical Society, I presented several papers on the subject that are now part of the book, and many colleagues contributed with their comments and suggestions. I also want to particularly thank Ester Palerm for having given me the opportunity to verbalise dark aspects of some passages of the manuscript, and participate in an enlightening dialogue. Seminars with students from the Institute of Barcelona have also been a stimulus.

I am also grateful to the IPA Publication Committee for having accepted the proposal of this book for its publication in the Psychoanalytic Ideas and Applications series, and in particular to their chair, Genaro Saragnano. I am also in debt to the translators, Caroline Williamson and Mary García, with whom I worked intensely to transform the Spanish manuscript into English, and to my English teacher, Maggie Evans.

Between the manuscript and the text that the reader has in his hands, there has been considerable improvement, thanks to the careful and excellent team work of Yvonne Doney, Anita Mason, Julie Collings, and Hilary Perry of The Studio Publishing Services. My thanks also to the Karnac team.

I also offer my appreciation to Dr Ronald Britton who, kindly and generously, agreed to write the preface to the book, which is a creative contribution. I must also not forget Dr Claudio Eizirik and Dr David Rosenfeld, who read it and gave it their support.

ABOUT THE AUTHOR

Antonio Pérez-Sánchez is a psychiatrist and psychoanalyst. He is a training analyst and supervisor of the Spanish Psychoanalytical Society (SEP) (a component society of the International Psychoanalytic Association) and he teaches at the Barcelona Psychoanalytic Institute. He was the president of SEP (2008–2011). He has worked in psychiatric hospitals and outpatients departments for many years and now works in private practice as psychoanalyst and psychotherapist. He is interested in the differentiation between psychoanalytic psychotherapy and psychoanalysis itself, and has written about this subject. He has also written on psychological phenomena from a psychoanalytic perspective, including envy, psychic truth, forgiveness, and time. He is the author of five books: *Elementos de Psicoterapia Breve Psicoanalítica* (Elements of Brief Psychoanalytic Psychotherapy) (1992), *Prácticas Psicoterapéuticas. Psicoanálisis Aplicado a la Asistencia Pública* (Psychotherapeutic Practices: Applied Psychoanalysis in Public Mental Health Care) (1996), *Análisis Terminable* (Terminable Analysis: A Study in Ending the Psychoanalytic Process) (1997), *Interview and Indicators in Psychoanalysis and Psychotherapy* (2012, Karnac; also in Spanish, Promolibro, 2006, and Italian, Astrolabio, 2014), and *Psicoterapia breve psicoanalítica* (2014).

He is now chair of the Sponsoring Committee of the International Psychoanalytical Association for the Study Group Nucleo Portuguese Psicoanalitico (Lisbon). He is a member of the European team of the *Interregional Encyclopaedic Dictionary* of the International Psychoanalytical Association.

SERIES EDITOR'S FOREWORD

The Publications Committee of the International Psychoanalytical Association continues, with this volume, the series "Psychoanalytic Ideas and Applications".

The aim of this series is to focus on the scientific production of significant authors whose works are outstanding contributions to the development of the psychoanalytic field and to set out relevant ideas and themes, generated during the history of psychoanalysis, that deserve to be known and discussed by present psychoanalysts.

The relationship between psychoanalytic ideas and their applications has to be put forward from the perspective of theory, clinical practice, technique, and research so as to maintain their validity for contemporary psychoanalysis.

The Publication Committee's objective is to share these ideas with the psychoanalytic community and with professionals in other related disciplines, in order to expand their knowledge and generate a productive interchange between the text and the reader.

Psychotic Organisation of the Personality: Psychoanalytic Keys, authored by Antonio Pérez-Sánchez, is a well-written, didactic and comprehensive study of the psychotic functioning of the human mind, which in just ten clear and well-organised chapters explores both the theoretical and clinical aspects of this fundamental part of current psychoanalytical thinking, starting from Bion's ideas about the co-existence in all human beings of both a psychotic and a non-psychotic part of personality. In this original study Antonio Pérez-Sánchez, a well-known and distinguished Spanish psychoanalyst, pays particular attention to the interactions between the two parts, their linking and splitting dynamics, and the way one type of pathological organisation or another will eventually emerge. The author also gives great importance to the concept of "psychotic pain" and to how the psychotic patient lives through it. The detailed description of the analytic treatment of a schizophrenic patient, in the second part of the book, adds a vivid clinical evidence to the author's conceptualisations.

I am sure this new volume in the IPA Psychoanalytic Ideas and Applications series will encounter the favour of all psychoanalysts and students of the human mental functioning.

Gennaro Saragnano
Series Editor
Chair, IPA Publications Committee

PREFACE

Dr Ronald Britton

This is a courageous book on two counts: Dr Pérez-Sánchez aims to advance theoretical understanding of psychosis and second, he does so based on his own psychoanalyses of schizophrenic patients. As a clinically based book it is timely with his update on Kleinian and post-Kleinian clinical theories of psychoses; we need to produce newer models of these mental disorders and this is a very valuable contribution. It is likely someday to be a meeting ground of psychoanalytic theories of the mind and neuroscientific theories of the brain.

The psychoanalytic theorising on psychosis did not start with Freud but with Abraham and Jung in the early days of analysis. Both of them worked at the time in the famous Swiss mental hospital, the Burgholzi, the medical director of which was Bleuler who first coined the term schizophrenia for what was then called dementia praecox. Having read Freud's *Studies in Hysteria* (1895d), Abraham posited that in dementia praecox the analytic explanation for the condition would not be the same as hysteria but would be based on repudiation and hostility to all object relationships. This has persisted as an idea ever since and resurfaced in a new form in Bion's notion of "Attacks on linking" (1993[1959]). Freud was impressed by this and also by Abraham's later analytic work with manic-depressive psychosis.

Abraham persisted in his notion that innate hostility to objects existed alongside attachment to them and as Melanie Klein's mentor and analyst bequeathed that thinking to her. Alas she also inherited the Viennese school's opposition to this idea of ambivalence: this started early in Abraham's writings, particularly in his paper on Segatini where he emphasised infantile ambivalence and the crucial importance of the infantile relationship to the mother. Neither of these ideas had a favourable hearing in Vienna.

Klein's analysis of children revealed that, as Freud suggested, there was a precursor to adult neurosis in childhood but she showed that there was a precursor to childhood neuroses in infancy. The infantile phantasies she uncovered she realised resembled the delusional ideas of adult psychotic patients, ever since they have been described as psychotic phantasies. These if retained and active it became thought, formed a core of psychotic functioning, in what Klein later called the "deep unconscious". Initially she thought of the earliest of these as harbingers of schizophrenia and the later ones the precursors of depression: the former became known as paranoid–schizoid and the later as depressive. These became the basis for what later she described as "positions": first the paranoid–schizoid and then depressive: as positions they were no longer thought of as simply developmental stages but as organisations within the mind that could exist throughout life. Bion later thought of them as being alternate states of mind in normal life, not only as pathological. He saw them as alternating mental states of un-integration and integration PS$\diamond$D. These alternations I have characterised as part of a series, $PS(n) > D(n) > PS(n + 1) \ldots D(n + 1)$, in order to emphasise incremental change, with n as the number of times it has been reached in life, whenever major new experience or new ideas required a new cycle of un-integration and re-integration.

The innovations in the practice of child analysis, begun by Klein, provided an opportunity to develop a psychoanalytic approach to psychotic patients and this was taken up by the next generation of analysts in particular Rosenfeld, Bion, and Segal, who were now described as Kleinians. It is from their work with adult psychotic and borderline patients that we have the variety of concepts used by Dr Pérez-Sánchez as a background to his study of the analyses of schizophrenia. Rosenfeld's concept of acquisitive projective identification; Segal's distinction between symbolism and symbolic equation;

Bion's introduction of his universal model of the container–contained, and the consequence of its failures and complications, and of his notion of a psychotic organisation in the personality hostile to the limitations of reality.

Once the model of PS<>D had become familiar, further explorations of the part it played in psychological disorders took place producing ideas such as John Steiner's concept of pathological organisations. These defensive systems and compromise formations were seen to provide psychic retreats from the dread of D(n) or the phantasies of the catastrophic consequences of PS(n + 1). In this book Dr Pérez-Sánchez uses the term psychotic pathological organisation and suggests that it rivals the non-psychotic version of reality. In view of our growing awareness of how much our "normal" perceptual world is a construct, it is perhaps best to describe the competition as between the psychotic pathological organisation and the common sense view of reality. Taking common sense as Bion does in its two references: common to our different senses of the external and internal perceptions and also as reality as perceived in common with others.

What is the competition for between these two systems or models? It is, I think, as rival claimants for the belief function that confers the psychic status of fact on perceptions, phantasies, and ideas.

We should thank Dr Pérez-Sánchez for giving us a stimulus to think further on these ideas but also a considerable contribution to doing so.

One great advantage of this book for our overdue reassessment of our models of madness is that the author not only gives us a most impressive review of psychoanalytic findings and theories but also a huge amount of clinical material on which we too can study and think about.

Introduction

"Though this be madness,
Yet there is method in't"

(Shakespeare (*Hamlet*))

One of the reasons I decided to write this book is my conviction that clinical experience is foundational to the knowledge and development of the theory and technique of mental pathology (and health). The other impetus was provided by the difficult experience of a psychoanalytic process shared with a schizophrenic patient, Ms B. Given the considerable effort invested in this treatment, both by the patient and by me, which for my part involved the detailed recording of abundant material in order to go over and rethink, on my own, what was taking place, as well as to ask the opinion of other colleagues, that it would be a worthwhile endeavour to divulge this material in case the experience could be useful to other professionals interested in psychosis. Furthermore, as far as I know, there is no detailed description of psychoanalysis of psychotic schizophrenic patients in current literature. Moreover, this experience has led me to reconsider Bion's ideas on "psychotic personality" and Steiner's on "pathological organisation", and to propose a definition for "psychotic organisation of the personality".

I am not claiming that psychoanalysis is the therapeutic method of choice for psychotic patients, but, whenever possible, in addition to the benefit obtained by the patient, it offers a unique opportunity to draw some lessons on the functioning of the psychic life in these types of patient in particular, but also in general.

Psychological approach to the psychotic patient comes up against the difficulty of the apparent incomprehensibility of their behaviour and thinking. Therefore, one of the first tasks is to demonstrate that, in fact, they are subsidiaries to understanding what a long psychoanalytic tradition has been attempting. There are various ways and means of achieving this. One, through scientifically substantiated pedagogic demonstrations, which offer a comprehensive and accessible view of the dynamics of the pathology of psychosis, comprising an entire array of convergent factors, from patient, family, and professionals to health care systems (see Tizón, 2013). Another route, which is the one I have adopted in this book, is to give a microscopic view of the mental functioning of the psychotic patient through the detailed monitoring of a psychoanalytic treatment. Both are complementary.

In order to convey the complexity of psychosis and the difficulties inherent in its treatment, I consider two factors necessary: one, the most detailed and wide-ranging exposition of psychotic functioning as it unfolds in the direct relationship between patient and analyst, which might be termed as "fieldwork", and two, to clarify the theoretical and technical assumptions that underlie our position from which we observe and act. Our theoretical assumptions allow the reader to know where we are starting from. However, as the theory does not always fully account for *everything* that we have been able to observe in our clinical practice, hence the exposition of the case material in the most complete way possible will enable us to keep sight even of those aspects which could not be adequately accounted for by the theories upheld by me.

I shall set out my concept of mental health/pathology, founded essentially on the Bionian model of the container–contained, and underpinned by the ideas of Melanie Klein and the contemporary Kleinian authors. I shall then provide a summary of the book's contents.

Mental health/pathology and psychic pain

One of the challenges we encounter with psychotic patients, particularly so-called schizophrenics, is how do we help them to verbalise experiences that appear to them as unspeakable, so that they are able to recognise them as their own and tolerate them?

Before entering into the realm of psychosis itself, let us go back. How do we understand mental health/pathology? There are many conceptions of mental health and, consequently, the definition of the inadequacies, disorders, or pathological organisations will also be very varied. For example, without leaving the psychoanalytic sphere, Freud summed it up very well with the idea that a person's healthy functioning includes a good capacity to love and work. At many junctures of his work he also refers, in a more general assertion, to the capacity to tolerate reality. Or, put another way, to bear the pain that contact with reality brings with it. Bion elaborated on this aspect, drawing a distinction that I shall take as the basis for this study. He tells us that one of the essential problems encountered by the psychotic patient is the inability to "suffer" psychic pain, not just to feel it (Bion, 1993[1970]). Bion does not mean that these patients are anaesthetised to such pain, but, rather, in so far as they "feel" it, they are not capable of tolerating it for long enough for the mental work to take place which would enable the modification of reality to make it more tolerable; in other words, to experience the process of transformation. The reality principle, as Freud already noted, has no other purpose but to attain the satisfaction of the pleasure principle, but under conditions that do not involve the risk of damage to the personality. This involves a detour, a wait. So, according to Bion (1989[1963]), psychic pain can be considered a basic element in the constitution of the personality and, consequently, of pathology, according to the various forms of defensive organisation of the personality to avoid "experiencing" such pain.

Furthermore, from the standpoint of a theory of the mind based on object relations, the key to a definition of mental health lies in the capacity for recognition of the needed object. Pathology, from this perspective, would, consequently, derive from any strategy leading to a denial or distortion of the importance of this relationship. In this respect, we would say that psychopathology has a common trunk constituted by narcissism, in the fullest sense of the term. It is no coincidence that, in his study "On narcissism", Freud (1914c) alludes to the severe pathologies, such as the psychoses, where narcissism would be extreme. Consequently, I consider the degree of tolerance to psychic pain and the degree of narcissism to be fundamental to the constitution of mental health of an individual.

The treatment and study of psychotic patients, together with child psychoanalysis, has allowed us today to have expanded our understanding of psychic life at archaic and psychotic levels, along with its psychopathology, besides affording us a broader approach to psychosis.

Health/psychopathology can also be understood in terms of the basic conflict between the desire to come to know the psychic reality—and, consequently, external reality—and the forces opposed to this. This opposition occurs as a result of the immediately painful and distressing nature of such knowledge. Faced with the difficulties of reality, summarised in experiences of frustration, Bion (1991[1962]) calls attention to two types of personality: one dominated by the impulse to *evade* frustration, and one governed by the impulse to *modify* it. As for the first, these are people who tolerate pain and frustration so little that although they feel pain they cannot suffer it (Bion, 1993[1970], p. 11)

In addition, Bion (1991[1962]) states that in every relationship an individual establishes with his surroundings there is a process of coming to knowledge, which at once constitutes an element of the link. He symbolises this component of the link with the letter K (knowledge). Two further elements inherent to any link are feelings of love (symbolised by L) comprising an entire range of feelings along this line (affection, gratitude, solidarity, respect, etc.), and the component of hate (H), with its corresponding shades of emotions (destructive aggressiveness, envy, resentment, etc.) The interrelationship between these three factors, knowledge, love, and hate can be regarded, then, as the components determining the dynamic nature of the object relation.

In addition, Bion took the concept of projective identification from Klein (1987[1946]) and developed it. This primitive mental process, according to Klein's description, consists of an unconscious phantasy through which the subject needs to expel or push out into a given object all those experiences from life that he cannot tolerate because they are too painful, thus constituting a particular kind of identification, the prototype of an aggressive object relation (Klein, 1987[1946], p. 8). Though Klein herself rounds out the idea by saying that there is also a type of projective identification whereby the identification is based upon the projection of the loving parts of the self, which, she adds, is vital to the development of good relations (Klein, 1987[1946], p. 9). The projective identification may be used for different defensive purposes: to control the object, to acquire its attributes, to evacuate the bad, to protect the good, or to avoid separation.

Now, with Bion, the concept of projective identification is elaborated with his statement that if the object can be projected into, this implies that it might be conceived as a containing space able to receive the projected contents. Therefore, in the unconscious mind of the individual who is projecting, the object is not something vague; rather, it has a very specific function, to contain what is projected into it, in other words, the metabolisation of the projected content so that he can take it back in a tolerable form. In this way, a mutually involving relationship between container and contained is established. However, for this relationship to be truly dynamic, it must be influenced by the nature of the link, with its components of love, hate, and knowledge. The container–contained relationship, likewise, occurs between different parts of the personality of the same individual: for example, when we say that a person is containing the psychotic part of his personality, we mean that a neurotic organisation predominates. Ultimately, Bion widens the concept of projective identification by considering it as the basis of a form of primitive communication, to make known to the object what one's own self is unable to metabolise, tolerate, or think—in other words, to contain. In this sense, he distinguishes a "normal" projective identification from a "pathological" one, which would be that described by Klein, although, in this regard, Bion adds an important caveat. When Klein speaks of "excessive" projective identification, this should not be understood solely to apply to the frequency with which it is employed, but to excess of belief in omnipotence (1993[1962], p. 114).

Another of Bion's contributions was to introduce several modifications to Klein's ideas on mental positions, which I shall mention briefly here. By the term "positions", Klein (1987[1946]. 1992[1940]) was describing two types of states or levels of the mind characterised by the specific way in which a constellation of basic anxieties, defences against these and the resulting type of object relation, are grouped together. The "paranoid–schizoid position" is a mental state predominant in the early stages of an individual's development, in which catastrophic and paranoid anxieties prevail, as well as the primitive defences of splitting and projective identification; this is a narcissistic object relation in the sense that there is a denial of dependence in relation to the object, even though it is put to use in the service of the subject: if the object is good, it forms part of the self, if it is bad, it must be rejected or eliminated. In the "depressive position", the predominant anxieties are the "depressive" ones, in so far as there is a grieving for the implications of the recognition of psychic reality. This involves several aspects: the acceptance of the object as someone upon whom one depends, but who might not always be there, as they do not form part of the subject. That loss must, therefore, be worked through: the object is a not-me, a new experience in regard to the paranoid–schizoid position in which the ideal object was, at the same time, me. Besides, in the depressive position there is the recognition that the loved and the hated object are one and the same. This means accepting oneself as the author of one's "actions" (in behaviour or in fantasy) and feelings, both hateful and affectionate towards the object, with the consequent damage inflicted; the result of this is the feelings of concern and guilt for the object. This recognition brings with it the unfolding of an act of reparation which initially involves returning to the object that which belongs to it, and which has been stolen from it, by accepting its autonomy and independence, thus re-establishing a re-valued image of it.

The acceptance of the object's independence also involves the acceptance that it sustains other significant relationships, in particular with the parental partner, with whom, moreover, there can be a creative capacity. There is one further aspect to our understanding of the depressive position, one that is perhaps not adequately considered, but observable in the advanced stage of an analytic process. This is the recognition by the patient that a more realistic or complete version of his "real" objects, internal and external (the parental figures in his history, and the analyst in the analytic situation), not only involves the acceptance that they have been disfigured and damaged by hostile projections, but that these external objects also did damage to the individual; his parents were not always good, at times being the source of traumatic situations, and the analyst is not the idealised figure and has his limitations. It is painful, then, to admit the conclusion that the good object did not always respond adequately or, indeed, that sometimes there was a "denial of normal degrees of projective identification", as Bion puts it (Bion, 1993[1959], p. 109).

To accept the depressive position brings in its wake the experience of loss of the idealised relationships, of the self and of the object, with the feeling of grief and mourning, but it also entails the recognition of the damage inflicted upon the object and upon one's own self, with the inherent feeling of guilt and the resulting task of reparation, as well as the recognition that the object is not ideal and was not always adequate or good. In this way, whenever one accesses the depressive position, psychic work can take place, transforming the internal world into something different to that which existed before, with new objects, partially or totally, new relationships with them, as well as new aspects of the self. In the paranoid–schizoid state, the predominant concern consists of the survival of the ego, while, in the depressive position, although there is also concern for the subject's wellbeing, this is bound up with the respective wellbeing of the object.

To these Kleinian ideas, Bion added that the overcoming of the more primitive position, with the dominance of the paranoid–schizoid, to proceed to the more evolved, predominantly depressive position, does not mean that this progress is achieved once and for all, in such a way that the return to the paranoid–schizoid would only take place in regressive situations. Indeed, the designation chosen by Klein, "position" over "stage", already reflects something of this. This is not a developmental sequence, in which the paranoid–schizoid would come before the depressive, in the sense that Freud talks of psychosexual stages of psychic development, with one succeeding the next. Rather, the idea of positions involves the coexistence of both mental states, and, moreover, from the beginning of life. So, for an adequate understanding of the functioning of mental life, Bion underscores the importance of a constant tension balanced between the paranoid–schizoid position (Ps) and the depressive position (D), expressed by the following graphical symbol: Ps↔D. Put simply, we could say that the organisation of the mind according to the paranoid–schizoid mode (→Ps) reflects the tendency towards the splitting and separation of contradictory components of reality, while the depressive (→D), involves the tendency towards integration.

However, as I have already said elsewhere (Pérez-Sánchez, 1997), Bion's proposal, according to the formula Ps↔D, taken literally would not allow for progress and mental growth; rather, we would find ourselves in a permanent state of flux and reflux between Ps and D, which does not match up with real mental development. Therefore, rather than a balance between the paranoid–schizoid (Ps) and the depressive (D), this can be understood as a constant interaction, whereby there will be mental growth if the state of mind organised in terms of the depressive position predominates; that is to say, if there is a predominance of those mental activities tending towards integration and the recognition of an object relationship that provides the opportunity for creative activity. Yet, predominance does not mean that this tendency towards integration is continuously in effect; rather, that its existence takes precedence, with alternations at moments where the tendency towards the splitting of reality, with the corresponding paranoid–schizoid defences, is present. In the case of the patient in treatment, this implies the predominance of a (positive) valuing of the relationship with the therapist, despite the annoyances or attacks out of frustration or envy that might also occur against him. When this relates to patients with a neurotic personality organisation, the "regression", or, rather, we should say the "retreat"—in consonance with Britton (1998, p. 70 et seq.)—into mental states with a predominance of the paranoid–schizoid (Ps) is temporary. Instead, in patients with more severe pathologies, with a pathological personality organisation, although there is a predominance of the paranoid–schizoid, also present will be aspects of the depressive, elements with a tendency towards integration, which ultimately create a certain tension so as to avoid catastrophic collapse. As such, the graphic expression most befitting the movement between $\rightarrow$ Ps and $\rightarrow$ D would not be backward to forward, and *vice versa*, *ad infinitum*, but, rather, that of a spiral movement, where each repeated advancement and backward movement does not take place at the same level of development.

I agree, then, with Britton (1998) who, by reconsidering Bion's Ps$\leftrightarrow$D proposal, ponders it more suitable for a chemical formula reflecting the oscillations between two unmodifiable substances, and, therefore, taken as a psychological analogy, suggests a reversible perspective rather than a psychic development (Britton, 1998, p. 74). He describes the progressive movement in analysis "from integration to disintegration, followed by reintegration" (1998, p. 73). Or, put another way, the analytic process involves cycles of progress and regressions, that is, from the renunciation of states of coherence and security (characteristic of D) for the incoherence of Ps, which one must tolerate.

Summing up, for Bion, mental life involves the existence of a container–contained (between the subject and the object or between one aspect of the personality with another) which allows the coexistence of that balance or dynamic interaction between the paranoid–schizoid and the depressive, in so far as the link that connects the individual's activities is influenced by the components of love, hate, and knowledge. If these components are not present, the link between container and contained will be a devitalised relationship which leads to the deterioration of relational and mental life. Or, otherwise, it can also happen that, in parallel to this dynamic in which mental activity functions positively, signified by the plus sign (+), that is, towards the individual's progress and growth, there is an analogous functioning, but as a minus sign (−), which is predominant. In this case, love, hate, and knowledge are active but in favour of negativity, of destructiveness. For example, in the positive sign relationship, +(K, L, and H), the patient–therapist pair experience feelings of affection and hate which can be expressed and worked through, making way for knowledge, to insight both of and for the patient. Instead, in the pair with a negative sign relationship, −(K, L, and H), the patient (and the analyst when he colludes with him), by contrast, seemingly shows evidence of a relationship in which he demonstrates affection or anger towards the therapist, but this is experienced from a perspective that tends to impede knowledge, and, consequently, insight does not take place. Even when the therapist believes that the patient has understood his interpretation, this proves to have been an understanding based on different premises, and, as such, knowledge has not been possible. This is what Bion himself (1989[1963]) called the reversion of perspective. He illustrates this with the image of the drawing that can be seen as a vase or two faces, according to the perspective adopted.

Summary and structure of the book

I have drawn upon the idea that in the mental life of each person there is always a part presenting psychotic characteristics, which coexists with another non-psychotic part. From the balance resulting from the interaction between the two parts a personality organisation takes place that is more or less pathological, the severity of which can vary from the psychotic to the neurotic. I attach special importance to the dynamics that are established between the two areas of personality; then, according to the nature of the link/splitting between the psychotic and the non-psychotic part, different forms of pathological organisations will be derived, with their respective particularities, which I describe in Chapter Two. While the term "pathological organisation" offers a good description of the psychic pathology, it should be taken as a common trunk, from which other pathologies originate, whose specificity should be stressed; this has certain conceptual and technical consequences. Bearing this conceptual framework in mind, I shall attempt to explore the specificity of the psychotic organisation of the personality.

The book is structured with the aim of showing as broadly as possible, and sometimes in detail, the analytical process of a unique case of a schizophrenic patient. The question that arises is how to articulate the clinical material with the theory. Obviously, the naked clinical account of theory is not enough, but the description of material limited to "illustrating" the proposed theory does not suffice either, since clinical reality always overflows with theory. In order to offer different facets of the psychotic reality, including perhaps those that have no answer from the theoretical assumptions supported here, I have chosen a system that includes abundant clinical material in four different areas or contexts.

1. Theoretical aspects on psychic pain in psychotic patients (an element to which I give significant importance) in several chapters; the conceptualisation of PsOP (psychopathological foundations, Chapters Three and Four; the limitations of symbolisation, Chapter Five; the delusional world, Chapter Seven).
2. The psychoanalytic technique with such patients; emphasising the difficulties in maintaining the setting and in the transference interpretation (Chapter Seven).
3. Sequential description of different moments of the analytic process, depending on the psychic pain and the predominant transference ("vertex"), where a progressive evolution can be seen (Chapter Eight). Obviously, this linear description is an artifice, since we know of the oscillating trajectory, with advances and setbacks, of any analytic process, and especially with psychotic patients

4. Diverse material from advanced moments of the analysis in which the "emergence" of the psychotic organisation is illustrated, by means of the selection of several themes (Chapter Nine).

This organisation offers a view of the patient and her relationship with the analyst from different angles. Sometimes, it is necessary to repeat material, but in different contexts of the analytic process and theoretical issues, which offers a new understanding for both the patient and the theoretical aspects developed.

The book is divided into two parts. The first, "Theoretical (and clinical) aspects", the parentheses indicating that, while I give relevance to theory, I also draw heavily upon clinical evidence. The second part, for the opposite reason, I have called "Clinical (and theoretical) aspects", because importance is given to the exposition of the treatment of Ms B with the theoretical elements I support.

Presentation of clinical material and confidentiality

Given that the book is largely underpinned by clinical material, I think it would be appropriate to make certain clarifications in this regard, in terms of the method of selection, as well as confidentiality.

We know how difficult it is to convey the clinical experience, arguably more so when we are dealing with psychotic patients. The translation of clinical work to text comes up against the limitation of confining a living, or multi-dimensional, "experience" within the boundaries of the word. Men and women of letters have made this very task their craft. And according to Ward (Ward, 1997, p. 6) clinical reports possess certain qualities of the literary genre. However, we analysts do not all possess the literary talent that we would wish. In our case, moreover, we cannot give free rein to our imaginations; rather, we must stick to the description of the facts, despite these being, to some extent, subjectively determined (Spence, 1997). Nevertheless, many analysts are increasingly convinced of the need to narrate our clinical work if we wish to lay the foundations for the development of psychoanalysis. Apart from the fact that every psychoanalyst who writes often has literary whims, even if he is an amateur, the limited literary capacity can be supplemented, to some extent, by the fact that it is an experience in which he actively participates, of which he is a witness, one that he is part of, and, consequently, an experience he has grounds to talk and write about; needless to say, with all the prevailing risks of excessive subjectivity.

Then, there is the question of which material to choose. When it comes to publications for journals, space constraints determine the quantity of material, since this must also be accompanied by the respective theoretical considerations. So, the possibilities for these formats tend to be various clinical vignettes, or a summary of several junctures of the patient's treatment, or the detailed description of one, or at most, two sessions. As we are dealing here with a book, I am able to select enough material to illustrate the dynamics of PsOP and the analytic relation, or that is my hope.

As Tuckett has pointed out (1993), the selection of material is also determined by the analyst's personal interests, both conscious, by emphasising certain aspects of the case which support the theory he is seeking to demonstrate, as well as unconscious, by avoiding those aspects that might undermine or call it into question. To this we might add the inevitable conflict, for any analyst who publishes, between fidelity to the psychoanalytic group he belongs to—without excessive deference to it—at the same time as seeking to be original, as pointed out by Britton (1997).

So, if the way in which the material is presented also conditions what one wishes to show, as I see it, we may observe psychoanalytic work from two perspectives. One would be that of a transverse section, and the other a longitudinal section. Or, put another way, from the first perspective we reflect upon the here and now of the session and from the second the analytic process. We can easily illustrate the first just by describing a session in detail. With regard to the analytic process, we must inevitably recount the history of what has taken place in the relationship between patient and analyst, and in order to do so we might have to summarise and condense long periods of the analytic experience, though for this account to reflect the process as reliably as possible, it will need to be underpinned by the detailed description of several sessions in a row, for example, a whole week's worth, at various stages of treatment. I have used both procedures.

In terms of confidentiality, I have adopted several measures. The first is something that has evolved from my way of working. Since I tend to focus on what is happening in the transference, or, more specifically, in the here and now of the analytic relation, the questions relating to the patient's history and external reality are, to a large extent, played down. My observation is essentially directed at the patient's internal world and her manifestations in the relationship with the analyst. Then, I have ensured that sufficient time has passed since the end of the experience and the time of publication of this material. In addition, of course, wherever reference is made to the patient's external or historical realities, I have modified these so that under no circumstances could her confidentiality be compromised.

PART I

THEORETICAL (AND CLINICAL) ASPECTS

CHAPTER ONE

Psychic pain, the psychotic part of the personality, and pathological organisation

> "Grief bunches up between my ribs,
> each breath I take is painful"
>
> (Miguel Hernández, quoted by Ms B (translated by Ted Genoways))

Theoretical considerations on psychic pain and psychotic pain

My analytic experience with a schizophrenic patient, which, as I mentioned earlier, will constitute the central clinical reference material in this book, made me see both the significance of psychic pain in mental life and the level of intensity that it can reach in these patients, making it easier to understand the enormity of the defences raised against it. Hence, my wider interest in the study of psychic pain, notably psychotic pain, as well as the resulting defensive organisation that acts as a pseudo-container for it.

The pain described by the patient is of intolerable dimensions, and tends to be expressed in terms of somatic pain. This does not refer to a metaphor, such as neurotic patients, at times, describe mental pain. The impression one has is that the patient is experiencing a painful sensation as if he had received a tremendous impact, a body blow, with the additional problem that it cannot be localised to any particular organ or body part. Thus, my patient speaks of a profound pain suffusing her entire body, which may be likened to the words of the poet, whom she quoted on one occasion, "each breath I take is painful", or when she says: "It hurts me deeply", or "It is so painful I can't take it any more." It is almost as though she were referring to the pain of a wound or lesion that occupies her entire being, which never fully subsides and which almost nothing can alleviate. Incidentally, the very fact that the patient quotes the poet indicates that her mental state, at that moment, was such that it allowed her to give (poetic) form to the pain, and, as such, it would have ceased to be the unspeakable pain that Bion describes. I would then anticipate that the fact that the patient is able to speak about the pain is an indication to me that she has a minimal capacity for psychoanalytic work.

From the perspective of psychic pain, and borrowing the two parameters used by Bion (1991[1962]), psychopathology can be seen as a way of organising the individual's personality in order to modify or evade the reality that generates that pain. To some extent, the tendency towards both the modification and the evasion of reality are present in every person, as it is not always possible for us to modify it, or we would be omnipotent, and neither can we avoid it absolutely, since this would signify death. That being the case, the degree of psychopathology in one's personality organisation will be all the greater the more one channels psychic activity in favour of the second term, in other words, the avoidance of reality. In more severe cases, the psychopathology entails deploying a wide range of strategies and defences that, while they achieve the avoidance of pain resulting from contact with reality, they generate another type of pain that, in turn, requires new strategies and defences, in a never-ending spiral, in order to not only *suffer* increasingly less pain, but also to *feel* less of any emotion. This leads to a certain depletion, distortion, or fragmentation of psychic life (both affective and cognitive). Within the affective sphere, the devitalisation can be so pronounced that it leads the patient to what Resnik has termed a "time of glaciation" (Resnik, 2005). This is the mental impairment we find in long-term psychotic and schizophrenic patients.

Before examining the nature of this type of pain, certain clarifications should be made regarding the expression "psychic pain". I think that it can be understood by considering two levels of categorisation. On one level, pain is a generic concept comprising any sensation that is unpleasurable to mental life. Freud was the first to use it in this wide sense (1911b), by using the term "unpleasure" in relation to contact with reality. Bion also tends to prefer using the term in this broad sense. (His English translation for "pain" appears to have been taken from Freud's "unpleasure".) In his case this includes any sensation of discomfort or malaise for the mind: mourning, grief, anxiety, guilt, and so on.

There is a second, more limited, level, essentially referring to situations of object-loss. Freud also uses the term in this sense, bound up with mourning, to the emotional impact (which would equate to physical pain) originated by the loss of the object (Freud, 1925d). Indeed, Bion also refers to pain in similar terms when he says that the absence of the object results in the presence of the no-object, which is accompanied by discomfort, and as such an experience of having bad objects, which incidentally, is necessary for the structuring of primitive thought. In this book, I will use the expression "pain" in the wide sense, because it is the use that I have encountered in clinical practice. When the patient speaks about pain this refers to a whole range of unpleasurable emotional phenomena that go beyond the loss of the (loved and needed) object, which might be considered as the prototype of painful psychic experience.

Another matter that requires clarification is the *quality* and the *quantity* (intensity) of the pain. As for the first, this is not always discernible. Ultimately, we could say, in a very general way, that pain arises as a manifestation of life forces in conflict with death forces (annihilation anxieties) that threaten to exert absolute dominance. However, this threat might be temporary, as is the case with the pain associated with growth, that is to say, with any mourning process. Equally, it might be instated as something perpetual, when it is the outcome of a certain type of object relation based on a pathological state of mind (a paranoid–schizoid state, for example, as we shall see later). The only aspect distinguishing "healthy" pain from "pathological" pain is arguably the sense of its duration, but in order to find out if it is temporary or not, we first of all need to tolerate it. The individual with very little capacity for tolerating pain will act quickly to get rid of it. By acting in this way, he will cut short the experience evolving with that pain, impeding the consequent strengthening of the personality.

In terms of the intensity of the pain, we might consider what quantity of psychic pain a person is able to tolerate. Let us say, for example, that the spectrum of tolerability for every person runs from just above zero (absolute zero would be incompatible with life) to n. The pain that any given person will be able to tolerate will depend upon the specific threshold he has reached (through his constitutional resources and the development of his personality in interaction with his environment). However, if this person is subjected to an intensity greater than n, in other words, which exceeds the threshold of what is humanly acceptable to him specifically, despite him being otherwise sane and well-balanced, this will bring about an inevitable distortion, reversion, or disavowal of reality. The psychotic patient will act likewise, albeit faced with levels of pain well below those acceptable to others, but always above his own personal threshold.

According to Freud, contact with reality entails pain because it denies access to pleasure. To which Bion adds that, in so far as this pain is felt as a threat to mental integration, the individual will try to evade it, thus jeopardising the necessary establishment of a good relation to reality and, along with it, the constitution of the personality. Thus, Bion continues, "pain cannot be absent from the personality" and, "I shall therefore consider pain as one of the elements of psychoanalysis" (Bion, 1989[1963], p. 61).

Klein also explored the idea of pain in relation to mourning, but gave it a broader definition, as she considers that all pain coming from any unhappy experience has something in common with mourning: it reactivates the depressive infantile position.

All pain, says Segal (1997[1993]), comes from the life aspects. The conflict between life and death can be stated in psychological terms. Faced with the experience of need, the drive might seek the object that satisfies it or, conversely, the impulse to negate the need itself, as well as the perception of the object, might predominate. Both tendencies can be merged. Freud points to the fact that although the death drive works in silence, in patients with severe disorders, such as psychotics (but not only in these patients), we might detect the working of the death drive in battle with the life drive (Segal, 1997[1993], p. 17). Later on, Segal tells us:

> The question arises: if the death instinct aims at not perceiving, not feeling, refusing the joys and the pain of living, why is the operation

of the death instinct associated with so much pain? I think the pain is experienced by the libidinal ego originally threatened by the death instinct. *The primary source of pain is the stirring of the death instinct within, a dread of annihilation.* (Segal, 1997[1993], p. 22, my italics)

Joseph talks of a specific psychic pain in patients with significant psychotic anxieties and a heavy use of projective identification. The pain arises, she says, in the periods of transition when the patient is emerging from a state of *quasi*-delusional withdrawal in which he experienced a fusion with the analyst through the use of projective identification. In her description, Joseph also notes the almost physical nature of this pain, although it is not psychosomatic, she specifies. The author also refers to the pain that brought the patient to analysis, but she only explores that which arises in the analytic process. This is a pain that is at a halfway point, it is borderline—she concludes—between the pain of fragmentation anxieties and the pain of integration or depressive pain (Joseph, 1989[1976]). We will have the opportunity to determine the legitimacy of these descriptions by Joseph in my patient's case material (for example, in Theme 3 of Chapter Ten).

Steiner remarks that the psychotic patient experiences intense anxieties of a catastrophic nature, requiring drastic and omnipotent defensive measures and that the loss of the pathological organisation entails the return of the uncontrolled panic with experiences of fragmentation and disintegration of the self and its world (Steiner, 1993, p. 64). Bott Spillius also talks about the existence of an intense component of the death instinct in these pathological organisations (1988, p. 6).

We can describe three types of psychic pain. One, related to the loss of the object (I will include pain owing to frustration here), another, owing to the integration of the mind (this would be the pain of the depressive position), and a third, relating to the predominance of catastrophic anxieties and the threat of annihilation (pain specific to the pathological organisations), to which, in particular, I shall turn now, without, however, disregarding the other forms of pain.

I shall return to Bion to refer to various stages of his work where he discusses pain and the organisation of the mind produced to manage it. According to his theory of schizophrenia, the patient experiences a conflict that is never finally resolved between life and death drives, with a preponderance of destructive impulses. Hence, the unremitting dread of imminent annihilation. Consequently, the patient is forced to attack the ego apparatus, in its function of internal and external reality perception, which he isolates and divides into multiple fragments to then expel them (by projective identification) into the object. These are some of the characteristics of the psychotic part of the personality, which, if predominant, cause an increasing divergence with the non-psychotic part, until a gulf is created between the two that proves to be insuperable. From that moment on, maintaining the splitting that deepens that divide between the two parts is an important condition of the perpetuation of the schizophrenic equilibrium or the psychotic organisation. At the same time, the minute and violent fragmentations of the self, and the corresponding projection of them, continues unabated (Bion, 1993[1957], p. 51).

I think that any approach between these two parts of the patient (the psychotic and non-psychotic parts) constitutes another of the most fundamental causes of mental pain experienced by the psychotic. The non-psychotic part of the personality is the fundamental marker of the predominance of the life drive. The psychotic part, as we have seen, is a marker for the destructive drives. Consequently, when there is insufficient consistency in the life aspects, the conjunction of the two can lead to total catastrophe, with a form of mental annihilation that would be completely dominated by the destructive impulses. Segal describes a patient who expresses very well the nature of the interconnection between madness and health, which became truly unbearable to her (Segal, 1981), which I have also seen for myself in my patient.

The most critical stages of my patient's analysis have taken place precisely when there has been a true recognition of the psychotic part. In other words, when she identifies it as an active part of her mind, although not a dominant one, and not just as something that is past. In these moments, in which the splitting decreases, the resulting experience becomes unbearable to the patient, and the way she defends herself against it is by attempting to translate the split to the analyst's function. Thus, she may value him, and even retain his help and affection for him, and so on, but all of this is detached from his therapeutic function. Although envy can also be operating in that defence, it is important to highlight the splitting fantasy of the analyst, in which he seeks to avoid the therapeutic relation with her, as a "person able to see herself as psychotically ill", as unbearable as this might prove to be for her.

I would like to emphasise the presence of the death tendencies as the basic problem, owing to the profound difficulties in containing them. In several passages of his work, Bion turns to the example of the baby or the psychotic patient who experiences the fear of dying and his need of an object to contain such anxieties. We find in "A theory of thinking":

> Normal development follows if the relationship between infant and breast permits the infant to project a *feeling, say, that it is dying*, into the mother and to reintroject it after its sojourn in the breast has made it tolerable to the infant psyche. If the projection is not accepted by the mother the infant feels that its feeling that it is dying is stripped of such meaning as it has. It therefore *reintrojects, not a fear of dying* made tolerable, *but a nameless dread*. (1993[1962], p. 116, my italics)

That means that the bases of the individual's first relationships is the need for an object to deal with the imminent "feeling of dying", which the baby's fragile mental structure cannot yet contain, and constitutes a fundamental element of the individual's early relations. Furthermore, by elaborating his "container–contained" model in *Elements of Psychoanalysis* (1989[1963]), Bion moves forward in the representation of this process with his simple but masterful description:

> The infant, suffering pangs of hunger and *fear that it is dying*, wracked by guilt and anxiety, and impelled by greed, messes itself and cries. The mother picks it up, feeds it and comforts it, and eventually the infant sleeps. (1989[1963], p. 31, my italics)

Here, the account he offers us presents bodily sensations (hunger) together with feelings (fear of dying, guilt, greed, and anxiety, bodily and emotional) which form a complex mesh that is impossible for the baby to differentiate and which must be taken in by the mother. In addition, I must reproduce the full text of the following paragraph in its entirety, where he gives us a more complete version of the process, clearly illustrating the transformation of the bad experience and bad feelings of the baby into another, more tolerable one, through the intermediary of the object. So we see

> The infant, filled with painful lumps of faeces, guilt, fears of impending death, chunks of greed, meanness and urine, evacuates these

bad objects into the breast that is not there. As it does so the good object turns the no-breast (mouth) into a breast, the faeces and urine into milk, the fears of *impending death* and anxiety into vitality and confidence, the greed and meanness into feelings of love and generosity and the infant sucks its bad property, now translated into goodness, back again. (1989[1963], p. 30, my italics)

Noteworthy is the clear description Bion gives of the primitive level of the mind, where soma and psyche are so closely intermingled. Thus, he groups physical elements (faeces, urine) together with emotional elements (feelings of guilt or fear of dying), indicating that the former are translated, by the adequate return of the object, into other elements that are also material (milk) but have the opposite physical effects (satisfying hunger), so that they bring about the transformation of those feelings of greed and meanness into other, benevolent ones: love and generosity. Once more, the fears of impending death, thanks to object intervention, can be turned into vitality and confidence.

In "Attention and interpretation" (Bion, 1993[1970]), Bion returns to the idea of the patient who is unable to suffer pain, either because there is a pathological projective identification, or because the normal projective identification has not been received by the object, and he describes with uncanny accuracy the intensely painful emotions that he needs to project "explosively". However, given the restrictive character of his reality and the dependence on projective identification, there is no adequate conception of containers into which the projection could take place. Consequently, this leads to the following dramatic situation:

The explosive projection is therefore felt to take place in what is, to the analyst, the realization of mental space: *a mental space that has no visual images* to fulfil the functions of a co-ordinate system, either the "faceted solid" or the multi-dimensional, multi-linear figure of lines intersecting at a point. The *mental realization of space is therefore felt as an immensity so great that it cannot be represented even by astronomical space* because it cannot be represented at all. (Bion, 1993[1970], p. 12, my italics)

That is to say, in so far as the patient has not been able to construct visual spaces, or, rather, he lacks the notion of precise limits, he has not developed the idea of a tridimensional container, and, consequently, his own mental space appears as a space of such immensity that it cannot be represented even by astronomical space; it is simply unrepresentable. Neither can he conceive of a tridimensional object able to contain it.

So, Bion continues in the next paragraph,

> Paradoxically this *explosion* is so violent and is accompanied by such *immense fear*—hereafter referred to as psychotic fear or psychotic panic—that the patient may express it by sudden and complete silence (as if to go to an extreme as far from a devastating explosion as possible). (Bion, 1993[1970], p. 12, my italics)

Therefore, the explosive nature of what happens to him is of such intensity that the experience of it is rendered impossible. There is no mental space to store emotions that would account for what is taking place. The only possible response is silence.

The accompanying mental state—Bion continues—would be one of mental shock, similar to surgical shock. In the latter, the advanced physiopathological process is that the blood vessels lose the muscle tone necessary to maintain the fluidity of the bloodstream, resulting in an enlargement of the vascular space in which the liquid is left stagnant and unable to access the interstitial spaces, starving the various organs of the body of oxygen. It is as though the patient were bleeding to death in his own blood vessels. The river-space through which the blood once circulated as been widened to the point where it has become a vast pool that is not strong enough to provide oxygen to the tissues around it.

Bion describes the analogy of surgical shock in reference to the state of mental shock experienced by the psychotic patient in the following way:

> Mental space is so vast compared with any realization of three-dimensional space that the patient's capacity for emotion is felt to be lost because emotion itself is felt to drain away and be lost in the immensity. (Bion, 1993[1970], p. 12)

Mental space, seemingly, has no limits to contain the emotions that circulate within it, or, put another way, it is as if the force of the emotions stagnate, drain away, and lose vitality. In fact, Bion comes to repeat, using other words and another analogy, the immense and unrepresentable nature of the psychotic patient's pain, just so we are in no doubt about it. I wanted to cite both paragraphs, thus to give prominence to that dimension of psychic pain which I observed in my patient. It should come as no surprise, then, that the patient should, time and again, use extreme defences and aberrant types of relation in order to rid himself of that unbearable pain. This, at the same time, might give us some idea of the difficulties involved in this type of situation for the analyst.

My patient manifested a delusion that caused her great anxiety: the aliens, who represented the idealised destructive aspects of her self, were condemned to eternity. The feeling of anxiety, projected on the aliens, resulted from the idea of limitlessness, as in Bion's description regarding astronomical mental space, but, in this case, in relation to time: eternity.

The patient had also alluded to this problem of boundary-lessness in her mental life when speaking to me about the unbearable feeling of being "in the most absolute void". Although the feeling of the void had many meanings in terms of the context of her lived experience, one of the states that engendered the most desperation in her was when she experienced something akin to being in outer space, the feeling of losing her entire self. If we once again take up the analogy of surgical shock, the risk to the patient was that if she ceased to be delusional, she would lose vital "tone", just as the blood vessels lose muscle tone and the patient bleeds to death internally. At an advanced stage of analysis, the analytic relation gave her evidence of solidity, permitting her to begin to surrender her delusions and trust in the consistency of the "tone" provided by this relationship to contain her emotional life. The problem lay in the fact that this transformation did not occur automatically, and this would give rise to states in which she felt the painful experience of being lost in a void. So, in the absence of the delusional structure, let us say owing to a weakening of the psychotic organisation, she ceased to feel "contained", as she was no longer being provided with an alternative immediate and omnipotent container, one that would rid her of any discomfort.

In Winnicott we also find other reflections that offer us an approach to the idea of what must underlie psychotic pain, when he lists the "primitive agonies" (he does not call them anxieties because he does not consider this a sufficiently strong word for what he wishes to show). These are the primitive agonies that he lists: "1. A return to an unintegrated state. 2. Falling for ever. 3. Loss of psychosomatic collusion, failure of indwelling. 4. Loss of sense of real. 5. Loss of capacity to relate to objects" (Winnicott, 1974, p. 104)

He goes on to note that it is erroneous to think of psychotic illness as a breakdown, when it is a "defensive organization" in the face of the "primitive agonies" (1974, p. 104).

Other features of psychotic pain are identified by the name chosen by some authors to highlight a particular aspect of it. According to Meltzer (1978), Bion's expression "catastrophic anxiety" is what lurks behind other minor anxieties. This would correspond with Freud's conceptualisation of "signal anxiety", as an alarm, which might anticipate the risk of something difficult to bear or dangerous to the person, or, in Klein's model of the mind, this would correspond to the pain underlying the paranoid–schizoid and depressive positions; in Bick (1986), the equivalent would be the expressions "dead end", "endless falling", and "liquefaction". Bion (1993[1962]) himself, in his early work, used another expression, "nameless dread", and Meltzer, for his part, formulates the "terror of dead objects".

About the component of death drive in psychotic pain, Rosenfeld describes a deadly force that functions surreptitiously (a secretiveness present in all problems related to the death drive) to collude with the destructive and narcissistic parts of the self. That deadly force, Rosenfeld continues, manifests itself in the analysis of certain patients as a chronic paralysing resistance to the analytic process, and in others, the patient is kept away from living and occasionally experiences severe anxieties about being overwhelmed and killed (Rosenfeld, 1987, p. 107). Consonant with Bion's idea, Rosenfeld talks about the destructive aspect of the self that attacks other parts of it. However, he adds that it is the idealisation of that part of the self, which is organised to obtain control over the patient's mind, which eventually renders the healthy and infantile dependent parts suppressed and even seduced by the tyranny of that destructive part (Rosenfeld, 1971).

Therefore, the libidinal, healthy, and infantile dependent life aspects act in conjunction with the destructive parts. The problem lies in the tolerating–containing of the pain resulting from a true integration of these aspects into the total personality under the guidance of the live aspects. The tolerance of this growing integration is what provides strength to the self to contain the different ranges of pain: that relating to fragmentation and annihilation anxieties, the pain due to the damage inflicted upon the object, and upon aspects of the self (some of these lost for good), together with the pain derived from the loss of the object.

The task of the analyst in relation to the pain that the patient brings to analysis, as Bion well notes, does not consist in alleviating it. The fundamental analytic function lies in helping the patient to increase his capacity to tolerate the psychic pain associated with recognition of reality in such a way, I would add, as to avoid unnecessary pain.

Feeling and suffering psychic pain

During the very early stages of life, during which there is not yet any distinction between psyche and soma, happenings are registered in the body until mental representation is possible (Bion, 1991[1962]). In this sense, I understand unconscious fantasy as rooted in the body (Isaacs, 1948).

For this to happen, one must tolerate the pain resulting from the undertaking of translating that happening to the mind. Herein seems to lie one of the problems of the psychotic patient.

As such, I consider the fact emphasised by Bion, that the psychotic patient "*experiences* pain but not suffering" (Bion, 1993[1970], p. 19) to be crucial, which he argues in this way: "The patient may say he suffers but this is only because he does not know what suffering is and mistakes feeling pain for suffering it . . . The intensity of the patient's pain contributes to his fear of suffering pain" (Bion, 1993[1970], p. 19).

In the next paragraph, he adds,

Suffering pain involves respect for the fact of pain, his own or another's. This respect he does not have and therefore he has no respect for any procedure, such as psychoanalysis, which is concerned with the existence of pain. (Bion, 1993[1970], p. 19)

These statements call for certain qualifications. First, and most notably, Bion uses the term "experiencing" as synonymous to "feeling", when he has theorised upon "experience" as the road to learning. In other words, that experience is not only linked to the sensory, that which is felt in somato-psychic terms; rather, it is something more elaborated. As for the second quotation, that the psychotic patient, unable to respect the fact of pain, cannot have any respect for the psychoanalytic method, this can be understood in reference to the psychotic part of the personality, but not to the psychotic patient as a whole who, as Bion himself maintains, also possesses a non-psychotic part. From this, as we shall see, emerged my hypothesis that the existence of a certain degree of interest in, and tolerance for, "experiencing" or suffering psychic pain might be regarded as a good indicator to consider the prospect of beginning psychoanalysis with a severely affected patient.

This idea of feeling pain without suffering it, characteristic of the psychotic patient, is found in other authors in addition to Bion. For example, from the perspective of ego psychology, Federn (1952) dedicates a paper to ego response to pain. The fact that an individual should develop a neurosis or psychosis is not merely a result of a quantitative difference in relation to the intensity of the pain; rather, we must accept that there is a qualitative factor. This, as Federn states, allows for a seemingly inconsequential, but very significant difference "between 'suffering from a pain' and merely 'feeling a pain'. Suffering is the direct experience, included in the ego boundaries, of the mental pain caused by the painful event or object . . . (Federn, 1952, p. 268).

Whereas the psychotic does not accept the pain (he feels it, but as something that comes from outside), "he feels the afflicting object as something that pains the *ego boundaries* from outside" (my italics). Attempting to find an explanation for this difference, he responds with an organic metaphor: "[in neurotics] the pain is consumed and digested by the ego" (Federn, 1952, p. 279). When the individual lets the pain pass through the ego boundaries, a process of digestion is able to take place and the resulting transformation of that experience, which will prepare him for new painful experiences. Instead, when the patient leaves the pain outside of his ego, the affliction is only felt on the ego boundaries, says Federn, and the pain is left as something outside of himself, without the possibility for modification. He goes still further, drawing a distinction between "feeling" pain and "suffering" it, by "daring" to base it on Freud's second theory of the instincts. So, he postulates two distinct types of mental pain. One based on the pleasure–pain principle and another based on the death instinct. And he says, "Beyond pain and pleasure which correspond to fulfillment or no-fulfillment of libido, there exists pain which corresponds to the fulfillment of the death instinct" (1952, p. 271).

Here, Federn is in consonance with the authors already mentioned above, who emphasise the presence of destructive tendencies as the source of the psychotic patient's pain.

We should also include Winnicott's reflection in relation to the fear of suffering a breakdown:

> I contend that clinical fear of breakdown is the fear of a breakdown that has already been *experienced*. It is a fear of the original agony which caused the defence organization which the patient displays as an illness syndrome. (1974, p. 104, my italics)

Here, the use of the word "experience" is equivocal, because we must assume that he refers to an event that a person has "felt" but not really "experienced".

More recently, Mitrani, taking Bion's idea, makes the distinction between something that has merely *happened* to an individual and something that has been suffered, *and that has subsequently entered the realm of awareness* (Mitrani, 2015).

The "psychotic personality": the psychotic part of the personality

Bion, like any psychoanalyst, considers that the interaction between a patient's environment and personality are necessary to the development of psychosis. What is explained in his two pivotal papers in which he also describes the characteristics of what he calls "the psychotic personality" (Bion, 1993[1957, 1959]), stating how it differs from the non-psychotic personality. A note of caution about the possible confusion between "psychotic personality" and "the personality of the psychotic patient": the first is a conceptual abstraction, in which Bion describes the fundamental traits of a psychotic personality based on the assumption that only the psychotic part exists. However, as he indicates elsewhere and as Freud has already shown, as well as what we are shown by clinical experience, the psychotic patient never withdraws entirely from reality, or, rather, the ego does not completely lose contact with reality. As a result, a non-psychotic part (associated with problems of a neurotic nature) will never be absent from his personality; it exists in parallel with, although obscured by, the psychotic part (Bion, 1993[1957], p. 46)

The characteristics of the psychotic personality, or of the psychotic part of the personality, are summarised by Bion thus:

> [1] preponderance of destructive impulses so great that even the impulse to love is suffused and turned to sadism; [2] a hatred of reality, internal and external, which is extended to all that makes for awareness of it; [3] a dread of imminent annihilation, and finally [4] a premature and precipitate formation of object relations ... transference, whose thinness is in marked contrast with the tenacity with which they are maintained. (Bion, 1993[1957], p. 44)

We could summarise by saying that we are dealing with the preponderance of destructive forces, as a result of the unresolved conflict between the life tendencies and the destructive tendencies. The result is the experience of catastrophic or annihilation anxieties that require extreme forms of defence to expel that inner destructiveness which threatens the individual's integrity.

The combination of these characteristics means that early psychic development takes place in a way that varies from the non-psychotic personality. In the psychotic patient, the mental disturbance is put in motion already in the paranoid–schizoid position, because a predominance of splitting and pathological projective identification, preventing the early forms of thinking from taking place, as the patient does not have the necessary capacity for balanced introjection and projection and a subsequent awareness (Bion, 1993[1957], p. 49). In essence, this pathological projective identification consists of the use of the fantasy of the fragmentary splitting off of his (internal) objects and his self, particularly the psychic apparatus for the perception of reality, and the expulsion of them outside of himself. The reason for acting in such a way is because the patient is attempting to detach himself from any awareness of reality, and the most economic way of doing so is to direct his attacks against the link that connects his sensory impressions to consciousness. The function of the psychic apparatus described by Freud comprises the negotiation of contact with reality by means of the execution of the following tasks: consciousness of sense impressions, attention, memory, judgement, and thought. The fragmentation of the psychic apparatus, then, involves the impairment or disablement of the functions that carry out this task, whereby the course of the subsequent development of the individual in whom a pathological paranoid–schizoid position has been established is very disrupted, lacking the necessary tools to cope with reality and having to resort over and over again to the same pathological "mechanisms", giving rise to "an ever-widening divergence between the psychotic and non-psychotic parts of the personality until at last the gulf between them is felt to be unbridgeable" (Bion, 1993[1957], p. 51).

As a result of excessive projective identification, this disrupts the introjection and assimilation of sense impressions, which are the basis for the establishment of a stable object upon which the beginning of verbal thought depends. The result of this projective identification, then, will be that "words *are* the actual things they name" (Bion, 1993[1957], p. 48, my italics), which Segal (1981[1957]) describes as a form of early symbolisation that she refers to as a "symbolic equation". Therefore, in the "psychotic personality" there is not only difficulty in accomplishing verbal thought, by not attaining the depressive position, but furthermore the alterations to the paranoid–schizoid position already imply a disturbance in preverbal thought, that is to say, in the very matrix of thought (Bion, 1993[1957], pp. 49–50).

In later works, Bion also addressed the matter of the problems the psychotic patient has in containing reality, in so far as this involves unbearable mental pain. One of the problems of the psychotic personality lies in the difficulty it has in creating a containing mental space. It seems that the source of this difficulty is twofold (Bion, 1993[1970]. In one sense, restrictions in the capacity to develop the alpha-function entail the absence of visual or mental images, and consequently the patient lacks the elements necessary to delineate a mental space. In another sense, in so far as there is a predominance of pathological projective identification, the patient has difficulty in recognising the object as a possible container into which he may project aspects of his personality. That is to say, the failure of the alpha-function has not made the construction of a mental space possible, and there is no conception of an external container (object) into which he can project what cannot be tolerated. Or, rather, the explosive projections take place in a mental space without visual images to fulfil the functions of a co-ordinate system. We have already seen the effects of this, in terms of the impossibility of creating a representable mental space, in the analogy of astronomic spaces and of surgical shock.

Therefore, the conception of the psychotic personality, from Bion's viewpoint, suggests a progressive movement towards the widening of the gulf that exists in relation to the non-psychotic personality, in a never-ending spiral. Understood thus, it would seem that we would return to Freud's suggestion, and the psychotic patient would still not be a candidate for psychoanalysis. Not because of their inability to establish a transference, rather the reverse, in fact; by establishing it in such an intense but fragile way that it would be impossible to develop the link necessary for treatment.

In spite of this, the experience of psychoanalysis with psychotic patients undertaken by several analysts—Bion himself among them—has come to show otherwise, as I also intend to argue in this book: at times it is possible to apply the psychoanalytic method to psychotic patients. That being the case, there must be some progression in the theory set forth thus far, as it appears that it cannot adequately account for this feasibility. In my opinion, one of the ideas that offers us a route through this theoretical stumbling block is the concept of "pathological organisation".

Pathological organisation of the personality

The study of narcissism has made possible a deepening in the knowledge of psychosis, and its subsequent development is what has given rise to the concept of pathological organisation. This clinical state was first investigated by Freud in his paper on narcissism (1914c), although he previously examined the question of narcissistic object relations in his study on Leonardo da Vinci (1910c). According to Freud's definition, the libido that should be directed largely towards the object is turned back almost entirely towards the subject's own ego. This is the reason why, argues Freud, the psychotic was inaccessible to the influence of psychoanalysis: by failing to recognise the object, he is incapable of establishing a transference with the analyst.

However, Freud would later qualify these ideas in order to once again open up the psychoanalytic way for psychosis. He says.

> Mental patients are as a rule without the capacity for forming a positive transference ... There are nevertheless a number of methods of approach to be found. *Transference is often not so completely absent* but that it can be used to a certain extent; and analysis has achieved undoubted successes with cyclical depressions, light paranoic modifications, and partial schizophrenias ... in many cases the diagnosis can

oscillate for quite a long time between assuming the presence of a psychoneurosis or of a dementia praecox. (Freud, 1925d, p. 60, my italics)

These affirmations have paved the way for the psychoanalytic view, today widely accepted on the whole, of the coexistence in severe pathologies of less severe aspects ("capable of forming transference") with the more severe narcissistic aspects (with an "absence" of transference).

It is in this latter sense that Freud concludes by saying that the therapeutic attempts made with such patients have given rise to valuable discoveries, such as ". . . the presence of the same aetiological factors and the same emotional complexes as in the neuroses". This is supported by several case studies published by Freud (1911c), as well as contemporary analysts, which he quoted himself: Jung's work accounting for the connection between various stereotypes of insane patients and their particular life histories; Bleuler's work also demonstrating the existence in various psychoses of mechanisms such as those found in the analysis of neurotic patients (the latter quoted by Freud, 1925d); and he later remarks that the understanding of the psychoses has provided the opportunity for analysts to make advances, "Especially since it has been possible to work with the concept of narcissism, they [the analysts] have managed . . . to get a glimpse beyond the wall" (Freud, 1925d, p. 61). After citing Abraham's work on melancholy, Freud concludes, "It is true that in this sphere all our knowledge is not yet converted into therapeutic power; but the mere theoretical gain is not to be despised, and we may be content to wait for its practical application" (Freud, 1925d, p. 61).

But what Freud did not suspect is that our knowledge of psychosis would enable us to broaden our understanding of neurosis.

We can find other contributions on narcissism in Abraham (1927), who explored the notion of the narcissistic character as a resistance to the psychoanalytic method; as did Reich (1933), with the idea of "characterological armour". Other authors have provided similar descriptions, although under different names, such as "highly organised system of defence" (Riviere, 1991), "pathological narcissism" (Meltzer, 1974; Rosenfeld, 1965[1964], 1971), and "defensive organization" (O'Shaughnessy, 1981; Segal, 1997[1972]). We have also mentioned that Winnicott discusses the "defence organization" in reference to psychosis (Winnicott, 1974, pp. 103, 104).

The New Dictionary of Kleinian Thought (*NDKT*) gives the following definition of pathological organisation:

> The term "pathological organisation of the personality" refers to a family of extremely unyielding and tightly knit defences. Their function is to enable patients to avoid overwhelming persecutory and depressive anxieties by avoiding emotional contact with others and with internal and external reality. (Spillius et al., 2011, p. 194)

To this I would add that these defences have become interwoven and entwined, in the sense that they function in articulation and with mutually cumulative effects. This endows it with the character of an organisation that guarantees a degree of psychic equilibrium, albeit a pathological one.

Within the concept of the pathological organisation of the personality, there are two fundamental and complementary lines of study. One is the existence of certain omnipotent "bad" and "mad" aspects of the self which prevail over the sane and dependent aspects, and which dominate the entire personality. For some authors, the existence of addictive and sadomasochistic components also constitutes an important element of this dynamic. The other line of investigation focuses on the ultimate aim of the pathological organisation in achieving a psychic equilibrium—as precarious as this might be—by means of the impairment of the faculties of the self, in order to avoid imminent catastrophe, if reality is *perceived* as wholly as possible. As the authors of the *NDKT* observe, Melanie Klein rejects the erroneous Freudian notion of a primary narcissism belonging to an objectless (an-object) developmental stage preceding any object relations. For Klein, this narcissistic stage does not involve the absence of the object, since from the beginning of life there has been an ego, albeit a rudimentary one, capable of establishing object relations. So, Klein's description of that very early narcissistic and auto-erotic Freudian stage is one of a mental state of the individual, which "includes the love for and relation with the internalised good object which in phantasy forms part of the loved body and self" (Klein, 1987[1952], p. 51).

The psychoanalytic experience with children provided Klein with the opportunity to sketch these early developmental stages of the mind. This dovetailed with the practice of psychoanalysis with psychotic patients by some of her followers, such as Rosenfeld, Bion, and Segal.

It was Rosenfeld who most succinctly described one of the dimensions of the pathological organisation: the existence of the narcissistic and omnipotent aspects of the self. He first outlined a "libidinal narcissism" (Rosenfeld, 1965[1964]), which he then rounded out with "destructive narcissism". Libidinal narcissism, Rosenfeld specifies, is the kind that identifies itself with the qualities of the object, it appropriates them, either through omnipotent incorporation or an intense projective identification. The authors of the *NDKT* (Spillius et al., 2011) warn against confusing libidinal narcissism with libidinal self. The latter refers to the aspect of the self stimulated by the life aspects, which tends towards the establishment and recognition of dependency upon the object, and constitutes the sane aspect of the self, whereas libidinal narcissism is the delusional aspect of the self that takes itself as the object. Libidinal narcissism, therefore, has destructive consequences, since it divests the object of its qualities and appropriates them for itself, while projecting its own bad aspects on it, thereby devaluing the object. As for destructive narcissism, there is an omnipotent idealisation of the destructive self. This is usually played out in dreams and fantasies by way of a "gang" or "band" of "gangsters" in which the various aspects of the self, including the sane and dependent aspects, unite and submit to the destructive self that tyrannically asserts its power. One of the primary objectives of the destructive self consists essentially in negating any dependency upon the object and exalting self-sufficiency, obliterating everything that runs counter to this principle.

An important contribution in the development of the concept of pathological organisation of the personality is that of Steiner, who coined the term, and defined it as a defensive complex against catastrophic anxieties of fragmentation of the self and of the patient's world, by which he attempts to avoid both the paranoid–schizoid (Ps) position and the depressive position (D), in order to retreat into a different form of defensive organisation (position) which constitutes a kind of refuge from the dreaded catastrophe of Ps or the unbearable guilt of D. And he considers that this defensive structure may occur in a wide range of pathologies from psychosis to neurosis, through to the borderline disorders. And even in normal individuals, the pathological organisation comes into play when the anxiety exceeds the limits of what is tolerable to the individual (Steiner, 1993, p. 5).

Therefore, the idea of the pathological organisation is a rich contribution to the problem formulated by Bion of how to overcome the progressive divergence between the psychotic and non-psychotic parts of the personality. From the moment we conceive of the personality as an *organised* entity, this implies the inclusion of psychotic and non-psychotic aspects in interaction. The problem is that while "the psychotic part" predominates, the links established with the non-psychotic part are pathological, and, consequently, the task of the analyst and therapist consists in how to transform these connections into healthy links.

However, it is possible to find in Bion's own work tools that help us to better understand the psychotic pathological organisation. Although Bion speaks of pain as an element of psychoanalysis, I have also taken it as an element of personality, bearing in mind his statement: "pain cannot be absent from the personality" (Bion, 1989[1963], p. 61); and I would say the same about the other elements of psychoanalysis (Ps↔D and ♀↔♂), which I consider to be constitutive of the personality. Regarding pain, Bion goes on like this:

> [Nevertheless] Pain cannot be regarded as a reliable index of pathological processes partly because of its relationship with development (recognised in the commonly used phrase "growing pain") and partly because intensity of suffering is not always proportionate to the severity of disturbance. Its degree and significance depend on its relationship with other [psychoanalytic] elements. . . . It will be necessary to trace its relationship with Ps↔D, and ♀ and ♂. (Bion, 1989[1963], pp. 62–63)

That is to say, the assessment of the significance of psychic pain (PP) must take account of the conjugation of the other two psychoanalytic elements of the personality already defined by Bion: the state of interaction of the positions (Ps↔D) and the container–contained relationship (♀↔♂). It is, in my view, the interplay of these three elements that will determine a degree of mental balance or, conversely, a pathological organisation. This is summarised by the chart shown in Figure 1.1.

Given this configuration of elements of the personality, according to the dynamics that take place, this will result in an organisational pole corresponding to the "psychotic part", or another that would be the "non-psychotic part". Depending on the nature of the interaction of these two poles, one type of pathological organisation will be derived or another; a subject I deal with in the next chapter.

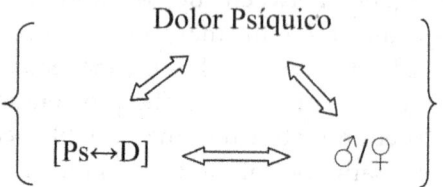

Figure 1.1. Interaction of the three elements of pesonality.

CHAPTER TWO

Communication and the psychotic part of the personality*

Taken literally, this chapter's title is contradictory. Communication with the psychotic part of the personality is, by definition, unfeasible if we understand "psychosis" as mental functioning which "attacks" (Bion, 1993[1959]) and/or severs and disconnects (Britton, 2015) from any link and which tends towards the prevention of integration and articulation of the various parts of reality, in order to evade painful knowledge of it. However, it is not a contradiction if we take the premise maintained thus far into account, of the coexistence, alongside the psychotic part, of a non-psychotic part of the personality that acts as a mediator of the analyst's intervention.

In this chapter, I attempt to expand upon the two questions framed in the previous chapter. One is the existence of that relationship between the two parts. The second question is that of whether the concept of "pathological organisation" can account for the entire psychopathology. With regard to the former, I shall deal with the

---

* This chapter is a substantially modified version, with the addition of new ideas, of the text published in *Temas de psicoanálisis* (Pérez-Sánchez, 2003–2004).

nature of the link/splitting between psychotic and non-psychotic parts of the personality. In the previous chapter, we revisited Bion's theory of "elements of the personality", three of these in particular: psychic pain, Ps↔D and ♀↔♂, leading us to consider that the personality might be organised on the basis of these elements in a psychotic way or, conversely, that it might take on a non-psychotic type of organisation. Since, both parts coexist, the respective progression of each will also coexist, with alternating moments where one or the other is predominant. The psychopathological course of the personality development as a whole will depend upon how one part is articulated with another; ultimately, upon whichever pathology of the link/splitting between the psychotic and non-psychotic parts prevails. On the basis of that pathology, we will get a type of personality organisation of greater or lesser pathology.

So, we come to the second question arising from the previous chapter, and that is, while the concept of "pathological organisation" is a common core for a wide range of pathologies, it would seem fitting to specify the different clinical forms emerging from the pathology of the particular link between psychotic and non-psychotic part. I shall put forward a rough psychopathological categorisation, with the aim of elaborating upon this aspect. This distinction drawn between pathological organisations will serve as a framework to deal more exclusively with psychotic organisation in the next chapters. For now, however, we will need to reveal some of the key characteristics of the psychotic part of the personality in order to understand the problem; some have already been described in the previous chapter, and others I shall come back to in the following chapters.

Finally, I present two vignettes: one showing the difficulties encountered by a schizophrenic patient (and by the analyst) in gaining access to the non-psychotic part, and the other a session with a non-psychotic patient in whom it became necessary to detect the psychotic part so that communication could be achieved. I end the chapter by setting out certain technical consequences.

Some general characteristics of the psychotic dynamics

One possible brief description of the fundamental characteristics of psychotic functioning might be: pathological splitting and pathological projective identification. Essentially, this consists of a disorder in one of the bases for the construction of the personality: the processes of projection–introjection or, rather, a disorder in attaining an adequate balance between the two. Both are affected from very early on in the individual's development, and, consequently, the construction of internal reality and how one manages external reality are considerably affected. One of the principal reasons for this, as I have contended, is intolerance of the mental pain caused by contact with reality; either because the reality is too traumatic and/or one's innate capacity for tolerance to psychic pain is minimal.

It is clear that, owing to the intense activity of projective identification, there is a progressive mental depletion, which can only be "refilled" with spurious elements (delusions, overvalued ideas, magical thinking, and so on). This "refilling" gives rise to a growing detachment between the non-psychotic part in relation to the object, hindering, if not entirely precluding, the introjections necessary to acquire mental "sustenance", whereby the feeling of emptiness and the recourse to new forms of "refilling" increase. If we add to this the feeling of imminent annihilation as one of the fears that threaten the psychotic part, it is clear that the feeling of emptiness—in as far as it is approximable to the former—can be regarded as a significant element of psychotic experience, for which reason the patient must resort once again to the activity of "refilling", thereby shifting further and further away from reality, thus perpetuating a vicious circle.

As a result of splitting and projective identification, the self-boundaries are also affected. In so far as the patient expects his own personality to comprise all those objects or part-objects which have been projected into, that is to say, to the extent that he considers the object or its qualities to be part of himself, reality allows the inconsistency of such a principle to be revealed by laying bare the fragility of the ego, which must now respond by distorting reality with new projections, which instils little faith in the patient's own ego-boundaries, along with the constant threat of being invaded by reality. Needless to say, both the sense of emptiness and the loss of self-boundaries will have a greater or lesser repercussion according to the prevalence of vitality of the non-psychotic part (aggressive tendencies in the service of the life tendencies), which is able to become aware of this, or the preponderance corresponds to the degree of vitality of the psychotic part (aggressive tendencies in the service of destructiveness).

In short, we could say that the central core of the psychotic personality organisation consists in the multiple splitting of the self, as well as of the ego-functions, in particular the capacity for perception. This splitting constitutes an attack that impairs the development of verbal thought, in turn hindering the relation to reality. Via projective identification, it then expels the various fragmented elements into the depended-upon external objects. This dependence could take on a dual character: that of a persecutory type, having to flee from the object, or of extreme fusion, or both at once, which tends to be the most common. The use of excessive projective identification, in turn, increases the difficulty in making contact with reality, and, consequently, both splitting and projective identification must become more pronounced in a pernicious vicious circle process, to the extent that the mind becomes little more than a device for projection. This dynamic creates a widening divergence between the psychotic and non-psychotic parts, in relation to the conception of reality, until there comes a time when the gulf between the two is felt to be insurmountable.

Yet, in so far as there is no "pure" psychotic functioning, in other words Bion's "psychotic personality" is an abstraction, an activity of the non-psychotic part must coexist at the same time. Therefore, the crux of any psychopathology must consist of how both parts are articulated, linked, and, ultimately, integrated within the same personality.

Linking/splitting between the psychotic and non-psychotic parts of the personality, and the Ps↔D interaction

The characteristics of a pathological organisation will be determined by the end product of the combination of the dual consequences of pathological splitting, which, on the one hand, tends to generate an increasingly wide gulf between the psychotic and non-psychotic parts, together with the bare minimum of links between the two, essential to establishing some degree of contact with reality, on the other. Consequently, I think that the potential for therapeutic progress, in both the neuroses and the psychoses, depends upon the gains achieved in establishing and maintaining communication with the patient. In order to do so, one will need to identify the patient's psychotic part and to uncover the type of relationship it has with the non-psychotic part.

In relation to the existence of a non-psychotic part in psychosis, this is an idea we already find in Freud when he says that in all madness there is a fragment of truth, and that "the delusion owes its convincing power to the element of historical truth which it inserts in the place of the rejected reality" (Freud, 1937d, p. 268). This statement appears alongside another, "there is method in madness", taken from the poet, whom I quote on the first page of the Introduction. He also says something that I believe to be significant to the treatment of psychotic patients when, after warning against the futile endeavour of attempting to convince patients of the error of their delusions, "on the contrary, the recognition of its kernel of truth would afford common ground upon which the therapeutic work could develop" (Freud, 1937d, p. 267). Or when he asserts that not even in the most severe cases of psychosis does the patient does not withdraw his ego entirely from reality as, even in acute episodes,

> one learns from patients after their recovery that at the time in some corner of their mind (as they put it) there was a normal person hidden, who, like a detached spectator, watched the hubbub of illness go past him. (Freud, 1940a, p. 202)

On the other hand, Klein's (1992[1935, 1940]) concept of "position"—the paranoid–schizoid and depressive—might provide the basis for the idea that behind any "non-psychotic" organisation there are elements with which, under certain conditions (internal and/or external), one could develop a psychotic organisation. The concept of position, as I have said, indicates states of the mind, or polarities around which the mind is organised to relate to reality, but which coexist without cancelling one another out; on the contrary, they interact, as Bion pointed out.

The borderline area between paranoid–schizoid and depressive positions

As the rhythm of toing and froing between Ps and D might be said to determine all mental functioning, inevitably there will always be "borderline" moments in the personality organisation of any individual. In other words, forms of mental activity that are on the border between Ps and D, or which share both. This borderline state of organisation might be transient or acquire a more permanent state, as a stabilised form of mental functioning. The first would be a "dynamic" state for mental growth. The second would be a pathological form of organisation in Steiner's sense. "Dynamic" signifies that while the immediate problem that mobilised the mind is resolved, this does not stop once this has been accomplished, as new problems will prompt it to dynamise once again to resolve them. So, what are these problems exactly?

According to Bion (1991[1962], p. 6), the sense impressions of emotional experience received by the individual from everything outside his mind need to be transformed into something "digestible", or, rather, into something that is later able to be used for thinking. Bion names such a task the "α-function" which, by acting on the "raw" elements of sense impressions of emotional experience, transforms them into what he names "α-elements". This alpha-function would correspond to what the mother does in her maternal function of reverie when she meets the needs her infant communicates to her, and which he cannot manage alone. The continuous activity of the alpha-function fosters the creation of a membrane constructed of thoughts, to which Bion gives the name "contact barrier" (1991[1962], p. 17); a space or area between the conscious and the unconscious where the interaction between one and the other takes place. The conscious and learnt becomes repressed and available for use whenever necessary (dynamic repression, Segal specifies in Quinodoz, 2008, p. 64). Instead, when the emotional experience of these "raw" elements perceived within external reality by the mind has not been worked through by the alpha-function, they are left as indigestible products, which Bion calls "β-elements" (1991[1962], p. 6). In these, as emotional experience is not transformed, this—as I understand it—leads to a dual outcome: either they are stored as a accretion of stimuli, but, unlike alpha-elements which are available for thought, that is to say, to be remembered, β-elements remain as "undigested facts", and differ from the alpha-elements in that this storage does not serve to connect the unconscious with the conscious, but, quite the reverse, it constitutes a "screen" (of beta-elements) which prevents communication between one and the other. Beta-elements also end up being expelled from the mind through splitting and projection, via various routes: projective identification, hallucinations, or psychosomatic states. Meltzer equates the "impressions of emotional experience" to

Freud's primary process, while he likens the Freudian "secondary process" to dream-thoughts, resulting from the intervention of the alpha-function (Meltzer, 1978, p. 41).

Accordingly, from this viewpoint, we must acknowledge the existence of a borderline area of the mind in which the transformation of stimuli of reality into emotional elements takes place, which are then available for thought; an area which, as Segal says, we are continually working on—not only we analysts in relation to our patients, but every person for their own personal growth and creativity (Segal in Quinodoz, 2008, p. 64). The problem occurs when remaining in that borderline area becomes a stable organisation, and, therefore, pathological.

Pathological evolution of the link between the psychotic and non-psychotic parts of the personality

In emphasising the common element of pathological organisations in a series of pathologies of different gravity, there is a risk that the differences between them may not be sufficiently defined. Lucas (2007) draws a distinction between "psychotic process" and "psychotic disorder" and considers that the borderline pathologies—subsidiary to psychotic process—would find their theoretical foundation in the idea of "pathological organisation", while the pathologies of "psychotic disorders" would find their basis in the Bionian concepts of psychotic and non-psychotic parts of the personality.

For my part, in another publication (Pérez-Sánchez, 1996a), I draw a distinction between greater pathological personality organisation (GPPO) and lesser pathological personality organisation (LPPO). The former, GPPO, would correspond to the classical personality disorders, *sensu strictu*, whose conflict is of an essentially pre-oedipal nature, or is narcissistically structured, along with the more severe pathologies, psychosis and borderline pathologies. The latter, LPPO, would include the principally neurotic organisations of a predominantly oedipal conflict. In that paper, where I study in particular borderline pathology, I also made a proposal for the formulation of its psychodynamic diagnosis, giving prominence to the following elements: a narcissistic object relationship, pathology of identity, the use of primitive pathological defences, and a continually renewed borderline experience, that is to say, a permanent state of being on the borderline. Now I shall turn my attention to the last factor in particular. By the expression "borderline experience", I mean that the patient lives in some ways caught on that border which we have just examined in the previous section.

However, I would now like to raise another possibility for considering that intermediate area, and not only with reference to the borderline patient, but to any organisation of the personality: not in reference to the border between the conscious and unconscious (Bion's "contact barrier"), or that which exists between Ps and D, but between the psychotic part of the personality and the non-psychotic part. That is to say, the borderline area would be situated within the conflict between the mode of organisation of the Ps↔D interaction by the psychotic part, on the one side, and its mode of resolution by the non-psychotic part, on the other. Although, to be more precise, we would have to consider, as I have already noted, the conjugation of three of the elements of the personality as described by Bion: psychic pain (PsP), the interaction of the positions (Ps↔D) and the relationship between container and contained (♀↔♂). Bion often expresses these symbols as follows: ♀, ♂ (container, contained). But his description that they both influence each other is better reflected by including the double arrow, symbolising the interaction between the two. The organisation of the mind, according to these elements, has different outcomes if it is carried out from the psychotic part or from the non-psychotic part of the personality. If as we have been holding, in so far as both parts must always be present in some way in any individual, it is inevitable that a conflict should arise between the two, owing to the differing way of dealing with pain: in other words, the tendency to evade it in the former and to modify it in the latter. It is that conflict between the two, the interaction, we might say, of those two modes of organisation of the mind, which situates us temporarily in a borderline area, one that we must tolerate until we find the means to resolve them and to lead to growth and creative activity. Or, there again conversely, it leads to pathological forms of organisation such as those described by Steiner, in so far as its prevalence rests with the tendency to evade pain, the result being a psychic functioning which does not motivate growth or creativity.

We could imagine approximately the interaction between PPP and PNPP by returning to the three elements of the personality represented in Figure 1.1 in the previous chapter.

In Figure 2.1, note that there is interaction between the psychotic part (PsPP) and the non-psychotic part of the personality (NPsPP) where they mutually influence each other, in the same way that Ps↔D can be said to do, according to Bion, and with the appropriate clarifications mentioned earlier with respect to the double arrow (Britton, 1998; Pérez-Sánchez, 1997). That is to say, that under favourable conditions, the tendency of such interaction leads to a stronger relationship with reality, enabling it to be modified instead of avoiding it, the results of which are creativity and growth. This is represented in Figure 2.1 by a thicker arrow from the non-psychotic part, indicating its greater influence, as well as that which links it with reality.

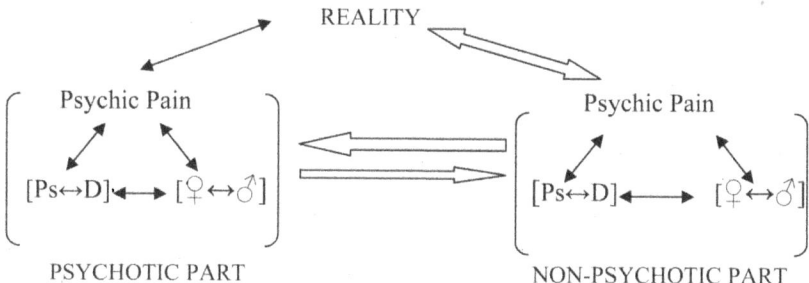

Figure 2.1. Non-psychotic organisation.

Taking the Bionian model, the illustration could be simplified thus: PsPP↔NPsPP.

However, another potential interaction between one part and the other could be reflected as shown in Figure 2.2.

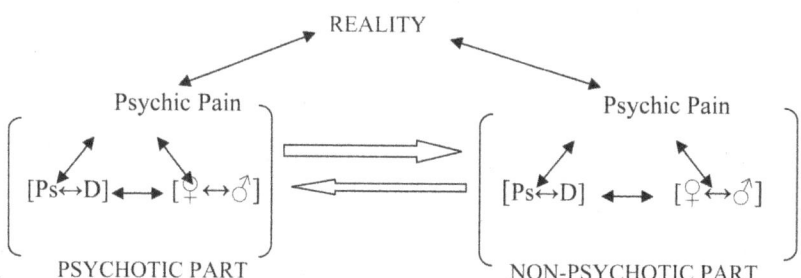

Figure 2.2. Psychotic organisation.

In Figure 2.2, we see that the arrows do not intersect, and there is a greater influence of the psychotic upon the non-psychotic (represented by a thicker arrow), which gives rise to a progressive separation between the parts, creating the growing gulf between them as Bion says (1993[1956], p. 38) if there is no intervention through therapeutic action (Figure 2.3).

One can imagine multiple possibilities for pathological organisations situated between one pathological organisation and the other, depending on the kind of interaction between the psychotic and non-psychotic parts of the personality. We might say that the different pathologies are result of different ways of resolving that borderline conflict. We can see in Figure 2.3, at one end of possible pathological organisations the tendency to distance between PPsP and PNPsP, and, at the other, the approach between the two with a predominance of the influence of the PNPsP.

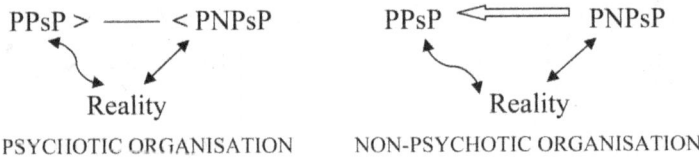

Figure 2.3.   Evolution of PPs↔PPNPsP.

Given this perspective and the clinical symptomatology, four broad areas of pathological organisation can be suggested: psychotic personality organisation (PsPO), borderline personality organisation (BPO), perverse personality organisation (PvPO), and neurotic personality organisation (NPO). (We note that no mention has been made of psychosomatic pathology; however, some authors, such as Green (1990[1986]), consider it to be part of borderline pathology.)

While they all share, to some extent, in the dynamics of the PO, it is worth pointing out which characteristics are more specific to each pathological organisation.

In summary, we could say that any PO faced with ridding itself of the emotional experience that one is unable to contain requires various defensive resources, which, in essence, revolve around the following three: the acting-out of what has failed to be mentalized (the acting-out dimension), the distortion of reality by passing off as good what is destructive (the perverse dimension), and the search for a space or system in which to flee from that reality; this escape might have a protective character (a "refuge"), or, in the case of psychotic patients, be a separate world (delusional dimension).

Psychotic personality organisation (PsPO)

I shall only mention a few characteristics in contrast with other such organisations. In PsPO, the processes of splitting and projective identification are very marked. Splitting has the character of intense destructiveness that brings about a mass mutilation of mental life and the ability to be in contact with reality, which avoids the complete view, that is to say, the integration of experience. A key feature is the part that is able to be in contact with reality is gradually weakened to instate a rift between the psychotic and non-psychotic parts, which progressively widens.

The basic mechanisms for relating with the external world, projection and introjection, will have undergone some type of impairment. Projection has been substituted by pathological projective identification; as for introjection, in so far as there is resistance to integration, it is not possible to accept what is received from outside as elements that can be used for thought and connection with reality, but, rather, as an accretion of "material things" in the mind, some bundled together with others and yet with no interconnection, which Bion refers to as "projective identification in reverse". Another form of pathological introjection is omnipotent projective identification: the individual takes what belongs to the object and makes it his own, as if it formed part of himself; in a true introjection there is a recognition of the origin of what has been acquired and the working through of its integration with the rest of the personality.

In other pathologies, there is a greater possibility of interaction between the psychotic and non-psychotic parts, and, therefore, with reality. Nevertheless, even in the psychotic organisation, while the non-psychotic part persists—however small this might be—there will always be the possibility for interconnection between this part and the psychotic part, as psychoanalysis with such patients shows. With regard to the most notable distinctive feature of PsPO in relation to other pathological organisations, it is the delusional dimension, that is to say, the creation of worlds as an alternative to the unbearable reality, without overlooking the type of splitting, characterised by its radicality and the tendency towards the fragmentation of reality.

Borderline personality organisation (BPO)

As we know, the term for this type of pathology refers to that intermediate position between the neurotic and the psychotic, as it shares the condition of both states. That is to say, it would be the type of pathology that exists most closely to that "borderline" position, as we saw before, but without resolving it. Here, the non-psychotic part of the personality would be more present, while the psychotic part is also active. One of the characteristics that have been described of this pathology is that of diffusion of identity. While there is a capacity for contact with reality as well as for achieving degrees of identity, there is not sufficient consistency of the self to tolerate the continuation of this identity, hence it must be replaced by another, or modified, which will prove to be equally unbearable, because what is unbearable is a continuous contact with the internal reality, needing to look for another new identity.

Considered from the standpoint of the interaction between the three elements of the personality: psychic pain (PsP), Ps↔D and ♀↔♂, the mobility between Ps and D is constant, unable to remain in Ps as the pain in the face of catastrophic experiences cannot be contained, and so it would attempt to move towards D, which also fails to tolerate the pain entailed by integration and the correspondent guilt, therefore arriving at a kind of compromise formation shared as much by Ps as by D, resulting in a new personality organisation: the pathological organisation. The differentiating feature here would be the predominance of the acting-out dimension, in the sense of an acting-out with auto- and hetero-destructive connotations and, alongside it, the characteristic of identity diffusion.

Perverse personality organisation (PvPO).

In this case, the link between the psychotic part of the personality and the non-psychotic part is made more tolerable in that the patient possesses greater ego capacities, which are in the service of the psychotic part, despite this part being very heavily disguised. That is to say, the linkage and integration of psychic reality and external reality are possible at the cost of establishing "links" contingent upon the triumph of the destructive part of the self. According to some authors, perversion might be considered as a defensive organisation against psychotic emergence (Bassols & Beá, 1981). In other words, in this organisation, reality is not attacked directly, as in the psychotic personality organisation (PsPO); rather, it disguises and "perverts" it to make it more tolerable. The prevalent dimension in this pathological organisation would be the perverse quality of the defences utilised: what matters most is to distort reality, passing it off as good, when it is known not to be so.

Neurotic personality organisation (NPO)

The problem here lies in the fact that the psychotic part is not manifest, since sane functioning enables it to be concealed and, thus, pass almost unnoticed, although acting surreptitiously. For example, some neurotic patients present with broad intact areas of the personality, facilitating appropriate contact with reality, albeit at the cost of impoverished social, professional, and even emotional capacity, arguably on account of suffering from very split-off subterranean psychotic processes, although the degree of splitting and projective identification does not acquire the dimensions it has in the psychotic personality organisation, where the consequences for the structure of mental life are much more devastating. When points of impasse in the therapeutic process are reached in the course of psychotherapy or psychoanalysis with these patients, it would be worth considering whether we have come up against the hurdle of psychotic levels which had not been adequately laid bare until now. The distinctive feature here would be that of a greater tolerance of contact with painful reality and, consequently, the temporary nature of the use of some of the other dimensions mentioned in the other pathological organisations, when, in certain situations, these are used as extreme defensive resources.

I shall present two clinical vignettes in order to illustrate the relationship between the psychotic and non-psychotic parts of the personality. First, in a patient with a greater (psychotic) pathological organisation, and then in another patient with a lesser (non-psychotic) pathological organisation. In other papers, I have shown the presence of the relationship between both parts in reference to the borderline (BLPO) (Pérez-Sánchez, 1996a) and the perverse (PvPO) (Pérez-Sánchez, 1991).

The psychotic schizophrenic patient: gaining access to the non-psychotic part of the personality

I shall now describe a clinical vignette regarding the schizophrenic patient, with long-term psychosis when she began psychoanalytic treatment, and that is the main clinical material of the book. I will attempt to make manifest the psychotic functioning and the routes of access to the non-psychotic part. For several years the patient suffered from repeated delusional psychotic episodes requiring successive hospitalisations as well as continued treatment with antipsychotic medication. However, some significant ego-capacities persisted in her, such as the capacity for observation of her psychic reality and of her interpersonal relationships, as well as her interest in knowing about herself, that led me to the indication of psychoanalytic treatment five times a week. I will cite a passage in which the difficulties encountered in dealing with her delusional world, by means of access to the non-psychotic part, may be appreciated.

The episode I shall recount takes place after a couple of years of treatment during which time the patient had made some progress, such as being more able to tolerate many aspects of her external and internal reality, and even to achieve some professional fulfilment. It is a difficult moment, and the patient is in the midst of a delusional psychotic episode. Suddenly, and without prior notice, she stops coming to the sessions. After a week has gone by, she calls me on the telephone. She informs me that she is worried about the international political situation, as it could be heading for a global conflagration of unforeseeable consequences. After listening to her for a while, I answer her with a direct interpretation: perhaps her worry and anxiety is related to the relational politics taking place inside of her, a situation she fears she will be unable to control alone. Her immediate reaction was to hang up the phone, without another word. Two hours later, she calls again. During this second call, in a somewhat calmer tone, she asks me how I am. She is worried about me, she says, about whether I will be able to tolerate the situation we were going through. This time I was very careful not to make the previous error of interpreting in terms of the patient's internal world, as it had proved evident that she was not able to bear it. Instead, I accepted her projection into me, that it was I who must be experiencing some kind of anxiety or distress. So I told her that certainly I was feeling some concern, owing to the fact that over a week had gone by without her coming to the sessions. She answered that it was true, that quite some time, a lot of time in fact, had gone by, and that too many things were happening, generating intense anxiety for everyone. I tell her that perhaps she is calling me to re-establish communication with me and to make me a part of this whole situation. She says yes, actually, and expresses her thanks.

I tell her that we could talk about all of this in her sessions, which, as she knows, are still reserved for her. She insists that the international situation is there, and it is going from bad to worse, hence little or nothing can be done at the sessions. With such clear evidence of that particular reality for the patient, I realise that I cannot introduce comments that might cast it into doubt. So I reply to her that I wonder how we might face this situation. Perhaps, I add, we could start by dealing with the immediate individual situation. You are right actually, she replies. She asks me what I am doing to achieve this, because to cope with all of this would surely call for artistic creation.

I tell her that perhaps in this very conversation I am trying to achieve something like that, a kind of art of relationships with people, and in this sense perhaps it could be considered somewhat creative, constructive, which contributes something or other to us. She says yes, it is kind of like that; that is what we are doing. Taking advantage of that moment of agreement, I try to progress a little further, and I say to her that we could take another step along this road if we had a session in which we could continue talking.

She replies that she could agree to us continuing to talk but not in the office, because psychiatrists' offices are prisons. I tell her that the office I am proposing we continue to talk is this office, where she and I have had many sessions for quite some time, and she has been able to come and go, express her feelings, ideas, and so on. Because I can only offer that chance to talk within the conditions of the therapeutic relationship that she knows.

She says that she is fine, actually, and that, as I said to her a while ago, she now feels as though she is walking in her own shoes. When I reply to her true enough, but there is still a way to go, she answers that she can now do it alone, and on that point we disagree. She adds that she hopes I am more radical in my approach, and that I take a vigorous and consistent stance. I tell her that I will think about what she is telling me about being consistent and that at this point in time

I believe I am trying to be. She tells me that I undervalue myself. I reply that, in fact, I try to make an adequate valuation of my work, although within the limits permitted by reality. She says that she takes issue with this, and that it is the point of contention between her and I. I continue by saying that I am not expecting her to agree with me; rather, I am trying to set out and defend what I consider to be my consistency, in my way of thinking and carrying out my work.

The patient answers, "The thing is I feel weak and depressed, and I don't have the strength to come to an interview . . . and besides . . . I'm very busy with things." I tell her that perhaps she is also busy with the many worries in regard to what we are talking about. And I can tell that, for my part, I am holding her session times and that perhaps I can share in some of all of that which is taking up so many of her thoughts. She thanks me for my willingness to do so and tells me that, for now, she does not feel able to come but that we will continue talking another time. I accept her decision and we say goodbye. Several days later, she comes to the session and resumes analysis.

Comments on the psychotic schizophrenic patient

This excerpt reveals the difficulties with the delusional patient in that it tests the analyst in his primary function: that of trying to get closer to the psychic truth of the relationship he establishes with his patient. With her delusion, the patient is proposing that the analyst be as untruthful as she is, either by him accepting the delusion, to some extent, although at this stage of analysis (a couple of years have passed) she should not expect the analyst to share it, if only in part, but above all, by attempting to stimulate an interpretative stance in the analyst that might be equally untrue, if not a lie. The latter is what happened with my intervention during the first phone call.

My interpretation, that it was inside her where these "politics" of warlike conflict were taking place, signified two things: first, and scarcely without "metabolising" (that is to say, passing it through my personal experience), that I had returned what she had projected into external reality and, therefore, she experiences it as a violent return. Yet, neither is it entirely true that the worry or concern is the patient's alone. When she says that we are worried about "the world war that's happening", there is a fragment of truth in this. Indeed, there is something of a war between her and me, owing to the fact that has interrupted the sessions, and there is, indeed, also some concern in the analyst for the "life" of this analytic relationship, as well as that of her family and personal relationships. However, interpreting it as I did, I am *absolutely* divesting her "reality" of the category of reality, even though hers is delusional, to impose another as reality—mine. It equates to telling her that the world that is shoring her up at that moment is false, untruthful, and of little consistency, when she needs it so much for her balance, as precarious as this might be. There again, if she is talking about world war, we must understand that the conflicts and death anxieties that she is experiencing are of such dimensions that she must place them on a planetary scale. We are reminded of the description given by Bion of psychotic pain as something that is unrepresentable. For that reason, trying to put all of that inside her, as my first intervention implied, constitutes doing real violence to her, in the face of which she responds with similar violence, by cutting off the communication abruptly.

However, two hours were enough for the patient to be able to resume communication with the analyst. I think that her previous therapeutic experience with the analyst has enabled a degree of trust to be deposited in the link with him—from the non-psychotic part—which, in spite of the violence of the last interpretation, has not disappeared. Although in order to re-establish the relationship at that time, the patient has needed to project massively into the analyst her concern for the situation "we were going through" (the war between the two of us). Additionally, the cutting-off of the telephone call constituted a radical splitting, in the sense of nullification or severing of the relationship with the analyst who interprets to her in such a way. And if she called back, it must be because "the analyst-with-the-violent-interpretation" has been set aside, while the relationship with the analyst with whom she has maintained a viable relationship for over two years has re-emerged.

So, after hanging up, instead of fleeing, she needs to call back to determine what the analyst does with what she has projected into him. This time, I respond by saying that, true enough, I am somewhat concerned, on that point we would agree: the psychotic part confers (projects) her intense anxiety into me in order to rid herself of the pain, which I accept. We might say that consensus is possible between the psychotic and non-psychotic part of the patient to the extent that each has given way on something: the psychotic part yields by agreeing to re-establish communication and the non-psychotic part by giving its approval to the massive projection into the analyst. But I go on to say that the reason for my concern is because of something that we both know: her absence from the sessions. Here, I distance myself from what the psychotic part is proposing, which would seek to mislead me, making me a part of that distortion of reality in which the anxieties we have are due to something coming from outside: "the imminent outbreak of world war". No. On that point I distance myself from the psychotic part to instead address the non-psychotic part, by alluding to the immediate reality of the therapeutic relationship which has been affected by the patient's absence from the sessions. Her reply is eloquent: "it is true", she says. She acknowledges the truth of what I am saying. This would indicate somewhat of a turning point in the attempt to access the non-psychotic part, with the predominance of the psychotic part diminishing. Now, her reply comes from the part of the patient able to acknowledge the reality being shown to her. And she adds, "So much is going on, which is cause for anxiety for everyone." This statement is ambiguous enough to be valid for both the psychotic part and the non-psychotic part. I answer her in a way that is also somewhat ambiguous, that perhaps her phone call is an attempt to re-establish communication between her and I, so that I would participate in this situation that is worrying her (now, in fact, I was able to draw her attention to the worry inside of her). Her response of gratitude makes me think that we are still in contact with the non-psychotic part that feels understood in her anxiety. This is what encourages me to try to take a step further and attempt to bring the communication within the therapeutic framework. However, the psychotic part reacts swiftly, taking the problem to the delusional reality, to get us away from the therapeutic relationship we were talking about, and, simultaneously, to magnify the dimension of the problem, in the face of which the "real", in other words limited, capacity of the sessions would prove to be totally inadequate.

Again, I am faced with the dilemma between collusion with the patient, giving my tacit approval to that version of reality, or rejecting it head on with all the violence this entails. I begin my reply by telling her that "I am wondering how we might deal with that", and with this I am indicating that the analyst is trying to *think* about what is occurring, even if this is a painful task. With this response, it might seem that something of a trap has been laid, as it is as if I had accepted the patient's proposition that an international conflagration was indeed afoot. This is not necessarily so, in fact, as what we can concede is that the patient's suffering is of dimensions similar to those that any person might experience in the face of imminent global catastrophe, as I said before. In that sense, the answer I give her is, in fact, true. In spite of the magnitude of the problem, I suggest a possible, albeit limited, response: "we could start with the immediate individual situation". The patient agrees. Yet, once again, faced with her inability to carry it through, she must project it massively into the analyst by asking him what he is doing to achieve this, going on to add that such a task would surely call for "artistic creation". This suggestion might be located along a borderline area between the psychotic and the non-psychotic part. Or, to put it another way, it could be seen from one or other perspective. Perhaps she is saying it from the psychotic perspective: one would have to put up an artistic creation of genius, magical, omnipotent dimensions. So, too, a non-psychotic interpretation could apply, such as the one I offer her, by speaking about what is taking place at that moment during the telephone conversation, as somewhat comparable to an "artistic" endeavour in the relationship between her and I. The patient is not only in agreement, but she includes herself as the co-author of that undertaking: "Yes, in a way, that is what *we are* doing."

By establishing a new point of encounter with the non-psychotic part, I decide to take another step forward by proposing her return to sessions, to which the psychotic part responds by accusing me, albeit indirectly (which is a point to bear in mind), of being just another repressive psychiatrist who only wants to lock her up. That is to say, the response by the psychotic part is milder than on other occasions by making the accusation in a generic way ("psychiatrists' offices are prisons"), identifying me as a psychiatrist and not as the person with whom she has sustained a relationship to talk about her problems for some time. By this, I am able to avoid entering into considerations over whether what psychiatrists do is repressive or not; rather, I simply remind her of the type of relationship she has had with this particular "psychiatrist", me, and which, moreover, is the only professional relationship I am able to discuss with her and I mention the freedom of expression that she has been able to experience in the sessions. But then I feel required to add that what I am able to offer her is only possible within certain conditions, which I need to do my job. Implicitly, the patient accepts my way of working, as well as the fact that I am not a "jailer psychiatrist", a stance which must supported by the non-psychotic part of her that recognises the reality of the therapeutic relationship we have had so far. However, it appears that this is not enough, as the psychotic part then acts in collusion with the non-psychotic part by saying that "she is fine". Yet, if the psychotic part had acted alone, the attack on the link with the analyst would have prevailed. Therefore, it is logical to think that it has acted in alliance with the non-psychotic part: it is not that she attacks the analyst, it is just that she does not need him because she is fine now. But, with this, she crudely denies a reality of which she was speaking to me only minutes ago, that there is a situation of "widespread" conflict—in her entire person—which is the source of intense anxiety. Furthermore, I think that the reasoning she uses to support her well-being by calling up an intervention made by the analyst some time ago—that she had begun to walk in her own shoes—has connotations of the perverse lie, by making inappropriate usage of the analyst's assertions with the aim of making his statements pass for agreement when they do not. That is to say, a functioning typical of perversion is operating when the non-psychotic part is placed in the service of the psychotic part to distort reality by passing it off as true. In the patient who is perverse in the strict sense, there is a greater consistency or solidity to the self in that its functions are not as deteriorated as in the psychotic.

At that point in the conversation, I attempt to establish what we are in agreement upon and what we are not. I admit that she has begun to walk in her own shoes, but I add that there is still a way to go. She contends that this is where we disagree. I thought it was good that the patient could point out and admit this without discrediting me, although she immediately needs once again to project her desire to have "more energy and consistency" into the analyst, elements that she herself is sorely missing to move her life and treatment forward. Here, faced with the psychotic part, once again in association with the non-psychotic part, which seeks to devalue me, I energetically defend my consistency, referring us to the particular moment we are going through. When she insists upon devaluing me, I do not point out her projection into me, but I hold firm in my stance, accepting, furthermore, the limits of the reality of my work. Whereupon the patient answers, obviously from the psychotic part, that here again there is a point of contention between us. At that point, it was clear to me that

I was not able to grapple with the psychotic part directly, so I make myself clearer by stating that I am not trying to convince her to agree with me; rather, I am simply trying to defend my work.

The patient's reply is significant: "The thing is I feel weak and depressed, and I don't have the strength to come to the sessions." It is significant in that, by my navigating around her perverse strategy, and avoiding confrontation with the psychotic part, she is able to come into contact with the non-psychotic part once more, which is capable of acknowledging her weakness, her depression, and her lack of energy; deficiencies that, a short time before, she was trying to attribute to the analyst. My reply is to refer this discomfort to her anxieties surrounding everything we have been talking about, that is to say, the interruption of treatment, precisely when she needs it so much.

So, while the analyst cannot accept the patient's delusional reality as true, the only appropriate recourse is to defend his own reality, that of his working method, without trying to impose it upon her. If the patient is launching an attack on reality in such an overt way, I am obliged to defend my truth, my coherence, as she is asking me to do, but without trying to destroy her delusional reality since, there again, this is what the psychotic part would seek to provoke with her crude attack on reality and reason, with her delusion, in such a way as to once again project her hostile and destructive attitude into the analyst.

I think that what has occurred is that the patient has been able to validate an aspect of reality, offered to her by the analyst, which, albeit different to her own, is not felt as persecutory. This lays the foundation towards establishing a relationship with the non-psychotic part, in spite of the opposition by the psychotic part, which would seek definitively to sever the therapeutic relationship. So, at the end of the conversation, the patient is able to talk about her depression. That is to say, the initial massive projection into the analyst, owing to the predominance of the psychotic part, has been transformed into a capacity to look inside herself and acknowledge her depression. However, at this point it is not possible to go further. It was necessary to wait a few days until the outcome of the communication established with the non-psychotic part prevailed in order to enable her to re-establish the therapeutic relationship by returning to the sessions

The non-psychotic patient: identifying the psychotic part

Let us now turn to the situation of the non-psychotic patient in which it became necessary to reveal aspects of a psychotic nature. This involves a patient with personality characterological problems, who has been in psychoanalytic treatment for several years. It is a Wednesday session, the penultimate of the week, of the four we have together. She enters the session with a grave look, which surprises me in some ways as I thought that in yesterday's session we had worked hard with good co-operation on her part, so I had been left with the impression that it had been a good—albeit difficult—session for her, too.

She throws herself on the couch and remains in silence for several minutes, which tended to be rather unusual for her. I wonder what can be bothering her. I wonder whether she has had some confrontation at work, although this did not square with my experience from other sessions, where, under similar circumstances, she immediately shared her concerns with the analyst. I then consider whether we have come up against another negative therapeutic reaction, such as at other times during treatment. Just yesterday we spoke a little about this type of reaction, and I thought that in some way this might have been useful to her; consequently, I stick to the idea that what is happening now must involve her difficulties in accepting good experiences with other people, in this case in her relationship with the analyst. As the minutes passed, perhaps five or so, but which, as I say, is not usual with this patient, I remembered that on Monday she had anticipated that this week would not be as beneficial as the last, quite the contrary in fact, for which reason this seemed to be a self-fulfilling prophecy. I question whether to make an intervention along these lines, but I also think that we have seen this on other occasions, so she might already know this herself. So, I decide to wait a little longer.

After almost ten minutes she begins to speak. She does so in a low, almost inaudible tone, drawing out her words a little, which would suggest that she is in a more typically melancholic mental state. I note that she is hardly opening her mouth, so it is difficult for her to articulate the words. Her behaviour was so pronounced that it made me think that she was theatricalising her state, which did not fail to irritate me somewhat, causing me to want to snap back at her by saying something like, "Stop making such a fuss and take the session seriously", which would be tantamount to telling her, "Stop making a scene like a wilful child and be a bit more adult". Needless to say, I kept quiet, and decided to pay attention to the content of her words, avoiding being side-tracked by the tone of them: perhaps the patient needed that artifice for reasons as yet unknown, so I should let her speak and listen to the content. If the container of the communication was sending a message that was difficult for me to tolerate, I should wait to find out the contained and try to grasp another message. However, even though she has started talking, I am hardly able to hear her.

P: Last Wednesday you said that I had hit rock bottom . . .
A: [Although this was my expression, it corresponded to the mental state that the patient described, which she herself confirmed to me by proceeding to recall the last verses of a poem where the poet spoke of "hitting rock bottom", and which I considered to be the outcome of an insightful communication between her and I. So, to now attribute the diagnosis that she was hitting rock bottom to me was as if there had been some intent on my part to put her in that place, which seemed to me did not fit the reality of what had taken place. But I understood that, together with the somewhat hostile tone, it was a version in keeping with the unease she felt towards me, the reason for which I had not yet managed to ascertain.]
P: Yes, last Wednesday I also told you that I wanted to kill myself [pause]. Today . . . [She says something in a lower tone of voice that is inaudible to me. Another pause. The effort the patient is making to speak is very evident: she is hardly opening her mouth, while displaying some difficulty breathing.]
A: You were saying that today . . . pardon?
P: That today . . . I wouldn't have come to the session . . . I would have brought about the breakdown of this relationship [another pause].
A: [I am surprised by this reaction, and do not yet understand what could have happened yesterday to provoke such a violent reaction. I cannot say anything to her so I continue to wait.]
P: On Wednesday I felt that I was sinking down into the depths . . . [I am not able to hear what comes afterwards very well] or I was on top of one hilltop but I couldn't climb up any further, as I would have to come down to climb up yet another higher one [an image that had arisen some sessions ago as a metaphor for the process of analysis and her personal growth] or I felt I was having trouble coping with things, well today I feel like I'm at the bottom of a foul well. [She pauses again.]

A: [I begin to glimpse that the foul well must be the session, owing to something that I said to her yesterday not being well received or being taken as something soiled or unclean, so that today she is coming back into this unbreathable atmosphere. Over half an hour of the session has elapsed and I am beginning to worry because I don't see how it will be possible to overcome this atmosphere in the time remaining, which is becoming dense, and, indeed, almost foul-smelling and unpleasant. Furthermore, seeing the patient holding her breath to such an extent, as if to avoid taking in the air of the room as far as possible, almost conveyed the sensation to me that it did, in fact, smell bad in there. But I still fail to see what could have prompted this state.]

P: All the effort I made yesterday to talk about the things I did was for nothing. You said some dreadful things back to me. I already told you yesterday that in Monday's session you said nasty things to me, and yesterday, well, it was more of the same, which just increased the feeling of a rift ... Anyhow, it'll just be less hard for me go off this Thursday [tomorrow, the last session of the week] and there'll be no dismantling [as a result of the separation]. [Pause.]

A: [My degree of incomprehension and bafflement is increasing. One of the things I said to her comes to mind, although I knew that it was not a matter of returning to yesterday's session to check what I did or did not say, as this would mean moving away from the present moment; although, as I said at the beginning, my general impression of the session was good and productive in spite of it being difficult for both of us. But I also knew that she is an extremely sensitive person and that any comment, depending upon the tone or the words used, could be felt as painful and produce devastating effects.]

P: [continuing to speak in the same slow, laboured tone, conveying the sensation of us really being in a contaminated and unbreathable atmosphere, talking with her mouth half closed, with long pauses—not at all usual for this patient, as I said—as if in this way she could breathe only the air that was absolutely necessary,] I am worried about a person I saw yesterday at work and I didn't resolve something with her, so now I'll have to wait until she calls. And at the weekend I have a company course and I don't know if I will be up to it, but on the other hand I wouldn't want to make a scene there. Depending on how things are going, I've considered the option of leaving halfway through the course.

A: [Now, the only thing I notice is that the patient feels unwell, and yet she is talking about how to face the weekend without any hope of us being able to do anything in this session—there are still a little over ten minutes—or all of tomorrow's session. So I leave what I have not yet understood to one side, regarding why she had come to the session this way, and I talk to her in terms similar to what was going through my mind.] I have the impression that you are no longer taking into account the time that remains to us in this session or tomorrow's session to try to cleanse the atmosphere that feels so squalid and foul-smelling in the relationship between you and I, and therefore all you have left is to imagine, with some desperation, how you will face the weekend with only the mental state you are in at the moment.

P: [Silence.] Well yes, I think you have sensed that well. [Her tone is not provocative; rather, an acknowledgement of agreeing with the analyst.]

A: [I consider that, in spite of the bad atmosphere, the patient has been able to appreciate my intervention: "you have sensed that well", which indicates a recognition of my perceptive ability. Therefore, something coming from the analyst might be "clean", in contrast to her perceptions of a moment ago. This encourages me to add something else in relation to the situation we are experiencing.]

A: It seems as though you are in a difficult dilemma. On the one hand, you feel as though you sinking down into the depths. But, as you clarified, it isn't the sinking feeling of last week because of the things that were happening, when you were, in fact, able to receive help from here. Now you have sunk down into the foul well of analysis, or, rather, the relationship with me. So how will you be able to come out of this sinking, if to do so you would need to talk and for me to talk to you, but it turns out that my words, and even the air in the room, are contaminated?

P: [After a pause.] Well, you've hit the nail on the head there. It's just that I have that sensation of not being able to breathe, I have to really struggle . . . [She pauses and doesn't seem to want to press the point, as if hitting the nail on the head of the matter had, in some way, clarified the atmosphere and enabled her to mentally "breathe" better, and continue talking.] This issue of having difficulty breathing reminded me that on Sunday I went to have lunch at my mother's house, and she explained to me that, when my sister was born, I got something wrong with my throat, quite suddenly, and that I was suffocating, so they had to take me to hospital. On the way, apparently, my whole body was moving around because of how panic-stricken I must have been. My mother was holding me firmly so that I didn't hurt myself, and in the struggle I ended up kicking her in the breast and as a result she got an abscess that had to be lanced, so she had to stop breastfeeding my sister. Anyhow, although the abscess was caused by the kick, apparently my sister was already having trouble taking the breast.

A: [We are winding up the session and, while I listen to the patient's account, I feel a mixture of astonishment and shock at the turn the communication has taken, but the patient seems keen to keep talking.]

P: And then mum explained something else. My sister, who was also at the lunch on Sunday, and I, we were joking because my mother always tried to get us eat more, and we were saying that she's done that all our lives. She remembered how we used to eat when we were small. Apparently, I took the breast well as a baby, but then, maybe after my little sister was born, things took a turn for the worse. My mum was saying that, as far as mealtimes were concerned, you should listen to your mother. I replied that no, what you should do is listen to your stomach, because if it's full, you can't eat any more. But she told me that she would be flummoxed by me, because there were times when I was really hungry, but after one spoonful I didn't want any more, as if the hunger had passed, so she didn't know if when I was refusing to eat it was because I wasn't hungry any more or because I was so hungry. The thing is, my mum was saying, it's very difficult to be a mother.

A: Perhaps now we can understand a little more about what has happened. There are many things today [I think I should avoid repeating what happened yesterday, by "returning" lots of explanations to her, which she was unable to digest]. It seems to me that you are underscoring the issue you spoke about yesterday as your "eating problems", the problems you have in "taking in or ingesting" what is given to you and so on. [Yesterday, we discussed the matter of the difficulties encountered at times by the patient in accepting the explanations and interpretations given to her by the analyst.] In this sense, perhaps being an analyst isn't easy either. Yesterday, you contributed many things and I tried to think on them and return them to you . . .

P: [She interrupts me.] Of course, so if I said dreadful things, you just returned them to me as-is. The thing is, if someone has diarrhoea, they're hoping that someone will clean them up.

A: I am saying that my impression is not that I returned things to you just how you formulated them to me; I believe I thought about them and formulated them in a different way.

P: [After a pause,] Well, yes, you are right, you did explain them in a different way . . .
A: Perhaps, then, the problem was in the ability to digest what we were seeing. The fact that you contributed many things might have given the impression that you were able to receive them returned without being entirely "cleaned up", but apparently this was not the case, and as they were difficult issues, they needed more clearing up so as to make them digestible.

Following this, the patient is able to express one of the questions that were not clear to her in yesterday's session, but which yesterday she was not able to communicate, and we ended the session.

Comments on the non-psychotic patient

Towards the end of the session, when I thought I had understood something of what was happening, I opted to leave the aspect of the attacks on the breast out of jealousy to one side, as it would have been too much for the patient to be able to digest. Furthermore, I now see that this was appropriate, in the sense of continuing along the lines of working on what it was that had made it difficult for her to accept and to incorporate what I said to her the day before. That is to say, it seemed more important to explore the problem of an analysis/well relationship that was foul, foetid, and full of "poop" or vomit, judging by the nasty things she felt the analyst had told her. The unpleasantness of these things, I believe, is as a result of them being returned to her immediately, even before entering a process of mental digestion, and, as such, they could not be assimilated; it is like a baby suddenly throwing up at the same time as they are being fed, or having diarrhoea.

That being the case, it is clear that the patient is attacking the nourishing breast, although not so much out of jealousy; it seems to me that, in the context of the session, the little sister represents the aspect of the patient who is able to accept a relationship of nourishing dependency, although with certain difficulties, as has been corroborated in the sessions for some time. But there is another aspect: the omnipotent and envious infantile self that would attack it until it resulted in the interruption of breastfeeding. Indeed, this is what she was trying to act out by introducing the theme of the analytic relationship as a foul well, that is to say, by making the relationship into something useless, such as a breast with a pus-filled abscess that cannot produce good milk. But, on this occasion, it seems to me that by not addressing this (psychotic) aspect directly and by having focused on the self that was suffering the consequences of such a state, this ultimately provided the opportunity for a reconciliation in the relationship, a cleansing of its atmosphere, and an acceptance of the analytic relation.

The session also shows the psychotic anxieties expressed by her material difficulties in breathing. Hearing the analyst's words as unpleasant does not just have a metaphorical sense, but, at that moment, acquires the character of material reality, perceived sensorially through the air, which was contaminated by toxic substances: the analyst's words. These are no longer merely words that convey meanings; rather, they have become real, actual, noxious chemical substances. We are talking about a psychotic experience, albeit a fleeting one, that makes use of the symbolic equation, in which her psychotic anxieties have not been able to be contained otherwise.

In this case, I think that the fact that I addressed the non-psychotic part of the patient, or the dependent infantile part, contributed towards the psychotic part diminishing in strength. The attack lost potency, both the attack on the analyst, whom it devalues and turns into a pestilent well into which she was sinking, as well as the attack directed at her own perceptive capabilities which were unable to pick up on an atmosphere that was similar to that of other sessions, instead perceiving one that was "truly" noxious. This progress in the session proved possible owing to years of work during which this infantile part has been able to feel recognised in the analytic relation and has been able to have more trust in the sane dependence upon the object, as much as—and, at times, more than—her trust in the omnipotence of the psychotic part.

In this instance, then, it has been necessary, first, to recognise the patient's psychotic experience, as well as the attacks on communication and on her ego-capacities. Once this psychotic functioning has been identified, the analyst's intervention avoids direct confrontation. I think the moment at which the analyst leaves to one side his attempt to find out why the patient arrives in that state of mental discomfort and hostility towards analysis is crucial to the progress of the session; instead, he draws attention to what was also evident: the patient's immediate desperation. It is after this, when the analyst is able to refer to the psychotic experience (by calling attention to her breathing difficulties) and is able to put it into words, that it is possible for the hallucinatory experience of the toxifying atmosphere of the room to be deactivated. From that moment on, verbal communication is re-established, which provides significant content contributing towards an understanding of something that had occurred in the previous day's session.

Conclusions

This chapter has been based on the premise that psychotic anxieties are universal. I am referring to the catastrophic anxieties: the feeling of imminent annihilation, of fragmenting, of disappearing, and so on, which I mentioned earlier. If world war is breaking out for the first patient, this might be said to be the expressive forms of such anxieties; or that of being "poisoned" in the second patient, with the commensurate psychotic defences. The type of object relation that is developed will depend upon how we come to resolve these anxieties, which have generated psychotic forms of transference. Yet, as has been acknowledged in psychoanalytic thinking for some years now, while the psychotic organisation as such only occurs in certain patients (those we would classify as psychotic in the strict sense), forms of psychotic functioning might, however, make themselves present in any patient at one time or another during the therapeutic process. The resultant organisation depends upon the dynamic, or, rather, the greater or lesser pathology, of the interaction between the psychotic part of the personality and the non-psychotic part, which, in turn, is determined by the interplay between the three elements of the personality noted by Bion: psychic pain, Ps$\leftrightarrow$D and the relationship between container and contained ($♀$–$♂$).

From this standpoint, how to reduce the intensity of this dynamic constitutes a fundamental question that has significance for both the psychotherapeutic and psychoanalytic treatment of psychotic patients, as, indeed, for any patient with moderate to serious pathology. The potential for affecting the therapeutic outcomes of these patients is based on the achievement of communication with the non-psychotic part of the personality, without disqualifying the psychotic part. Herein lie the difficulties inherent to any psychoanalytic or psychotherapeutic attempt, since, by definition, the psychotic part will take exception to consenting to the non-psychotic part establishing a link with the therapist. First, because any link implicitly carries the threat of a connection with the reality from which it is attempting to escape; second, because the link with the therapist is, moreover, created specifically to work "against" the intentions of the psychotic part.

CHAPTER THREE

Psychotic organisation of the personality: psychopathological dynamics and foundations

In Chapter One, we examined the idea of pathological organisation as a useful concept, as it sets out a defensive personality structure that can be present in a variety of pathologies, from the psychotic to the neurotic patient. This, we suggested, has the advantage of offering a more approachable conceptualisation of serious pathology. This way, we do not "marginalise" that which pertains to psychosis, to be banished to a conceptual terrain of its own. Furthermore, this is in keeping with the traditional psychoanalytic line of thought, beginning with Freud, which blurs the rigid divisions between the normal and the pathological, with the aim of making the latter more understandable. However, as we also noted, we run the risk of diminishing the specificity of each individual pathology encompassed by the term "pathological organisation". For this reason, in Chapter Two, we indicated some of the differences between the pathologies, paying close attention to the type of link that exists between the psychotic and non-psychotic parts of the personality. In this respect, I believe, it is possible to speak of a "psychotic organisation of the personality" (an expression taken from Steiner (1993) in his description of one of the distinct forms of pathological organisation) as a particular form of pathological organisation which goes beyond the dominant dynamic in other pathological organisations. The rest of the book is devoted to this.

One way in which we might conceive the dynamics of the PsPO is in terms of its huge limitation in the management of the pain associated with contact with reality; in other words, in its containment. As we said, the patient feels pain, but there is difficulty in tolerating its experience, so he needs to resort to primitive pathological defences.

By the way, we should undo a frequent misunderstanding, by which the use of primitive defence mechanisms and pathological defence mechanisms are considered equal. I have already said that Klein's description of phenomena of the early psyche resembles that of the functioning of psychotic and schizophrenic adult patients, without this involving pathology in the former. On the contrary, they are necessary for an acceptable psychic development. Consequently, Klein herself, and, to a greater extent, the contemporary Kleinians, clearly established the difference between the ordinary use of primitive defences and their pathological counterparts. Caper (1988) considers the normal primitive mental states contain omnipotent fantasies, which are accompanied by a sufficient sense of reality to enable to the child to learn through experience (Bion, 1991[1962]). By contrast, in primitive psychopathological states, the omnipotent unconscious fantasies (delusions) persist owing to a failure in learning from experience. I agree with Caper's criticism of the Freudian theory of psychopathology as a regression to, or fixation in, primitive mental states, as it implies a notion of the "normal" child as an abnormal mind (Caper, 1988, p. 541). In other words, all adult pathology suggests the previous existence of an infantile mental life with poor contact with reality and capacity for learning from experience, in whose development the early mechanisms of functioning have not only persisted over time, but have also modified their initial nature; in effect, they have become pathologised.

Psychopathological foundations of the PsPO

In that a sufficiently containing mental space has not been constructed, the patient needs to resort to primitive pathological forms of functioning, such as pathological splitting, pathological projective identification, and the predominance of omnipotence. I shall consider each one of these, albeit paying unequal attention to each, not on the basis of the importance accorded them, but because some have already been studied extensively, as is the case of projective identification. For others—while also discussed elsewhere—I shall seek to emphasise certain other aspects on the basis of my experience, as is the case with pathological splitting.

Pathological splitting

Splitting is an essential psychic process involved in coming to terms with the complex and difficult reality in which the newborn finds himself at the beginning of life. This is a life clearly shaped by the pleasure–pain principle; to survive it he will have to avoid pain and attain pleasure, where pain is synonymous with death, and pleasure, the total absence of discomfort. Consequently, there will be a world of pain and a world of pleasure that must remain clearly separated, and in a radical manner. This is binary splitting, and forms part of every individual's development. This division can fail for various reasons: some originate in the individual's extreme intolerance of the inevitable pain of the reality testing that goes hand in hand with development, others because of the excessively demanding environment, which exposes the individual to painful situations well above what is bearable to him (be they situations of lack or trauma). Therefore, when there is a failure of binary splitting, that is to say, the world of pain–death (and the anxieties related to these) is not separated off from the world of pleasure–life, but is present within it, even invading it, that particular parcel of reality will, as a result, need to be split again, in an attempt to separate the pain. This process will be repeated countless times, so that what had been a "mechanism" conducive to the protection of the developing life becomes a fragmentation of reality in order to lessen the painful impact of it. The result is, therefore, a fragmentary and radical—and, thus, pathological—splitting of reality, external and internal.

When it happens that there is a predominance of pathological splitting, reality amounts to a source simultaneously of pain–death and pleasure–life, bringing catastrophic experiences in its wake, hence (nearly) any direct connection with reality must be avoided, as well as connections established between the fragmented elements of it. This is what Bion (1993[1959]) described as the attack on linking, the maximum expression of which is the attack on one's own perceptive capacities that register impressions of reality, as I have already reminded us. This generates a state of multiple splitting, or fragmentation of reality, of the object and of the self.

Here, I would like to bring in Britton's recent ideas (2015) questioning the suitability of the expression "attack on linking" for the phenomenon it describes. He begins by quoting Bion: "an omnipotent phantasy that is intended to destroy either reality or the awareness of it, and thus achieve a state which is neither life nor death" (Bion, 1993[1957], p. 46). He adds the following commentary: "the eradication of awareness of an object by elimination of its psychic representation would mean the actual link, the sensory connection to an object, would be *wiped out*" (2015, p. 88, my italics). Along this same line, he wonders, "Is the individual's disconnection from the outside world and the internal representatives regression or destruction?" (2015, p. 92). Before answering this, he calls to mind the current controversy over the different perspectives on narcissism, considered as defensive and libidinal, or as destructive. He is of the view that the difference disappears if, instead of considering narcissism as primary and loving object relations as secondary, we see them as concurrent and in conflict from the very beginning. We might consider narcissism "not as a force in [its] own right but as a negative reaction to connection to objects because they are not identical and thus arose an *immune response* of hostility" (2015, p. 92, my italics).

Britton's suggestion, regarding the immune response to that which is not the self, is appealing, but it is, none the less, a metaphor. What is demonstrable in biological terms makes its translation to psychic life very plausible. However, we should question the psychological significance of an immune response. One explanation might be the concept of envy, but I think that Britton is referring to something else: simply to whatever it is that is different from the self, and, looking to the clinical approach, we can agree with this. The psychotic patient seems to be saying that which is different to me is implicitly not-me; as such, it is a threat, until proved otherwise, and only by unifying my ego or self with the not-me or not-self will I be able to resolve the problems of my relation to the world. This constitutes the basis of the work with all patients, and, very particularly, with psychotic patients: the aim is not for the patient to learn to tolerate being differentiated from the object because he needs it, which would also correspond to a more evolved psychic level (that of the depressive position); rather, it is for him to be able to acknowledge (and tolerate) that he is distinct from the object, in terms of the threat this represents to his psychic life. Consequently, the patient says to himself, "I cannot introject what comes from this object because it is 'something else' [in the sense of a foreign body, to follow Britton's metaphor of the immune response]. My psychic dynamic is not used to it, it does not know it . . . even if it can see that I need it."

My clinical experience, and particularly the work with my schizophrenic patient, Ms B, supports Britton's idea. This takes the perspective of the unbearable nature of the psychotic pain experienced by these patients, which leads to the response, by means of omnipotent phantasy, which changes the subject–object relationship into one of subject–subject, in other words, *fusion instead of connection* (Britton, 2015). In my view, this is a crucial point in our discussion of the psychotic patient: fusion with the object, as opposed to any connection which would mean acknowledgement of difference, that is to say, to be tied to something foreign to me. The Bionian expression, "attack on linking", indicates an aggressive motivation, and, therefore, Britton suggests the term "severance", which leaves questions of aetiology and possible reasons for these reactions open (Britton, 2015, p. 93). Although I wonder if it would be sufficient to use the well-known expression of "splitting", whenever referring to psychotic patients we add the adjective "pathological": pathological splitting. As fragmentary splitting has been studied more, I shall refer to another type of pathological splitting that I have observed in my patient.

The theme of "the twins"

In psychotics, the omnipotent character of the splitting, even when it does not act in a fragmentary way, has a radical, extreme quality. For example, the patient who acknowledges feelings of affect and hate towards the analyst must keep them radically separated, to the extent that he loves the analyst as if he were the only person in the world he wishes to be with, or he hates him as the root cause of all his suffering. This radical splitting of the object was evident in my schizophrenic patient, Ms B, on the subject of "the twins"; a secondary delusional idea, in the sense that it was less present than others, but arose in certain conflictive moments of the analytic process. The subject emerged, notably, after a long analytical holiday. After the first long interruption from analysis, the patient told me that I felt cold and distant, and the explanation that she found for this was that I must be the twin brother of her psychoanalyst. The *messages* told her this: the person seeing her in the session at that time was not Dr PS but his twin brother, and she continues, "Dr PS is a psychiatrist, a psychoanalyst, he is married and has a family, but you, that is, the person who's seeing me now in the session, you are not a psychiatrist, or a psychoanalyst, nor are you married or have a family; you are alone, which is why you need to live with your twin brother." At other times, resorting to "the twins" would fulfil another function. During a time when the eroticisation of the relationship had been intensifying, the patient claimed that this erotic component was the element that was lacking to complete her cure. So, if there is a Dr PS who helps her and cures her mind, but is not willing to give in to her demand of completing the "treatment" through the physical consummation of the relationship, we could turn to Dr PS's twin brother, who, at such moments, is present in the session, who could, in fact, perform such a function and thus cure her body also. The theme of the "twin" also had another sense: the analyst is her own twin brother. This I shall refer to now.

To illustrate this last aspect in relation to the pathological splitting, I shall present a detailed report of two consecutive sessions. Clearly, other phenomena of the psychotic personality organisation are implicit, and these I shall likewise consider. For example, the patient's attempts to attack the setting and the analyst's analytic function, the analyst's assertive response, and the patient's later introjection of this assertiveness, as well as the use of pathological projective identification.

A particular form of splitting/fusion of the analytic relation

The first session, although difficult, provided the opportunity for analytic work that brought about a change in the patient which could be seen in the following session. These sessions take place during a time when Ms B was insisting upon the legitimacy of an eroticised relationship with the analyst and her irritation at the analyst's response of limiting himself to the application of the psychoanalytic method.

It is a *Wednesday (s-395)*. (The numbering indicates the session number from my notes. I include it to give the reader an approximate idea of the stage of the analytic process.) The patient sits on the couch, just as she did yesterday, with a demeanour of determination to stay in that position. In her attitude there is a mixture of provocation and inability to lie down, in other words, to lose sight of me. She remains alert to any indication from me in this regard. The subject of the couch is quite frequently a conflictive one, as I shall go on to consider when discussing the setting with these patients. As on other occasions, I accept her inability to lie down and wait to find out something more.

She says that she is not doing well at all and that, as she revealed to me yesterday, she was with J (a male friend we had talked about at other times, associated to the analyst. This is a delicate subject to deal with, as by making an interpretation which addresses the displacement there of the type of relationship she hopes to have here, a relationship of reciprocity which would provide her with all the affection she would hope for from a romantic relationship—she understands it as a censorship). She was not doing well even before seeing the friend, because of the "disastrous" literary prize that she was not awarded, and, as such, was hoping to find comfort, affection, and love in him. (On Monday the patient informed me of this disappointing result.) But it did not go as planned. Seeing that he was not responding affectionately, she asked him for an explanation. He replied that he loved her just as a friend, because he is married with a child. She replied that this was not what he had led her to believe at other times, as he would take particular interest in her. The friend did not remember any such show of affection, and she was very hurt by this.

While she is explaining all of this to me, the patient appears very anxious and distressed. She needs to get up and walk around the room, as she often does in similar situations. Right off, she warns me not to repeat the same old things to her, when she is feeling low like this. As I am learning, this type of warning is often a preview of what for her will be confirmed later on, whatever I say. So, for quite some time, I confine myself to listening to her. But I also know that if I merely listen, she will become increasingly distressed.

Sure enough, Ms B is feeling increasingly desperate because she finds herself alone after this disappointment. Neither does she find the support she was hoping for from her conversation with a friend with whom she has been talking things through lately. Besides, she is scared of, and dislikes, the homosexual component of her feelings towards this girl. For example, a few days ago she went back to having "against the rules" masturbatory fantasies, as she calls them, in which the girl performed cunnilingus on her. However, the fantasies were more complex, as she also fantasised that she performed fellatio on the male friend, and at one point the image of the analyst was present as a figure that put a stop to these fantasies. At this point, I intervene to tell her something to the effect that perhaps it has become difficult for her to hope that here she might be able to find the help she needed, when she felt so disappointed and unloved.

She replies that this is quite right, and that here the only thing I am able to do is repeat the same old things, and she does not want that. What she needs is affection, to be loved, while I only give her a professional relationship, and she does not know what she is going to do feeling so alone like this, without anyone to love her. She wishes she could die, that she could throw herself through the window . . . She does not want this type of relationship any more, as it is always the same. (She is raising her tone of voice, until she is shouting in absolute desperation. I feel increasingly unable to do anything, but my hesitance to do anything other than listen to her makes her more desperate. As her shouting gets louder and louder, my concern is if the situation escalates further and somehow spills over into her doing some kind of violence to herself; not so much to me, although I cannot rule it out entirely . . .) She continues to shout at me, telling me that I do not help her.

I try to tell her that, right now, the help I am able to offer her is being there listening to her and, in some way, sharing the difficult time she is conveying to me. She contemptuously dismisses the idea that what I do for her serves any purpose whatsoever. (At that moment I do, in fact, feel that I am nothing; she returns everything that I try to do for her, made into nothing. Thus, I must take a step back so I can observe the reality and grasp that my doing nothing is not true: it is not easy to attend to the patient's desperation, and to remain next to her without adopting an attitude of rejection, rather than trying to think of the best way to help her. Therefore, I feel as though I need to demonstrate an assertive attitude to curb that tendency to attack me by devaluing me and which she cannot control herself.) So I say to her, in a clear voice, that it is not true that I do nothing for her; for the entire session time (almost forty minutes have passed) I have been trying to listen to her pain and desperation that she is bringing to the session.

Ms B sits down on the couch, lowering her tone of voice a little, although immediately goes back to expressing her desperation. "So what am I going to do, now? Where do I go? I don't want to go home." She adds that she has not felt understood by her mother, because of other issues. And before coming to the session she told her father that she would like to have a conversation with him when she got back, thinking she would explain about her disappointment with the friend, although she had her doubts, as it could be a cause for concern for her parents, as they disapprove of the friendship because he is a married man.

I tell her that it seems that today she was not expecting me to be able to help her; her mind was made up that I would also disappoint her. Anticipating that the session would not be adequate, she had already arranged to speak with her father later.

Her reply is one of irritation. "See? It's true. You always tell me the same things, you always repeat yourself. Always the same old thing. Tell me something new. Tell me something different." (The patient gets up and paces, anxious and upset. She raises her voice again, shouting.)

(For my part, I acknowledge that in some ways she is right, that I do not tell her anything new. Maybe she needs me to help her to understand her acting out in the relationship with her friend, and what this means in relation to transference.)

I tell her that she has come to the session very disappointed because her male friend did not respond as she had hoped. Perhaps it is difficult for her to accept the fact of knowing, judging by what she has told me, that this is not a relationship that can develop, because the other person already has his own family life. Perhaps she might need to keep hoping that she was going to find, in that relationship, the reciprocity she does not have here, because she also knows that it would not be appropriate here, possibly as a way of keeping the relationship with me within a professional context.

She replies, very annoyed, because what I have just told her is that her male friend does not want her and neither do I. So, what is she to do. "Why go on living like this?" She cannot return home like this. She wants to die. (We are about to finish up, and I have another patient shortly afterwards, so I am under pressure in that she seems determined not to leave if I do not offer her some concrete response to her demand.)

I say that we have experienced similar situations of desperation before and it was possible to overcome them, because there is continuity to the sessions. She replies that it is not the same, that today is worse than other days, and that today is worse than ever.

I show my agreement, that each session is never the same, and that the pain is so intense every time in situations of desperation that it is not useful to point out that she has gone through this before. And it is true that having to finish here is very difficult now, but she has been able to use this session to express her pain, so perhaps this affords her some hope that tomorrow we can continue with this.

I am still not entirely sure how all this is going to turn out. We go over her hour by a few minutes. The following patient rings the buzzer and she sees me push the automatic door entry system. She stopped shouting when she heard the buzzer. Shortly afterwards, I get up and say that we can continue tomorrow. She picks up her bag and leaves without saying goodbye. I am left slightly uneasy, and annoyed at the same time. I am left with the bad feeling that the session has not gone well, and that I had serious difficulties in thinking and offering her other explanations or comments that could have helped her more. I do not know where she will go, but judging by what has happened at other times, I do not have the impression that she would harm herself. It would appear that the important thing is to make me feel as bad as she feels, although I also think that lately our experience has been that when misunderstandings occur between us, or she feels upset by something in analysis, causing her to become depressed or desperate, her recovery is often much quicker than it was at one time.

The following day, *Thursday (s-396)* at midday, the patient calls to tell me, calmly and carefully that she does not know if she will be able to come to the session because she feels weak, with little energy, as she has her period at the moment. I tell her that, as there are still three hours or so until her session time, we can wait until then and see if she feels up to coming.

When it is time for her session, she arrives punctually. As is her habit, she starts looking for the packet of cigarettes in her bag full of things. I often wait on foot for her to finish. When she finally finds the packet and leaves the bag on the chair, I sit down, but she gets up again to take off her jacket and goes to lay it on the chair. She looks at me and smiles, saying, "You got tired of standing up." (I smile slightly. I think that she must be worried by my tiredness with regard to yesterday's session.) She sits on the couch and, looking at me, she remarks, "Let's see if I can . . ." while she lies down.

A few minutes go by, two or three, in silence. This is not usual, since normally she begins talking immediately. She seems calm to me, which I find surprising after yesterday's session. But I did understand the telephone call as an attempt at reconciliation on her part, as well as a way to check my state of mind after yesterday's difficult session: would I be angry, or even aggressive? Would I turn her away? Could she be sure that she would not come to any harm from me? She also anticipates her state of physical weakness, perhaps as notice that she is not up to continuing her attack or for me to respond forcefully. I also feel that the silence during this time is a continuation of that desire for reconciliation. Although I do not know what has happened to everything that was mobilised in yesterday's session.

P: So, when I was silent just now, I was thinking about how before, as soon as I arrived, I would need to start talking. It is as if there has been a qualitative change. [Qualitative? I ask.] Yes, because before coming I felt the need to talk about things, about what I've been thinking about. Once I got here I see that I can be quiet [she pauses].

A: It seems that you are more able to be with your feelings, your experiences, and to tolerate them. Unlike other times, when you need to express them immediately, as if in that way, you establish a kind of continuity between you and I, and what is inside of you passes immediately to me.

P: Yes, I wanted to talk to you about just that, after everything that happened in yesterday's session . . . I felt so bad and so desperate when I came out of here that I didn't know where to go. Remember that I told you that I didn't know what to do, that I didn't have anywhere to go? So I started walking. I remembered that the day before I had also walked a little to get to the date with J [the male friend who had let her down]. So I started walking, thinking about the session, and I started to calm down. I was thinking that I had felt so bad with you because I could not bear seeing you so calm and quiet when I was in such a bad way. And thinking about it, I realised that my intention yesterday was for you to be like me. For you to go through what I was going through . . . I don't know if you understand me . . .

A: In other words for me to take in your experiences, your discomfort, your feelings.

P: But not just in the sense of you listening to me. No. But as if you were me. For you to experience everything that I was going through . . . The fact is it drove me crazy seeing you so professional . . . Although I still think that what you were saying to me may have been inadequate, as I wanted more . . .

A: And, as such, the pressure that you put on me, pressing the point of how desperate you felt and how I could not do anything for you, was a way of making me feel your desperation, above all at the end, when you insisted that you did not know where to go.

P: And when I thought it through I calmed down. So I kept walking. I thought that it would be good for me. And that today I would come here and explain that I was able to walk a long stretch of road by myself. [Walking to the session is a challenge she had rarely even considered.] When I arrived at what I consider to be the beginnings of my neighbourhood I thought I had already walked quite enough, as there is a slight incline and the going was difficult. I waited a little while for the bus, but as it was taking a while I decided to carry on walking, and that's how I made it all the way home. Imagine, getting home from here on foot! It's the *first time* I've ever done that [she pauses].

A: [This was moving, because it constitutes an important achievement, seen from the patient's perspective.] Perhaps the fact that I was able to resist the pressure you needed to place on me yesterday, for me to go through what you were going through, allowed you, once outside, to also be capable of walking alone.

P: [She pauses.] Yes . . . but I actually also saw some shoes I liked in the shop window. [I had already noticed that she was wearing new shoes today and I thought that she had actually needed them.] I remembered when, the previous year, I had bought some shoes and I told you about it, because I didn't know if it was a whim, and you asked me if I needed them. And it was true, I did need them. So, yesterday, I was able to see that I also needed them now and so I bought them. And I was happy. Besides they were cheap. And I like them.

A: So it seems that it is possible for you to be able to walk in your own shoes, that is to say, to be in silence at the beginning of the session with your own experiences, without the urgent need for me to go through your experiences with you, for both of us to be in the same shoes, perhaps. Because, if not, you would feel alone and abandoned.

P: Actually, that's the impression I've been left with this week. When I came here on Monday disappointed over the prize, I had the sense that I would have to do the session by myself. And that was what I felt on Tuesday, too. And on Wednesday I just couldn't take it any more . . . It was as if I needed . . . it occurs to me now, *to have a twin*. You know what I have told you before, that you have a twin brother or that I have a twin sister? Well, it wasn't that this time, but rather *you would be that twin brother* of mine, so that everything I go through you also go through . . .

P: [Pause of several minutes.] I was remembering a conversation with someone who talked about drug addicts, about the fact that when they are cured of the addiction, they enter into a stage when they feel monotony and boredom. So now, as I feel better at this point in time, it is as if there is that fear of entering into that state.

A: Perhaps you prefer to call boredom and monotony what may be, in fact, just the opposite. Because you are telling me that this is the first time you have walked home from here. And lately you have spoken from time to time about new feelings you are experiencing for the first time. Which, in one sense, is cause for satisfaction, but, in another, for concern, because of your difficulty in tolerating these new emotions.

P: [Brief pause.] Today, I came by taxi, and the taxi driver was a man who was really quite unpleasant, a bit rude, and I thought, "Well, look, things in reality are like this, it's not all poetry". And then I went on to think, "Well, perhaps the fact that not everything is poetry allows there to be poetry".

A: So it seems possible that the fact that not everything is always fine, not everything is the same, not everything is poetry, and I don't think or experience exactly as you do, this is what enables "poetry" to emerge. In other words, it enables something new to be understood to emerge here, and, in that sense, even a kind of creativity.

P: [Pause.] I am thinking now that you, by being different to your patients, and we all of us have our own issues, that really must provide you with the opportunity to be creative . . . [Pauses.] [Although at times the patient has to turn her head, she is able to stay lying down. At this point, she also turns around to say] Anyway, I wanted to thank you for everything that happened in yesterday's session . . . [pause].

A: I am now thinking about the fact that you needed to call before coming, because you doubted if you could, as you did not feel at all well physically. But physical discomfort that stops you from attending is something that has happened at other times, after sessions during which the experience of aggression here has been very marked. Perhaps you needed to call to find out if I was willing to see you.

P: Actually, I was hoping you would tell me to come to the session, and when you left it up to me, it was a bit more difficult. It was hard for me to come. I was in my room feeling, I don't know . . . just tired, weak, thinking of the effort it would take to get here. Then, I saw the new shoes. I put them on and I felt good. Then, I thought I could get dressed. And I did. And once I was dressed, I started to feel better physically, well enough to come to the session. But at the same time I was thinking that if I was better, I didn't need the session. [She is silent for a few minutes. She asks if it is time. I tell her that there is still a little while left. She remains in silence for a few minutes more until she gets up when there is one minute remaining. And, smiling, she says] OK, well, that's fine for today. [She thanks me, sincerely, as she usually does when there have been difficult points during the session.]

Comments on the two sessions

These sessions reflect, in one sense, the patient's tendency to breach the analyst's boundaries, not only in regard to the conditions of the setting, but also to the barriers between her ego and mine. Establishing a relationship, a link, is not possible if there is not that *co-experience* of her within the analyst. Any response of mine that does not coincide with this is received as a rejection, or, even more so, as leaving her out in the cold, in the desert, the void, and so on, to use expressions that she herself has used at other times.

However, as I do not let her destroy the "office partition walls", as she once remarked, both in standing firm on my setting conditions, devoting myself exclusively to her during her session time, and in not allowing her to invade me with her emotional life, her reaction is to reject everything I say.

This is what happens in the first session. The tremendous frustration involved for her in not being one of the winners of the poetry competition made clear first the extent to which there was a delusional conviction that she would win it. Consequently, the problem that arises in Wednesday's session (and in the two previous sessions) is her statement that when she communicates her huge and indescribable feelings of frustration, my response is not to also become depressed along with her, and neither do I respond in an omnipotent way, but I am "calm and very professional" in trying to help her in so far as I am able. That is what is unbearable to her, experiences like this that reveal, as we see in Thursday's session, that she and I are not in the same shoes, or, rather, both in mine. Or that is what appeared to be the case, that she could not bear it, according to what she tried at all costs to let me know at the end of Wednesday's session, with the idea that she did not know where to go, and how could I let her leave in that state. However, and to her surprise and mine, not only could she tolerate it, but it also gave rise to certain internal changes in her capacity for containment in her own psychic life. Indeed, once she leaves, the result of that relationship in which I have not let myself be invaded by her, is that she has been able to introject my assertiveness. It speaks volumes that, for the first time, she is able to make the journey home on her own two feet. Not only that, but she is able to buy herself some new shoes, to walk by herself.

With this, she reflects her ability to separate herself from the analytic relation. Walking home alone, with her new shoes, means truly becoming aware that each step she takes of her own volition involves increasing the distance between her and me. On Wednesday, she tried to remove that distance between us, by trying to make me feel what she was experiencing: turning me into her twin brother. I did not accommodate this; rather, I provided the experience of the possibility of sharing, in some way, her suffering, but with me staying in my own "shoes". Thus, I was not driven to despair along with her and neither did I, by contrast, try to trivialise her desperation, and I think that that was what, outside of the session, allowed her to introject that capacity and, thus, to shore up her tolerance of separation. The purchase of the new shoes unmistakably symbolises the matter. She had been trying to put herself in my shoes-mind so that I would experience her emotions, and when I did not accept this, she learns to change her "old shoes-mind" for new ones. In other words, she changes her old mental functioning, where space is always shared, for a new one in which she can begin to have her own mental space. She also demonstrates this by being able to remain in silence at various times during Thursday's session, thus tolerating her own feelings. In spite of how difficult this new experience was at Wednesday's session, the patient was able to return on Thursday, overcoming her concerns (reflected by physical weakness) regarding whether she would be able to face the analytic relationship. Admittedly, she needed to call to receive my support to come to the session, which, curiously, she took for granted; that is to say, she did not fear my rejection in spite of her devaluation or attacks on what were, as she clearly stated, inadequate responses on my part. But, in the face of the fact that I was continuing in my own "shoes" by letting her take the decision to come, she was then able to put herself in her own shoes and assume responsibility for the decision.

Her description of how her decision to attend the session came about is very eloquent: she saw the new shoes and put them on, then she got dressed, and once she had done this she felt strong enough to come to the session. Admittedly, she still needs to turn to concrete objects that represent actual events, in this case, being able to separate herself from the analyst, from his office to her house, and these are what now enable her to tolerate the re-encounter with him. In this sense, the patient still needs that form of pathological symbolisation, of the object's equivalence to what it represents. There is also something else: her tolerating lying on the couch, without seeing me and being silent with her feelings, which would indicate a capacity for introjection of an analytic relationship "separated" from the external, the concrete. Also her sincere thanks, afterwards, for everything I had to bear for her to be able to learn from this experience. The patient has been able to achieve a more evolved form of symbolisation during the course of the session, which allows her to understand the transference interpretation regarding being in her shoes and not in mine; being in her mind and not in the analyst's.

Returning to the theme of pathological splitting, one of my reasons for presenting this material is that we can see that this is a very particular type of splitting related to her tendencies to establish a fusional relationship. In the first instance, the patient fails to achieve a fusional kind of relationship, the one that she refers to as a relationship of "reciprocity". The subject needs the object, in the same way that the object needs the former. To the extent that such fusion fails, it is when that particular form of splitting—the "twin experience" with the analyst—arises, which is what she claimed had happened in Wednesday's session. The twins (she is implicitly referring to identical twins), although they experience the same emotions, are no longer part of the same whole; rather, each has his or her own physical individuality; they are two bodies that occupy different points in space. That is to say, there is physical splitting (two bodies) and, at the same time, emotional fusion. Thursday's session is when the patient becomes aware of this; it is an insight into this particular pathological splitting/

fusion. This is possible to the extent that I do not accept the role of twin and keep myself in my own shoes-mind. So this forces her to go somewhat further and accept that neither is it true that I am her twin. She must then go with her own shoes-mind, which she had to buy since the old ones—trying to be in the analyst's mind—are no longer of use to her. Therefore, she needs me to clarify nothing more. She does need my intervention when, straight away, the psychotic part attempts to disparage that achievement, anticipating a state of boredom and monotony, such as with addicts after treatment. This allows me to expose the fallacy of that argument, as she has spoken to me of how exciting it was to walk in her own "shoes", as well as how moving it was to gradually discover new feelings.

So, one of the problems in technique arising through working with this type of patient is striking a balance, which is not always possible, between the assertiveness necessary to prevent psychotic organisation from drawing the analyst into enactments to save the patient from coming to terms with what is his responsibility, and showing that this does not signify rejection.

Drawing upon the material from these two sessions, there are other possible factors that demonstrate the dynamics of the PsPO: for example, the question of the setting, which I shall deal with in Chapter Seven. We see that, in the first session, the patient does not lie down on the couch, whereas in the following session, she does, although I do not refer to this subject in these particular sessions. However, it is the patient herself who, as a result of the change that took place in her after the experience of the first session, who makes the effort to lie down during the second session. My interventions here show two elements that I consider significant in the treatment of psychotic patients. One, that of defending one's statements when there is conviction within the analyst to do so, without seeking to convince the patient; the reality that I observe and work through is the one I am able to defend. If I am then mistaken, I will have to put it right. It is not true, as the patient was claiming, that I was not doing anything during the Wednesday session. The other question is that of trying to interpret in the transference whenever possible. Precisely because of the extreme intensity and fragility of the relationship established by the psychotic patient, time and time again it was necessary to show her what was taking place in her relationship with me. Thus, in Wednesday's session, I had to relate her acting out with her male friend to the analytic transference, in spite of her irritation with, and devaluation of, my intervention. Perhaps what fostered the patient's capacity to tolerate "walking home in her own shoes" alone were not merely my interpretations but, and perhaps above all, my attitude of tolerating her pressure.

In the clinical material I have just presented, we can pick up on various forms of projective identification. In Wednesday's session, it seems clear that communicative and evacuative PI are present at the same time, so it is very difficult to clearly demarcate them. The patient is experiencing an exceedingly painful episode owing to the combined disappointments of the prize she did not win and her male friend's rebuttal of her romantic aspirations, compounded by what she considers as a rejection by the analyst in the sense of him not accepting a relationship of reciprocity. The pain is so intense that she must apply almost all of her leverage (she does not lie down on the couch, she walks around the office, she screams, and devalues any intervention I make as inadequate). Through that attitude she truly makes me feel how painful the situation she is experiencing is for her; I am able to make contact, to feel her desperation. However, this does not mean that I must consent to her aspiration to resolve it her way.

At the beginning, she communicates her pain to me (communicative projective identification), but the necessary response of containment from me, by tolerating the pain she is transmitting to me, attempting to metabolise it and to think about it, no longer interests her. Hence, she must keep up the pressure to cause me to act (evacuative projective identification?). In fact, her motivation behind the intention of making me act is somewhat different to what I propose to her: it is not that she is causing me to feel her pain, thus freeing herself of it, which would correspond to evacuative PI; rather, she hopes for more. We know that, by means of communicative PI, the patient is seeking to inform the object of her discomfort or need, but this alone is not sufficient; it is also necessary for the object to provide some response to alleviate or meet her need. The difficulty for the psychotic patient is that she is hoping for a particular reaction as the only valid response in order to meet her need or alleviate her discomfort, not the one most appropriate to her need. The patient exerts tremendous pressure on me to experience her desperation up until the very last minute of the session, when her intention is to make me believe that she feels so bad and so misunderstood by everyone that she does not know where to go. This is an attempt to make me allow an exception by lengthening the session time, including postponing my obligation to my next patient. The session ends, and, clearly, the patient has left me with much of her discomfort. So, here we could say that the patient evacuates her desperation into me. Yet, the patient's response, once out of the session, offers a different perspective, in the sense that she has been able to take on board my attitude of assertion by not giving way in the face of her pressure to achieve a particular kind of return of her projective identification, and little by little, as she moves away from the analyst, she has been able to introject that assertiveness. Therefore, the projective identification that began as communicative, then turning to be an attempt at control (the only response of any worth was the one she wanted from the analyst), and eventually evacuative (she leaves me with her despair), now, outside of the session, finally transforms once again into a communicative PI, by accepting what I return to her. In other words, a capacity for containment that she has introjected.

In terms of the delusion of the "analyst as twin brother", it is clear that the way the patient portrays trying to make me into her twin brother is an attempt to make me feel precisely what it is that she is experiencing. So, although to all intents and purposes similar to projective identification, here, in contrast, there is a clear understanding that these are feelings that she acknowledges as her own. It is not that she is seeking to rid herself of them, but for me to also experience them alongside her. Thus, we are faced with yet another modality. We have already drawn the distinction of this "twin" state in relation to a fusional state; in the latter, the subject's aim is for subject and object to be one and the same, for them to be in the same "shoes". By contrast, in the twin state, there is a clear distinction between two bodies, but those bodies feel the same thing. Here, the aim would seem to be that if there is someone who lives everything I feel, even in another body, I will not feel so alone, which is a source of relief.

Negative therapeutic reaction (NTR) and splitting of the corporal self

In order to explore the idea of pathological splitting in more depth, let us take a look at the following, which significantly continues from the previous material. In this instance, the splitting is referred to the actual corporal self. At the same time, it will enable us to observe the negative therapeutic reaction.

Before this, I would like to note that the publication of the previous material in a journal would illustrate the patient's internalisation of the analyst's assertiveness in the fulfilment of his analytic function, highlighting one of those moments of analytic insight possible in psychotic patients, and which justify the potential for analytic work with them. The space limitations of a paper do not allow for much more. By contrast, the breadth of a book gives us room to go further and to reveal the complexity and difficulty in maintaining this breakthrough, owing to the workings of the psychotic part, which seeks to hinder and destroy it. Hence, the immensity of the task of psychoanalysis with these patients, which requires infinite patience to make and remake, time and time again, that which the psychotic part attempts to undo time and time again.

The following day (to s-396), Friday, the patient calls saying that she has not been feeling well since earlier that morning. She feels weak, and she checked her temperature, which was 37.5 degrees, which gave her reason to decide not to come to the session. Although the unwellness she feels is physical, it worries her to what extent this might relate to the situation she is going through now, but above all in relation to analysis. Quickly, before I have the chance to say anything, she goes on to tell me how things went yesterday with two friends she was looking forward to seeing but in the end their meeting did not take place. In this way, there is an attempt to do the session over the phone. After this she adds that she is concerned that analysis does not seem to be particularly contributing anything to her. (I feel surprised, following what, by all accounts, seemed to have been a satisfactory session yesterday, for which she even thanked me.)

I tell her that I wonder what could have happened yesterday to make her grateful for the strength she seemed to have acquired, whereas today she says that the session had not contributed anything, and she feels weak.

She says that when she left the session, she wondered what she had got out of it but could not find anything. That what she felt was boredom. It is true that she felt gratitude, but it was for what I put up with in the session the day before, and it was as if she had to force herself to express it, even if it was, in fact, heartfelt. But the sensation of boredom had stayed with her. This morning she felt so-so, which is the state that is least tolerable to her. She prefers being either very good or very bad, but not in between. She had thought a bit about the time when she had been very down and had considered suicide, when she had been admitted to psychiatric hospitals, but that she thought she had not been as bad as that. While at times it is a thought that she has, at others it is like a strong feeling that she is unable to control. (The patient speaks calmly and sedately, as if she were confiding to a friend on the phone about certain relatively importance reflections about herself.)

After five minutes or so, I see that the patient is still prepared to continue talking. Then, I tell her that I understand that she is concerned by this whole situation, in which, on the one hand, she feels grateful for our relationship here, but that this relationship is weakened, on the other. As such, it is something that we would need to talk about, and we would have the opportunity to do so on Monday, since today she has decided not to come because it would require a great deal of effort.

She replies that it seems that I do not want to talk on the phone. I tell her that it is more appropriate in the session, which is where we have been doing it. Somewhat put out, she says fine and we say goodbye.

Comments on Friday's phone call

The truth is that the patient's reaction had caught me by surprise. At first, it occurs to me that there might be some kind of perverse component in that response. I do not think the tone she uses, with such calm, necessarily reflects worry or concern, despite professing to feel it, so perhaps, instead, she is trying to induce it in me but, at the same time, she does not come to the session. In other words, she denies me access to the proper conditions so that I can help her. All of this, in point of fact, after a session in which she felt helped, which forces me to question if the session really was of help to her.

Initially, Thursday's session seemed to help her to understand the previous day's session. We might say that it was an extension of the previous session, and, as such, did not produce anything new. With this in mind, could it be said that everything we addressed on Thursday had been false, because it was not based on her immediate experience and, therefore, did not contribute anything new, as the patient says? Or was it a deception by the patient to make me believe that I had helped her in Wednesday's session? Did she need to make me believe it in order to appease me so that she would not feel in the wrong for how she had treated me in that session? Yet, I continue to believe that the patient's response to the difficult session on Wednesday was as a result of having introjected the analyst's assertiveness, without rejection, in spite of her attempts to pressure him. Therefore, I stand by my idea that the experience of Wednesday's session was positive, with her being able to separate herself from the analyst, and later express her sincere gratitude. This capacity for somewhat more strength was also reflected by her being able to remain in silence at various times during Thursday's session, tolerating her own feelings without needing to pour them out into her "analyst-twin".

Consequently, might Friday's phone call be understood as a negative therapeutic reaction? I think so, that it is an "attack" originating in the psychotic, envious part. In Wednesday's session, as she explained on Thursday, she could not bear my serenity, my professionalism, while she was suffering. The complaint is not that I am not receptive to her suffering, rather that I am able to take it in and tolerate it without being overcome by it. This is what is maddening and intolerable to her. So, perhaps, we might think that it is out of envy of my mental state that she wanted nothing more from me. What she did want is to destroy my mental state of calmness, by transforming it into her own. However, precisely the failure of her acting out of this envious aspect during Wednesday's session allowed her to incorporate the assertive and containing analyst, as demonstrated in Thursday's session. The problem is that, the very next day, on Friday, the envious aspect has been reactivated, to the extent that she tries to invalidate all of the work we have accomplished, both her and I, saying that I have not contributed anything to her, and what she feels is boredom and weakness. This confirms what she had already anticipated in Thursday's association with the plight of addicts who experience boredom after treatment; this in spite of her predominant feelings during the session being wellbeing and satisfaction. Today's telephone call, with the intention of having a session over the phone, I think is an attack on the setting motivated by that envious reaction. Because she does not even raise that possibility with me, she simply calls me thinking that we can just do the session over the phone. She has modified the setting and has tried to impose her own. Hence, I think we can talk of a negative therapeutic reaction.

Yet, if we return to Britton's (2015) idea regarding "severance" to rid oneself of a foreign body that proves to be unassimilable, we could consider something else. The patient introjects an aspect of the analyst, his assertiveness, but that means accepting the separation from the object: this is not an omnipotent introjection through which she becomes the analyst; rather, she merely takes on an aspect of him, and, thus, of someone who continues to be different to her. Could we not then understand the feeling of boredom on Friday as a form of severance and rejection of that particular aspect with which she had identified? The outcome is clearly a state of weakness, as she has rejected the strength she had acquired from the analyst. So it might be that in the NTR the envious attack is combined with the need to reject something that she cannot make her own yet, as she perceives it as foreign to her and, as such, threatening.

The material that follows may help us to further understand the situation.

The following Monday we were talking about her absence on Friday. It seems as though Thursday's session, in which we saw that it was possible for her to begin to walk in her life with her own shoes-mind was perceived as a huge demand on her. Consequently, her bodily response was one of debilitation, preventing her from walking to the session, so as to avoid being asked to continue to walk alone. This is another reason for the NTR, to add to those already given.

On *Tuesday (s-397)* she sits on the couch as she did yesterday, because she feels unable to lie down. She explains that she is giving up smoking, as she had already told me yesterday. It is really hard, and it is making her depressed (although she says this with a mixture of satisfaction and some humour). She insists that I believe that not smoking is making her depressed. Indeed, she is now lighting her second cigarette of the day, she explains to me (it is one o'clock in the afternoon, when she normally smokes more than two packs a day, and between four and five cigarettes each session). She says that this is making it very hard for her to quit. She feels a little disorientated, as if she is lost. As soon as she got up this morning she needed to call friends without knowing why, simply to talk to someone. What is more, she is alone at home as her parents are away. Yesterday, before her parents left, she had an argument with her mother and she is concerned that she might be having a bad time.

As she was coming here by taxi, she had a sensation like a longing for her legs to be cut off, so she would not be able to walk. She noticed a pushchair in the door of a shop, but you could only see the little girl's legs sticking out. And it suddenly struck her, she had been somewhat surprised by the fact that the little girl had legs. (I keep thinking about this association.)

She returns to the subject that giving up smoking is making her feel unwell physically, when, in fact, the initiative to attempt it has come from wanting to be physically well for the summer and go to dance classes which, according to her friend, will be good for her. But she has this feeling of being boundary-less, disorientated.

I tell her that, perhaps, the fact of having discovered that she has legs, that is to say, that she can begin to walk in her life by herself, in her own shoes, as we have been discovering, is something new that causes her some disorientation and bewilderment. Where to go? This difficulty is compounded by her giving up smoking with all that this appears to involve for her, as if it is something to cling to, and if she does not have it she feels disorientated, needing to find a friend to talk to, or now, here, sitting up so she can see me with her own eyes and thus find the physical reference of my body. But, perhaps, this deprives her of the possibility of looking inside herself to find her own internal references.

At first, she listens to me attentively, then becomes agitated. She says that I give her a hard time, that I do not value the efforts she is making, what it means for her to stop smoking . . . She gets up and storms out of the office, very irritated and shouting. After a couple of minutes, she returns. She sits down and cries, and then immediately lies down on the couch. She remains in silence.

I feel it is necessary for me to repeat the interpretation, although this time I nuance it slightly differently. I tell her that I am thinking about the image of the little girl, whose legs she had come across by surprise, and that this must relate to her own discovery of having legs; in other words, certain mental capacities to enable her to begin to walk in her life. And then it was as if I had told her, well, you have legs, you can walk by yourself, and whatever you do is simply a reflection of the effort you put in. And it seems to her that I do not sufficiently value the effort she is going to.

She listens to me, calmer. Every so often she cries. After a while, she sits up and apologises for sitting, but she cannot continue to lie down to talk to me.

She says that she surprised herself with her reaction a moment ago, that she must be more tense and depressed than she thought, and it must be because of how much she is affected by giving up smoking. She says that I can have no idea of what cigarettes mean to her, that she had never imagined she would be able, or even attempt, to quit, that smoking is something that forms part of who she is. I attempt to describe this effort in terms of how it relates to a situation of loss of something of herself, in the same way as the loss of the functioning of walking in the shoes-mind of another.

Comment on s-397

I think that acknowledging her capacity to "walk" in her life has been felt with sheer panic over what it means to have to accept that the possibilities of separation are also dependent upon her. Walking might involve her walking *away* from the object, in other words, detaching herself from it. She has just been complaining in her life about how it is the object that walks away, and separates itself from her. She frequently interprets this as an expression of rejection, and cannot conceive that separation is part of reality. Now that she sees that she is able to walk in her own "shoes" she is faced with the reality that separation from the object might also be dependent upon her. She cannot bear it when I make the recognition of this new capacity explicit, hence her reaction to cut (attack/sever) the session, walking out and returning, as a way to erase what I have said, although now she can lie down on the couch and listen to what I say.

In addition, there is the fact that she is giving up smoking in order to be fit enough to take dance classes this summer; that is to say, to be prepared to better tolerate the absence of analysis.

In the following session, *Wednesday (s-398)*, she continues with the subject of giving up smoking, which is causing conflict with her mother. Ms B is complaining that I have not been helping her lately, that she has to reach her limits to force me to respond and tell her anything, that it seems as though I do not realise what a bad time she is having and all the efforts she has been making, and so there comes a time when she simply cannot control the situation, such as what happened yesterday, and then she feels bad, which is why she apologised, in all sincerity. She acknowledges that she needs a wall, a limit, to put a check on that discontent, and that this is brought about by affection, which is something that I do not give her. The patient makes a direct and strong complaint regarding her dissatisfaction with what

I bring to her, turning it into almost nothing. Her complaint now relates particularly to my not giving her an explanation for why giving up smoking is affecting her so much. She insists that quitting smoking is one of the most difficult things she can imagine, and if she were able to do it she would be up to resolving other problems in her life. Smoking is something that has always been closely bound up with the relationship with her mother. It has been the main "sticking point" between them. After her intervention, she urges me to tell her something about all this.

I tell her that she is talking about the issue of smoking, which is bound up with the conflictive relationship with her mother, perhaps in the same way that, here, the fact of her lying down on the couch or not appears to be. I might have a particular interest in getting her to submit to me, perhaps. Then I would not see the efforts that she has been making, both in giving up smoking and when she lies down, as a form of starting to walk by herself.

She says that I only tell her what she has told me, that I do not tell her anything new, or very little. "And you are there in your armchair without batting an eyelid while I am going to such huge efforts."

I feel, as in many other similar occasions, that the patient is unfair to snub the effort that I am making. I tell her that my impression is that I have indeed told her something different. I think it is necessary to adopt a firm tone, to set a limit and not let myself be invalidated. "It is true that you are making an effort, but I can tell you that, for my part, I am also making an effort. [At this point, the patient, who had been sitting on the couch, lies down.] But if what I have said is received by you as meaning little or nothing, I think there must be a disagreement, a gap between you and me."

The patient continues to listen carefully to me. I continue, "I am thinking about what has taken place over these past few days since your disappointment over not being awarded a prize, or not gaining recognition for your writing. Prior to the prize, you had the experience of feeling like a genius; perhaps it is that genius aspect that you are able to acknowledge yourself which is acting with strength, and, from the particular viewpoint of genius-you, it is difficult for you to value and to acknowledge my modest effort."

P: [She is silent for a few minutes; she continues to lie down, without turning her head.] Well, the thing is you have not valued all the effort that I am making, especially with the issue of trying to give up smoking. It's making me depressed ...And the thing is, I need affection.

A: Perhaps the affection you are able to receive here, to the extent that I acknowledge and value your efforts?

P: [She nods.] I think that this whole thing of quitting smoking has been like a way to try to overcome the problems that were affecting me, my depression over the prize, the fact that the relationship with J [the married friend who is only interested in friendship with her] is not working, the fact that we are having problems here. And if I stopped smoking I would be able to overcome all that. But by stopping smoking, I feel disorientated, I'm all in disarray, as if I had lost my bearings.

A: In other words, perhaps I have not been sufficiently able to appreciate all that your attempt to give up smoking signifies, in terms of a deprivation which causes you to relive many other experiences of deprivation and lack.

P: Yes, I have been feeling like I did during the time when I was unwell. As if I had gone back to then, when I was disorientated, as if I had lost everything that I gained here since I've been coming ... Last night, I had a feeling a bit like when I was unwell in that, although I was smoking, I had the impression that the tobacco was missing, because I thought that they had sold me a packet of cigarettes that they had removed the nicotine from. And that would manifest into a state similar to the one I had last night, though not quite as strong. I had the sensation that I was lacking blood flow to my brain and airflow to my lungs ... So, I wanted to ask your advice. What do you think, should I give up smoking, or not?

A: And so, the fact that you are attempting to give up smoking is rather more serious than it seems; it is a deprivation that you experience as the loss of something vital, like the blood to your head, or the air to your lungs, but it is as if it were something that you also need for your mental life.

[The patient listens carefully. And when I stop talking, she remains in a reflective silence.]

A: And, therefore, I think that you are hoping that I can truly realise that when you contemplate some kind of change in your functioning, in your habits, this involves a tremendous effort towards mental change. [In this session, the patient has been smoking, as if she were returning to her habitual frequency.]

Comments on s-398

I think that when the patient asks me to act as a wall for her, it is because she is extremely anxious, and truly fearful of going crazy. Trying to give up smoking has involved losing a pseudo-containing substitute object. I now think that her devaluation of my contribution (albeit to a certain extent) does not come from the "genius" narcissistic aspect to the extent expressed in my interpretation; rather, it reflects her need to provoke me, to take me to the limit, as she herself says, so that I respond assertively, thus putting limits upon a situation that she is not capable of doing.

I think that, at this point, the patient's panic is related to the fact that her projections are not finding an object to project into, so that her experience is, therefore, that they would get lost in infinite space, plunging her into catastrophic anxiety. Hence, she needs to provoke in me a forceful and intense response that contains her. The limit or boundary that she is asking for at that moment would not so much be to control her destructive acting out as for her not to lose herself, so that her mental life does not end up scattered into the projections of aspects of herself which are then not returned to her, or are returned inadequately. In other words, the panic could be more closely related to her catastrophic anxieties, in the sense that we have already seen, in terms of disorganisation, disintegration, or liquefaction. Hence, her need to control the object, not so much to triumph over it, but to verify that it is strong enough to contain what she has projected into it.

We have also seen, as I tell her, the tremendous effort that any psychic change involves for her. Changing might mean losing her frames of reference that allow her some control over her projections. Any new situation, in that it is unknown, is more difficult to control.

Another question that emerges in this session is the fundamental significance of smoking to the patient's mental life. Her description of the organic state she finds herself in when she feels that she is lacking the active substance of tobacco, nicotine, is very expressive. Either through delusional experiences, such as those that occurred some time ago, when the nicotine was being removed from her cigarettes, or now, giving up under her own volition, it is as if the nicotine were a basic principle for the functioning of her brain and lungs, the element that provides "blood" to her brain and "air" to her lungs. So, nicotine would become akin to the nutritive principle that she gives herself for her mental functioning. Like the addict, if she does not have the drug this produces a profound personal and organic disturbance within her; she feels disorientated, disorganised, lost, and with fears of disintegration. However, in contrast to what would occur in her delusional states where it was others who intervened so that she would give up smoking (by giving her cigarettes without nicotine), it is now she herself who is deciding to quit, who is wanting to use her own "legs", so to speak, or mental resources, to come to terms with her decision to change something.

At the same time, smoking involves a conflict in the relationship with her mother, which is substantiated by the idea that it is something that goes against the nourishing object: the patient attempts to make her mother feel that the substance that she extracts from the tobacco is more important to her life than what her mother is able to provide her. By making it so obvious for her mother to be aware of this, she achieves making her feel attacked, through her devaluation and contempt for her as a mother. Perhaps her mother might also feel continually accused, as smoking becomes an act that reminds her of what she has not given to the patient. Hence, what the patients says in terms of what her mother goes through with her smoking is something that goes beyond a mother's worry about the damaging effects of smoking on her daughter. In the mother's attitude in the face of her addiction to tobacco, the patient perceives hatred towards her; in all likelihood this is all of the hatred directed towards her mother, implicit in her smoking. It is then a situation in which the patient can easily project her own hatred, as she finds very suitable terrain in the mother's hatred, always concealed. Although her mother makes efforts to neutralise her hatred, adopting reasonable and sensible attitudes, the patient's insistence on smoking in front of her makes her end up showing her feelings of hatred against her daughter.

This situation is closely connected to what the patient has made me experience frequently in the sessions. Although not in regard to tobacco, despite her smoking throughout the sessions, one cigarette after the other, in all probability to test if I, too, might take the bait of it becoming a "sticking point" between us. However, as I have never said anything to her on this matter, there is no problem, although, at times, when she has smoked less during the session, she has drawn my attention to this with satisfaction, the implication being that this was because the session went well. By contrast, the "sticking point" with me has arisen over different ground: the transgressions of my working method, such as insisting over and over again on reading her writings during the session, and above all in her not lying down on the couch.

The issue of giving up the cigarettes is also an example of putting the experience of separation of the object in terms of concrete reality. However, my answer is to translate it into interpretative terms, that is, a more advanced symbolisation.

Pathological projective identification

Just as with splitting, the same thing happens with the unconscious fantasy of projective identification (PI). As I have already said, although first described by Klein (1987[1946, 1952]) as a defence, it has later also been recognised as a psychic phenomenon which is indispensable to the individual's development and to communication. If we consider it from the perspective of the beginning of life, this involves relying on a process that enables communication with one's environment to make it known when there are needs which call for the participation of others so that those needs can be met at a time when the individual cannot yet use verbal language. Here, we are talking about projective identification in its function of primitive communication, first described by Bion (1991[1962]). Again, as in splitting, when there is a failure in its functioning, the mechanism is forced in a pathological way, taking on diverse forms in the psychotic patient. PI, therefore, acquires the character of malignancy owing to the omniscient dimension of the fantasy, the massive nature of it, and the frequency of its use. What once constituted a psychic process in the service of the development of the individual's psychic life ends up becoming an anti-life, anti-development resort to pathological defences.

Rosenfeld (1988[1971]), in studying psychotic states, distinguishes several types of projective identification, giving them unequal importance. Initially, he differentiates between two: *communicative* and *evacuative* projective identification. Although, at times, they might manifest themselves together, it is important to distinguish when one or the other is predominant. To this end, Rosenfeld tells us, the analyst should be attentive to the patient's response to the interpretation: either by integrating it into associative discourse, in the first instance, or with rejection, in the second. He later adds three more. One that

Steiner (2008) refers to as possessive, in which the patient's aim is the control of the object, and another in which the patient experiences the fantasy of living within the analyst. This can take on two forms: one in which he experiences a delusional world that is completely absent of any pain and with absolute freedom to do whatever he pleases, and another, which he names parasitic, involves the patient behaving like a parasite living at the expense of the analyst's capacities. I believe that these two latter forms of projective identification, as set out by Rosenfeld, are particularly significant in the psychotic organisation, and we will be able to observe both in my patient. Earlier, when discussing s-395 and s-396 sessions, I gave a description of different types of IP.

Omnipotence and omniscience fantasies

In the psychotic patient, fantasy does not serve as a form of trial thinking, an early imagining of the possibilities of reality to be confronted, and which will then need to be checked and tested. Rather, fantasy takes the place of reality. In this case, we talk about a delusional idea rather than a fantasy. Yet, the delusional nature of the fantasy is clear at times, and less so at others, although even in the less serious patients we always find a level of fantasy invested with that character of conviction that takes the place of the reality, at least temporarily, and it will become a true delusion if this "fantasy" persists even after repeatedly checking it against the reality which contradicts it.

One of the consequences of the predominance of the omnipotent dimension in the psychotic patient's mental life is that it becomes a double-edged sword. On the one hand, the psychotic patient lives in the conviction that he can "master" reality in order to evade it. On the other hand, reality is perceived (through projection) with that omnipotent, maximalist, and absolute character, so that it ends up becoming a limitless reality, without measure, unfathomable ... and when things go wrong, and it becomes a persecutory reality, it does so in similarly absolute terms. The limitlessness and incommensurability of reality are elements that are sufficient to reactivate the catastrophic anxieties that were intended to be evaded with the psychotic defence mechanisms.

CHAPTER FOUR

Consequences of the dynamics of the psychotic organisation of the personality

First, I provide an overview of the consequences of the dynamics and psychopathological foundations presented in the previous chapter. I go on to present clinical material which gathers together several such repercussions almost simultaneously. This will take up the entirety of the chapter. The detailed description of these consequences, accompanied by the corresponding clinical material, I shall leave to the following chapters.

The consequences derived from a particular dynamic of the PsOP are merely alternative forms of making up for the limited mental container in order to manage the inevitable psychic pain of contact with reality. I do not intend to provide an exhaustive list of all the possible clinical manifestations resulting from psychotic functioning. I shall limit myself to those I was able to observe in the patient on whom this book is primarily based. Consequently, neither will I dedicate equal extension to each mentioned.

I shall draw a distinction between two areas: consequences on the personality itself, and "relational" effects. In terms of the effects on the personality, these can be seen in three significant areas: thought, the body, and acting out, which will acquire a presence and prominence that differs from what is usual in a personality where there is greater capacity for containment of psychic reality.

Consequences for the personality

Effects on thinking: limited capacity for symbolisation and predominance of concrete thinking

All symbolisation involves a painful element through the mourning implicit to the process of abandoning the object for the symbol that represents it. Capacity for symbolisation will be limited, to the extent that there is diminished tolerance to pain. Concrete thinking evades this process by perceiving an unmediated reality, that is to say, without representation. As such, reality *is* equivalent to that which is named or thought.

Delusional thinking

This is the other important consequence of the limited capacity for containment of psychic pain. When there is a predominance of non-psychotic functioning, thinking is the necessary detour to be able to conceive of the reality we perceive, with the tolerance of the pain concomitant to this conception. In the PsOP, there are grave difficulties in tolerating this process, and, consequently, the individual must organise his mind by way of the predominance of a conception of reality which is more tolerable: delusional thinking.

Somatic manifestations

When a personality with adequate capacity for containment predominates, we could say that the relationship between psyche and soma is psyche–soma in that order; in other words priority is given to the former over the latter. By contrast, in the psychotic organisation, when the use of the two previous areas has not been sufficient, at times the order is reversed: priority is given to the soma, in order that the body can become the receptacle of whatever has not been able to be contained in the mind. Thus, it manifests itself as hypochondriacal symptoms which, when they are intense, become somatic delusions.

Acting-out

To move to action is necessary in any non-psychotic organisation of the personality in order to cope with reality and transform it, but it includes a prior phase mediated by thought that anticipates and prefigures the action. In the case of the PsOP, thought activity is limited as a result of the reduced capacity for containment, making it necessary to act out as a prerequisite, in order to alleviate this pain, and to deny or attack the unbearable reality, afterwards. Otherwise, acting out takes place in terms of delusional thinking in an attempt to omnipotently modify the unbearable reality.

Relational consequences

Here, we come up against difficulties in communication, in both the patient's own internal communication and externally; in particular, we are concerned with those encountered with the analyst. The form of communication will also be affected with regard to the use of both verbal communication and the style of free association, as well as the use of extra-verbal communication. Likewise, it is worth noting the patient's perceptive hypersensitivity, in particular in relation to the object.

Other consequences

I shall also set out some of the other consequences that have been salient to me in my clinical practice, particularly the experience of mental void.

Clinical material. Plurality of channels of expression: emotional, somatic, and delusional

Ms B, as I said, has been diagnosed with paranoid schizophrenia. The following material summarises a month of sessions (from s-415 to s-424) after she had been hospitalised for three weeks, when she had been in analysis for just over three years. I shall set out the circumstances around her hospitalisation and its consequences, which were felt as a genuine trauma by the patient. Another question that will become clear from this material is the difficulty in maintaining the analytic setting.

During the weeks running up to the holidays, we had been talking about what the separation meant for her, as, judging by the experience of other years, we knew how difficult this was for her. I have had to limit my holiday period each year with her. The patient was reasonably in contact with this reality, in a depressive and anxious state in response to the fear of not being able to bear it, and with doubts over whether it was worse to talk about it, as she would become bad even before the holidays, and then there would be no way of not being depressed during and after them, too.

A week before the interruption, the patient begins to stop coming, with the idea that she did not need analysis, and she could cope on her own. On the first day of my holiday, she calls me to tell me that she had decided to go to the psychiatric hospital where she had previously been an inpatient, to see if Dr X, who had treated her then, would like to make love to her. As I must leave, I refer her to Dr M (the psychiatrist who is monitoring her medication), and I remind her of our scheduled sessions for after the two weeks' hiatus for my holiday.

On my return from holiday, the day before our first planned session, she calls me to inform me that she is doing badly; she has tried to attack her parents with a knife. At that moment, she was waiting for Dr M, whom they had told about it, and she was afraid they would hospitalise her. I remind her that the following day we have a session and we agree that she would try to come. That day, Dr M informs me that he saw Ms B yesterday afternoon, after she spoke to me, and that he accompanied her to hospital without any resistance on her part, contrary to what they had feared. Indeed, he opted to be accompanied by a male nurse in case there was any necessity to take her by force.

The week following her hospital admission, we arrange with colleagues at the hospital to grant the patient permission to leave, accompanied, on the two days a week already planned for her sessions during her hospitalisation, which was expected to be for two weeks. In view of the patient's significant physical impairment, the weakness and exhaustion that prevented her from moving around, I suggested coming to visit her at the hospital, which she readily accepted.

In my visit to the hospital, Ms B was rather drowsy and having difficulty getting her words out, probably owing to the prescribed medication, in seemingly high doses, since her state of anxiety and insomnia had not subsided easily. Nevertheless, she was able to explain her concern about the fact that she had had another breakdown. She was experiencing, or, in part, this was how I understood it and got her to see, that the hospitalisation many things in her life seemed to have been damaged, including the relationship with me and our joint analytic work, and it seemed as though she felt unable to overcome this situation. She explained it to me in delusional terms: humanity had gone through harrowing times, such as when there are wars, and after that it becomes difficult to overcome catastrophes. She did not have the strength. Leaving the hospital, she goes on to say during this interview, involved confronting the reality of the failure of the work we had done. She was hurt because her rage at feeling left alone by the analyst during the holidays had, in some measure, contributed to this failure; also, there was the huge difficulty of once again facing life's day-to-day struggles. Nevertheless, we agree that analysis might help her to take up this work once again, if we take it step by step. We arrange for her next visit to be at my office.

The patient does not come to the session, or to the next two planned sessions. When I was just about to suggest that we arrange another visit at the hospital, she calls me herself to say she is coming to the session.

This *first visit (s-415)* at my office is a Tuesday, with nine days since our last meeting at the hospital following her admission. She brings me a copy of her book, which has just been published. It has been twenty days since she was first admitted. She appears relatively calm to me. "*Uff*, there are so many things . . .!" she says. However, she spends the session talking about me. She sees that I am suffering a lot, she says, and that I am very alone because of everything I have to bear on my own. She senses a lot of loneliness in me, she insists. I comment that if she sees me as alone, she must doubt how I can accompany her in the many things it seems she would need to share and I to bear, as a result of everything that has happened during these interruptions. She protests a little, that no, this is about me, whether I wish to continue agonising alone. At another point she says that she feels like a hyena barking at the moon and adds, after a pause, "And you so proper and well dressed [I am wearing my regular clothes!] and me all dirty, with these clothes." I tell her that perhaps she is able to recognise my effort to give her companionship, while a part of her barks at me. And the other part, she asks? "Well, that is the part that knows I am, in fact, trying to give you companionship," I reply. She answers that she does not want to return to hospital, and the decision comes down to me. I explain to her that this is true to an extent, in the sense that it comes down to us, here, achieving more freedom of expression and her not feeling confined. But in another sense, I continue, there is the fear that she spoke of in the hospital, of the abruptness of leaving to suddenly find herself once again facing the things in her life and whether she really feels prepared for it. We arrange to meet at the next scheduled meeting, on Friday.

Friday's visit does not go ahead because she finds the door closed. I am left waiting for her at her session time. Shortly afterwards, I receive a call from her parents, who are worried as they doubted the patient's version of events; that she came to the session and that I did not want to receive her. I am puzzled, so I ask them to have her call me to clarify what happened. She calls back immediately, and when I ask her what happened, she replies that I know it perfectly well and hangs up. She calls again later on. In the meantime, I have spoken to her psychiatrist and I inform him of the situation, for him to pass this on to her, as he will be seeing her that afternoon. When Ms B tells me again that I know what has happened, I explain to her what must have happened, as far as I know. It would appear that a carer accompanied her to the session, as her parents were unable to do so. They found the lobby of my office closed, as the porter must have been out at that particular time; she must have left, but not for the hospital, as she had agreed, but for her parents' house. I acknowledge that this must have been very difficult for her, finding the door shut after all the efforts she has made in coming from the hospital. So an untimely coincidence had prevented her from having a session, but it seems as though she would prefer to think that it was me who, by choice, had not wanted to open the door to her.

The following days, *Thursday, Friday, and Monday*, the patient does not come to the sessions, although she has telephoned every day to explain why she is unable to come. At the beginning, she said it was because she felt physically weak. I mention that perhaps she felt that the relationship with me was also weakened after the bad experience of finding the door closed, but that if we did not have a session, the relationship might weaken further. Her response is that she is very depressed. I tell her that, to some extent, I can take responsibility for what she is going through because, after such a difficult month, when there was a chance to pick up on things here, as we spoke about, it would seem that I put a stop to it.

On Monday morning, she calls me to tell me that the financial situation at home is disastrous and, as a result, her parents will not be able to continue helping her to pay for treatment. Therefore, she will have to cancel the analysis, because she cannot afford it. I tell her that in any case this is something we can talk about, that even if financial circumstances made continuing psychoanalysis impossible, she should not have to interrupt her analysis right now, because, as we know, she is going through a fraught and difficult time. Apart from all that, I have the impression, I add, that when she talks to me about ruins, perhaps we can also understand this as referring to the ruined state of her relationship with me, as well as all of the work we have been doing over these years, as if all of this had been lost, with the sense that there is no way of getting it back. Although I think, I continue, that, in fact, because of all the work we have done, we can try to see what can be salvaged. Somewhat more animated and calm, she replies that perhaps yes, but she needs time to recover, and that we would be in touch. As I am afraid that this is a form of evading the "ruinous" relationship with me, I mention to her that precisely if she does not come, it might deteriorate further, so I would be there at her session time. She replies that she is not in such a hurry (in a pleasant tone), that she needs to recover and restore our relationship here, and that we would be in touch.

On Monday, shortly after her session time, she calls to tell me that she was unable to come because she had things to do, and that she would see how she feels tomorrow.

On Tuesday, she telephones halfway into her scheduled session, and, in a very weak voice, she tells me that she has been unable to come because she is still very depressed, and that she can hardly get out of bed, although she did manage to get dressed. I remind her of the ruinous relationship we had been talking about. She does not think that talking alone will get her out of this depression. I talk of the last session we held here, when she was still in the hospital, that she was worried about the difficulties facing her after her discharge, but willing to address them, although perhaps the depression of the relationship with me is making that task somewhat more difficult. She replies that she finds it hard to see how she can get out of this state, because the only way would be if there was authentic interrelation between her and I, and she does not see how this is possible now. At one point in the conversation, and in contrast to other difficult occasions, she expresses that she feels bad for me for not being able to come to the session.

Comments on the situation around the hospitalisation

The patient was unable to bear the separation of the holidays, in spite of the care taken to schedule less of an interruption than the previous year, but, even so, this was still a lot for her to cope with. Her initial reaction is to deny the separation—she no longer needs analysis—and to stop coming before the separation takes place. And just the day before the start of my holidays, it is she who rejects me, and I am replaced by the hospital psychiatrist whom she is going to ask to make love to her. That is to say, that faced with the intolerable reality of the separation from the analyst, she substitutes him for another professional with whom, in her fantasy, she might be able to consummate a complete relationship, including physically. To some extent, being hospitalised continues to be a way by which she "penetrates" wholly into the physical sphere (the hospital), which represents the psychiatrist substitute for the analyst. Of course, this announcement is tantamount to an ultimatum that she will make the analysis fail with a new hospitalisation if I continue to take my holiday. If I do not give in, she will also leave me with the concern of an immediate breakdown, thus projecting her discomfort into me, so that I cannot leave with my mind at ease. In order to deny the painful reality of the inevitable separation, she departs from the assumption that I am willingly abandoning her. So I refer her to the psychiatrist, who sees her for management of her medication, and I remind her of the dates we have scheduled for my return, thus assuring her of my commitment to be here then. Interestingly, the patient was able to last the seventeen days of the analytic holidays without breakdown. She did not need to go to "make love" with the psychiatrist at the hospital, by getting herself admitted there, as threatened. Yet, precisely on that penultimate day, the breakdown takes place, which she is at great pains to let me know.

It should be clear that she puts up no resistance to the hospitalisation because this is an acting-out directed against the analyst, to let me know that the analytic work that we have been doing has failed if this includes separation for the holidays. This is a vengeful reaction with perverse components, by her intention to make me suffer what she considers I made her suffer by "leaving her" to go on holiday. Waiting until the following day and coming to the session would have been to concede that I was right and that she had been able to wait until I returned, albeit with a great deal of effort. Admittedly, she is simultaneously troubled by this predominance of psychotic functioning, and feels bad for the damage she has done to the analyst and to the joint analytic work (the "ruin" she speaks of). Threatening her mother at knifepoint might have several meanings. First, she knows that physical aggression, and in particular against her mother, has been cause for her committal on other occasions prior to analysis, and, hence, with that acting-out, she "guarantees" her internment. So, too, her parents may be regarded as representatives of the analyst.

So, if "provoking" her hospitalisation involves an attack on the analyst, the patient cannot come back to my office because she feels very persecuted by me. By contrast, she is able to receive me in the hospital, where she considers herself more protected, as this is not the analyst's "turf". At the same time, she is worried by the state that the analytic relation is in, expressed via her delusional ideas with regard to the crisis of humanity, as well as her weakness, which is also expressed bodily, and which precludes her from dealing with the whole task of reparation of the ruined psychoanalytic work. She does not come to the following sessions as planned at my office, though she needs to maintain communication with me by phone. The "pretext" she adduces is her physical weakness. When she is eventually able to move around, the session centres on her concern for my suffering in solitude. In other words, not only does she project the suffering and loneliness that she has undergone during the holidays, but she places me in the position of being the one who really needs help and her as being the one who could give it to me. Through this, she attempts to make herself available for manic reparation for the damage she has inflicted upon the analytic relation.

The unfortunate incident of the closed office door when she comes to the following scheduled session, in an attempt to restore some trust in the analyst, convinces her that, sure enough, I did not want to receive her, because I have acted out my revenge, so she can now in turn feel hurt and cautious.

Before her return to the sessions, during the month of September, she called almost every day. She felt weak, tired, with little appetite and difficulty in digesting what she eats. She presents symptoms of a depressive, regressive state. Towards the middle of the month she calls to say that she has decided not to come back to the sessions because they were of no use in avoiding hospitalisation, although she acknowledges that they have helped her in other things. During those calls, I connect her difficulty in returning to analysis with the incident of having found the door closed the last time she tried to come to the session. Ten days later, she calls again and announces that she is weighing up the possibility of resuming treatment. That day, Monday, she does not come, but she does come the next day.

Later, hours before her *Tuesday session (s-418)*, I find a message from the patient telling me that she has an appointment with the doctor (the internist) as she continues to have "low [blood] pressure" [translator's note: in Spanish, the expression low *"de presión"* describes the physical condition of low blood pressure, but it is equivalent to the word "depression"], but she intends to come if she does not get any worse. She arrives on time. She looks rather well. I would even say that she has put on some weight. She is well groomed and has light make-up on. She gives me the second short book of poetry that has been published. She explains her motivation for thinking about returning to therapy. It is related to the matter of impossible love: her tendency to fall in love with people who are married and with whom there is no chance of having a relationship. She ended up making the decision to talk about it in the session.

A lot of things have happened over this time, she says, the worst being the "trauma of the hospitalisation". It has been very hard on her and very painful. Furthermore, this incident has come to show her the existence of aliens and the little machine and she would no longer stand for being misled by being told that they do not exist. I acknowledge that a lot of time has passed, and in difficult circumstances such as her hospitalisation, which we were unable to avoid from here, and her difficulties in resuming the relationship with me. She remembers when she called me on the telephone (the day just before the holidays) with such a strange—or crazy—idea, she says, of wanting to sleep with the psychiatrist at the hospital, and that is why she wanted to be admitted. I tell her that I remember it, and that it was precisely on the first day of my holidays. During the week that she did not come, and on my return, I was here, which she knew but perhaps felt that, by my leaving to go on holiday, I was abandoning her, and, consequently, it is she who then leaves me and brings on her hospitalisation.

She protests that, in any case, what she told me in the last session is still valid, that she was not prepared to be lied to over the existence of aliens (I did not remember such a thing). She goes as far as to say, "I think that you had something to do with my internment. Although later on I didn't think it was actually you, but Dr M [the psychiatrist who manages her medication] who interned me." I reply that so much time has passed, two months or so, with so many difficult experiences, without my being present with her, that I must have become someone very distant, like a stranger, to a certain extent. Perhaps my connection with her internment might be because this originated from me deciding to take a holiday, which created an unbearable situation for her. She replies that actually she thinks that I must be an alien myself, and she asks me if I am one. She also recalls that what she has mentioned beforehand, regarding whether I am the double, the twin of Dr PS, has been on her mind lately. That is, that there is the Dr PS that helps her and the Dr PS who rejects her. Perhaps the latter must be the alien, she concludes. I comment that if I were to tell her now that there is still a Dr PS who has been with her for several years, trying to help her, for example, in walking in her own shoes (she nods her head, and acknowledges that this is true), I do not know if this would make it possible to recover this Dr PS, although it seems as though the distant Dr PS, the stranger, is more present, even after so much time, the one who did not prevent the hospitalisation. I conclude by saying that, in any case, perhaps she will give it the benefit of the doubt and try to ascertain if it is possible to recover the Dr PS who helps her.

"Yes of course," she replies, "but if you were to tell me now that you are not an alien, I wouldn't believe that at all either." She is afraid, she adds, of getting involved with me again, and going back to the same old impossible story. On top of that, during the time before her hospitalisation, she was able to survive and to gradually regain her capacities and make use of them, or at least some of them. The publication of her second book has helped her. She came into contact with people who flatter her, and all of that, although she does not think they will stick around if she does nothing more. Neither does she want to come here every day and think that her afternoons are already filled up with the sessions, and be hung up on coming here all over again. So she thought that we could reduce them to two or three, so that the other days are for her, for her to make use of. Because if not, it would be like going back to being a child and an invalid, when lately, albeit with some difficulty, she has been able to use what resources she has to pull through and to survive. And she concludes, "But as now at this point in time there are so many things, perhaps we could continue with the daily sessions [five per week], and then gradually reduce them over a month, or something like that." I agree to leave this open. At the end of the session, she tells me that she has brought me her published short work with a great deal of excitement because, in some ways, it has been written from here, from the things we have been talking about.

Comments on s-418

During the whole month of September her low pressure [*bajada depresión*] has persisted, that is to say, her depression expressed somatically, although, immediately after her hospitalisation, her absence from the sessions seemed to be prompted by persecutory anxieties, by the fear of my vengeance for having made the treatment fail; the incident of finding my office door closed was a confirmation of my rejection. She needs several weeks of calling by phone, to see just how disposed I am, even threatened with the interruption of treatment. It is curious that the reason she adduces for returning should be her problem of falling in love with married people. In a way, the patient has been able to experience that my commitment is to my working method. To put it another way, my commitment is to the reality upon which this relationship is established. Ms.B is, therefore, able to recognise that she has a problem accepting her commitment to reality, and it is, in point of fact, here where, in analysis, it would be possible to examine this question.

Once in the session, she needs to go back over the "trauma of the hospitalisation" and the role that I played in it. It is still impossible for her to accept the reality of what happened: the analyst took a holiday in spite of how painful this separation was for her. She cannot conceive that the Dr PS who helps her would have been able of "abandoning" her, knowing what this interruption means for her. Therefore, there must have been some outside intervention, from aliens perhaps, and even I myself might be one of them. But in order to retain the Dr PS who helps to keep her intact, she must once again invent the twin brother who rejects her, the alien Dr PS, by means of radical splitting. She accepts my interpretation of reintegrating the Dr PS who helps her into the analytic relation, without diminishing her conviction of the existence of the other one, the one who left to go on holiday, the distant, almost alien-like one who was not able to avoid her hospitalisation. The theme of the analyst's twin brother—already mentioned when talking of pathological splitting—here takes on a different hue. On that particular occasion, Dr PS's twin was not a psychiatrist, was not married, and did not have a family. Whereas now, both twins are doctors, one who helps her and another who rejects her, both present, although I would not be able to say in what proportion; perhaps in equal parts or alternating, depending upon the point of time in the session. For example, she expresses her excitement in bringing me the short work she has had published because of what it signifies in terms of the fruit of our labours here; of course, with the Dr PS who helps her. She had not been able to get her writing published until she first came to analysis. Now, her second book is published. This splitting is different from the one we also saw in the previous chapter, in which I am the twin who lives the same feelings as she.

For Ms B it is unacceptable that Dr PS, who has been helping her for more than three years, even in so many moments of despair, is the same as the one who leaves her during the holidays. Therefore, the splitting has a radical character, in the sense that the part of reality experienced with the Dr PS who has helped her has been erased, while the part that she perceives—although not in exclusivity—is that of the alien, inhuman Dr PS because only this alien Dr PS would be unable to understand her pain in the face of the separation, or, worse still, that, understanding it, he sadistically persists in abandoning her in order to make her suffer. Of course, she would not believe it if I told her that I am not an alien. But neither would she believe it if I told her that I am one. In any case, she returns to the session, and, therefore, in some corner of her mind—in the non-psychotic part—the Dr PS who helps her persists.

In a *Thursday session (s-419)* of the following week, she says that here she has learnt to experience her childhood, but she has encountered not the mother who rejects, but the mother who does not reject, and, smiling, she specifies, "Although that's not entirely true either, but there it is, broadly speaking you could say that it is." Here, she has also been able to encounter the assertive father, she adds, instead of the frail, housebound father. For which reason she now sees her mother in a more realistic way, in the sense that she has her limitations. I reply that, consequently, she will be able to also make more realistic demands, that is to say, more attainable demands, of both her mother and of me.

Several days later, a *Tuesday (s-420)* after a long weekend owing to a national holiday on the Monday, the patient arrives concerned that I help her to understand what is going on with her body. She is interested in knowing why illness (she is referring here to the physical) is something that has formed a consubstantial part of herself throughout her whole life. She would like me to help her to understand. True enough, here we have seen many partial responses, she says, but she would need something more comprehensive. Perhaps the issue of the autoimmune illness, which is the provisional diagnosis issued for her symptoms of persistent diarrhoea, which she has been suffering from since her hospitalisation, has something to do with all this, she adds. She became annoyed when, the Friday before, I suggested that perhaps the autoimmune illness might have something to do with the question of her envy, which she herself had been talking about as one of those bad feelings that she has discovered in analysis, and would like to be rid of. She wants to know, she insists during the same Tuesday session, what is happening to her body. And she tells me her thoughts. She has always wanted to be slim, and, consequently, has, on the whole, eaten little, for various reasons. As an adolescent, she was a little more chubby and busty, but then she wanted to be like a famous fashion model of the time, although also "I must have had a problem coming to terms with my femininity", she says. Later on, she stopped eating out of solidarity with the poor hungry children of the world and she starved herself to the point of becoming delusional; though not just because of that, she clarifies, but partly, yes. She does not know if the issue of her illness (of the body) might also be related "to the ambivalent way my mother fed me as a child: not like those mothers who willingly feed their children, with interest, with pleasure." Although the problem now seems to be something else, she says that it is hard for her to assimilate what she eats so, consequently, she suffers from diarrhoea. As a matter of fact, she continues, for a year or so (I remind the reader that we have spent a little over three years in analysis) she has been eating more, even picking out what to eat, unlike before when she would just eat anything. But the problem now is that with the autoimmune illness, she does not assimilate it.

She comments in the same session that perhaps she is talking a lot so as to avoid talking about how painful last weekend was, when lots of things happened. In truth, I tell her, she cannot talk about everything, about this and that, as at times she would try to, and that the session has a limited time. She says yes, but when she is at home it will feel painful to have gone without talking all about the weekend. I acknowledge her hunger for knowledge of her illness, but there are so many things that she needs to go about it more slowly. Precisely because the problem now is not one of hunger (as it was before and after the holidays when she did not want to come here), her problem now is one of assimilating what is said to her, which needs to be done at a suitable pace.

Shortly before finishing the session, she comments on what was painful for her on the weekend. After Friday's session she wrote a short story, after going four months without writing, and she came up with a beautiful one. She explains the story to me. A man tells of how he has fallen in love with a woman. The man turns into a child and asks her to become a child as well, so that they can go and play in the rain. She made a sculpture out of the rain, a girl—herself. The painful thing was the tepid reaction of her family, as it seemed as though they did not like it very much. Later, she was alone, feeling unwell with diarrhoea and vomiting. I tell her that perhaps she felt that not hearing praise for the story was as if they had rejected her, as if they had vomited up her writing and she herself, bot just because they did not give it the literary value it might have deserved, but for not acknowledging the effort she had gone to in writing after so many months without doing so.

Comment on sessions s-419 and s-420

In the first instance, the patient is concerned to know about her bodily illness, that is to say, about how it might be influenced by her emotional life. It is also clear that for a year she has been more "hungry" and is eating more. It is likely that the analytic experience is enabling her to come to more of an acceptance of her need for "food" and to recognise the object-analyst who provides her with this "food", although we should exclude the period around her hospitalisation. The problem now lies in her difficulty in assimilating it, in particular whatever she may be receiving in the sessions. It is likely that her limited capacity to "digest" what she receives has existed for some time (as, in her early interviews, she informed me that as a child she would be fed milk by the "teaspoonful" because, if not, she would bring it up again), but it seems that now this is more manifest in that her acceptance of her need has grown. Before, she would go so hungry that she would become delirious. In other words, the denial of her need would underlie her denial of the object that can satisfy her, to the extent that it would be the delusion that would come to sustain her. Now, she is able to accept the nourishing object, so the problem arises of her poor capacity for assimilating what she has ingested, which is rejected, perhaps like a foreign body.

On the other hand, the patient's idea in regard to how analysis is helping her is intriguing. In the transference, she is learning to experience her childhood in such a way that the analyst is not the maternal object who rejects, "but instead here she is encountering the mother who *does not* reject". She does not speak of a receptive object, rather an object who *does not reject*. That is to say, she places the emphasis upon not being rejected. This is precisely the problem she is now faced with: her rejection of the food provided to her by the object because it is regarded as something foreign to her, which comes from the other and with which she is unable to identify. Thus, we might venture the hypothesis that in patients who are so sensitive to psychic pain, owing to their low tolerance of the frustration of reality, they cannot accept what is not like themselves. To learn to gradually accept what the other provides them—albeit by the "teaspoonful"—first they must have the experience of a relationship with the object who tolerates the projective identification of rejection. Only in this way, when the object has made it clear that she is accepted, will the patient be able to reintroject that potential for acceptance of that which is other, which comes from the object. I think that the incident of the closed office door is better understood from this perspective: when the door to the office closes because there are holidays, she does not tolerate it and responds vengefully by bringing about her hospitalisation. By contrast, when the analyst's door does not open on the day of the session, it does not occur to her that some circumstance beyond the analyst's control might have arisen. Here, she is convinced that this is a deliberate act of rejection.

On the other hand, there is a recognition of what she has learnt in analysis which is not underpinned by an idealisation of the analytic relation and a devaluing of her primary objects, mother and father. On the contrary, first she plays down, rather drily, that here there is no rejection, but she must qualify this with, "well, broadly speaking", and then she is able to take a second look at her mother in a more realistic and less demanding way, and, thus, without devaluing her.

The following sessions are still part of the month following her hospitalisation. Let us take a look at a particular *Friday session (s-422)*. Some sessions ago, she had commented that there is something painful that she did not wish to talk to me about, but today it seems as though she would be willing to try, even though the decision is not at all clear. This involves the delusional experiences of her last hospitalisation. "And when I explain it, you will think that I am completely crazy," she adds drily. Some days before her hospitalisation, she was convinced that two acquaintances from a bar, whom she had helped to resolve some business some months ago, were, in fact, aliens. Ms B expected they would abduct her and one night she stayed up, waiting for them. At this point, she clarifies that the fact of being aliens entails certain characteristics that she had never described perhaps so openly: they are evil beings, that is to say, they cause harm, they have the ability to take on multiple personalities, and possess certain abilities such as making objects appear and disappear. At the same time, they are doomed for all eternity. I am rather surprised by such a description, as, up until this most recent hospitalisation, the "aliens" were entities which "made life easier": they sent her messages relating to the feelings of friends and family, whereby she did not have to feel responsible for her perception of the feelings of others, still less for her own feelings.

With regard to threatening her parents with a knife, the patient continues in this session, it happened so she could defend herself from her mother's physical contact, which she had the feeling was completely homosexual—and, therefore, incestuous—contact. She goes on to relate her extremely painful experience in the psychiatric hospital, where she was panic-stricken and terrified at the thought of the aliens propelling her into the void. I comment to her that perhaps she had not explained all of this until now as she did not feel there was sufficient trust between us, since the relationship had been damaged with the holidays and what followed afterwards.

Comments on s-422

The effort that Ms B goes to explain in detail her delusional experiences prior to her most recent hospitalisation is significant in a dual sense: as an expression of trust in the analyst and of her capacity for contact with the painful element of acknowledging her delusional thinking ("you will think that I'm totally crazy", she jokes to soften it). The content of the delusional subject matter is also noteworthy. On other occasions, the aliens are agents who help her, and on this occasion they become persecutors. It is as though the sane part of her felt trapped in the hospital, and she states that she fears being catapulted into the void. It is likely that being thrown into the void refers to the mental void, the state of being devoid of mental contained and its container, as well as of conscience, that is to say, of the non-psychotic part which connects her to reality. For a long time, her consciousness has been substituted by the mediation of the delusion of the aliens. The problem is that if she now expelled her non-psychotic part, this would mean ending up in the most absolute mental void, as, at that time, she did not feel capable of recognising an own psychic life without mediation by the psychotic part. We see here that a significant change has taken place in her internal perception of the delusion. For a long time, the aliens constituted an organisation in which she took refuge in order to deal with the harsh reality. We are reminded of Rosenfeld's conception (1988[1971]) of the organisation of the personality as a Mafia gang led by the destructive part of the self which intimidates the sane and dependent part, which then submits, but that destructive aspect was never revealed by the patient, as she was protecting it. It is now that she describes them as beings who do evil, by whom she feels persecuted, and who could even "catapult" her into absolute nothingness.

The following *Monday, (s-423)*, at the beginning of the session, she cries. She gets up from the couch where she was seated, walks around, continuing to cry, saying that it would have been better if she had not come, rather than just crying and wasting time. I tell her that perhaps she feels required to communicate only by talking, as on Friday, and that she could not also express her tears. Having been talking last Friday about her most recent hospitalisation has made her think that she now experiences the hospitalisation in a different way to previous episodes, she says. Before, as soon as they had happened, she would erase them from her mind. Now, she is aware of them, but in a threatening way. At the same time, she feels depressed and wants to cry, but not in an "epidermic" way. Now, she is able to observe her depression from a certain distance; she is more aware of herself, which makes it harder for her. She continues that when she left the session on Friday, she fought with various people, with her psychiatrist, with her mother, and so on. She is worried by the doctor's suggestion (the internist) of admitting her to hospital to run tests for the issue of her diarrhoea, which has not yet resolved, and, furthermore, she still has her period, which has lasted for eight days. (This comment is connected to something from Thursday or Friday's session, when she said that when her period arrived, her diarrhoea stopped.) I remarked that it seemed as though her body were expressing that there are continual losses, at times with menstruation and at others with diarrhoea. Now she complains that the losses are double, as her diarrhoea has returned, even though she has her period: anal and vaginal route. That's why she is expressing her desperation now, in response to so much loss.

She also comments that after her psychiatric internment, her body has been affected, referring to her diarrhoea. It was difficult for her to come to the session because she was afraid of spending the entire time crying. Coming here by taxi, she thought that her exhaustion and weakness is the same as what she had last autumn when she thought that that state must be a consequence of the side effects of the chemotherapy treatment she was receiving remotely. During that time she had some idea that she had cancer, though she was not told about it, and that it was probably me who carried out that treatment.[1] [The numbers in square brackets refer to the comments I will make after my description of the session.]

I tell her that perhaps Friday's session was felt by her like a chemotherapy session because of how excruciating it was to remember her hospitalisation. And she feared that today would be just as intense.[2]

She replies that this is probably true, and that she has had a dream about me. "I was in front of you, right up close to your face, but I had the impression that although it was you, you were a woman, like the feminine part of you or something like that, and that you were experiencing a state of sexual arousal in relation to me, although there was no kind of contact. But at the same time it was like you were behind me, and then you were in fact a man, or your masculine part."[3]

The patient goes on to talk about the relationship with a female friend with whom she also had a fight. She went to a concert, because she did not want her parents to find her at home crying when they returned, which she had been doing from three until five in the afternoon when she left for the concert. And she feels hopeless, as though she has no future. Then she says, "Lately, we seem to have been talking about my [physical] illness and today I am unwell" (she means depressed and only feeling like crying). It is clear that the patient is experiencing some degree of confusion. Some sessions ago, we spoke about the illness (of her body) and today she arrives feeling unwell (in her psyche), but she does not draw any distinction between the two. Throughout the session her crying has gradually abated. I have the impression that this is the problem now facing her: how to find the optimal distance to be able to recognise and experience the sick part, but without feeling overwhelmed, either by depression or by the delusional part.

She says that she would prefer for me not to say too much to her today, as she does not feel strong enough to think about and accept what I might say to her. In truth, as a friend had said to her, assimilating her hospitalisation is something that cannot be assimilated. I understand her fear of the side effects of a session of analysis-chemotherapy, as well as her fear of analysing the dream she brings to the session. But bring it she has, so I think that I should say something: as the man in the dream, I am behind, as when she is lying on the couch. When she is seated, face-to-face, opposite me, I instead become the woman who could become aroused. These are two types of distinct relationship, which should be looked at in small doses, I conclude. Towards the end of the session, she asks for my opinion on whether she should be admitted to hospital for her medical tests. When I do not respond, however, she does not push the matter.[4]

Comments on s-423. Comment 1

She begins the session by crying, and regrets coming as it will prove to be a waste of time. Another waste, or loss, to add to the many others she is experiencing at that time, such as her physical losses. This occurs after a session in which she was able to talk about how painful her delusional episode was, which now, unlike before, she does not erase, but instead keeps it in mind, just as she is more in contact with the depression that it engenders. But it becomes so painfully unbearable that she might have to get rid of as much as possible from inside herself, from both her mind and her body. In order to do this, she has to greatly expand all of the expressive, expulsive, and evacuatory routes for all of that internal discomfort: blood (her menstruation, which has gone on longer than usual), faeces (the diarrhoea, which is also protracted), and tears . . . and, perhaps, words, if they are converted into something evacuatory. But, in so far as these evacuatory expressions have a pathological character, that is to say, where the emotional levels are confused with the physical, the result is a feeling of emptying or depletion, as if her psychic life were spilling out of her bodily, through her blood, faeces, and tears. It is as if her tendency to rid herself of anything inside of her that she finds unpleasant had led her to indiscriminately "evacuate" anything coming from within, in such a way that the consequence is the experience of loss of her internal world. Menstruation is part of her female condition, although admittedly there must be a reason for it currently to be going on longer than usual; the diarrhoea can be said to express in a concrete way her difficulty in retaining what she has ingested for long enough to assimilate it, hence, it must be evacuated when it has not yet fulfilled its nutritional metabolic function, and, last, the tears she considers as something useless, because these must be in the same register as evacuation–emptying, and not as an accompaniment to an emotional state.

In other words, after her psychotic episode, the patient continues to be in contact with consciousness of the disastrous consequences of the psychotic functioning, but precisely because she knows that this has not disappeared, she perceives it as a threat. Perhaps this contact becomes very painful, to the extent that she must evacuate it, in the same way as she must evacuate the depression. Nevertheless, after a brief intervention from me, showing tolerance for the tears that she is able to express in the session, she explains how she is experiencing the delusional episodes in a different way compared to some time before. Likewise, she notices the difference in her tears, which are not superficial ("epidermic"), as at the beginning of the analysis; instead, she is able to distance herself somewhat, that is, to observe herself, to be conscious of her state, which becomes very painful for her. Here, therefore, we observe the internal struggle in Ms B's personality, between either feeling the pain and getting rid of it as far as possible, or really undergoing the experience that accompanies the pain.

Faced with the difficulties in managing this pain emotionally, her body must also take part. And certain somatic manifestations, which, in another, non-psychotic patient, might be unavoidable "partners" of the painful emotional state, or even temporary vicarious channels, in her become an essential expressive route to rid herself of all of this, with the attendant consequence of being fearful of depleting or emptying herself. From this, it follows that she is able to assert that this hospitalisation has had dire consequences on her "body".

Comment 2

It is meaningful that the patient associates her state of weakness and fatigue to the one she had a year ago, when she thought that it was a consequence of the side effects of the chemotherapy that the analyst was dispatching to her from a distance. Certainly, in part, in the sense that the therapeutic effect of becoming aware of her psychic reality has painful consequences, but the patient confuses the various painful elements. She does not discriminate the pain inevitable to her cure, in which she is actively participating, from that which proceeds from other sources external to her, such as the analyst with his remote treatment, or the aliens sending her messages. Now there is pain because there is more awareness of all of this. Given what I have just discussed in regard to her indiscriminate "evacuation", I think that there is something more: that her fatigue and weakness might be a consequence of this evacuation of *almost* all of what is inside her; though not entirely, as indicated by her later being able to put into words what is happening to her, and even with some degree of insight.

Comment 3

Once the patient has expressed the painfulness of the situation she is experiencing by means of her body, this does not stop there, but, rather, I would say surprisingly, she contributes a significant dream. That is to say, she also uses this other channel of expression, in this case in the service of *communicating* something of her internal world. The dream conveys the two fundamental types of transference relationship (psychotic and non-psychotic) that are active at that time. In the first instance, it refers to the psychotic transference of the face-to-face encounter, when I become the female figure who is aroused in front of her; a projection of herself who needs to visualise me in order to receive the sensory stimuli transformed into sexual arousal, or a projection of the internal maternal figure who needs that arousal (we should remember that what caused her hospitalisation was her aggression against her mother because she feared an incestuous approach). In contrast, when she places me behind her, while she is lying on the couch, I once again regain my male analytic function of firm assertiveness and capacity to maintain the conditions of this analytic method. Furthermore, this dream sheds more light on the conflict involved for the patient in accepting the conditions of the setting: lying down on the couch means accepting me in my male analytic function, which, according to her, places her in the position of child and invalid, and these are just the two dimensions she needs to acknowledge for analysis to be feasible. None the less, she believes that I would take that position to the extreme of not regarding the adult and sane part of her, whereas, with the tendency to face me, seated on the couch, I become for her a female figure, but not the receptive and nourishing female figure who does not reject her, but instead one who needs her to satisfy and relieve my sexual arousal. When she says, "Lately we seem to have been talking about my (physical) illness and today I am unwell" (she means depressed), once again her tendency to create a certain degree of confusion between body and mind is apparent. She refuses to recognise the distinction between them, in order to evade psychic pain.

Comment 4

Towards the end of the session, the psychotic part of the patient tries to get this confusion to prevail, and sets out to confuse the analyst. When she asks me if I think that she should be hospitalised for her physical examination, she tries to place her bodily "illness" in the foreground, thus rendering the psychic work that we have been doing useless, at the same time as she seeks to make me complicit in this confusion. In all likelihood, this is also a way of testing me to see if I will be able to respond like the male figure in the dream, by firmly maintaining the conditions of the setting and, therefore, not answering her question, since here we are tasked with exploring her emotional life. Or otherwise, if I had replied, would I act like that female part of mine in the dream, which now would become excited by everything she has spoken about, including the dream, but which would not be of any further use, as all significance would be placed upon the body. Fortunately, the analytic work carried out in the session allows her to tolerate my not responding to the question, in tacit approval of my stance in treating that which relates to her mind, not to her body.

A week later, in a *Tuesday session (s-424)*, she continues to be concerned by her bodily ailments, with her persistent diarrhoea and menstrual losses. Furthermore, a delusional transference is activated. The patient is seated on the couch. She thinks I am being cold, and she cries. Yesterday, she read some texts that she wrote shortly before I "rejected her proposal to go out to dinner with her" (a year or so before). While she was reading them, she had the sensation "as if it were you who was reading them; I was interested in finding out what you thought of the text and there was a moment where I had the sense that you didn't like it." This is the part where there is a boy who does not acknowledge the teachings of a man, whom she identifies with me. She adds that I must think she is completely mad as a result of these things she is telling me. She then explains, almost as an aside, that as she had an itching sensation on her genitals, she decided to apply oil to the area and, while she was doing this, a notion occurred to her, which she has had before at times (I do not remember such a thing!), that I might be a nymphomaniac, and she imagined that I must have been aroused looking at her, so she tried to satisfy me by letting me watch her while she touched herself until I ejaculated. I say that perhaps she views me as distant and angry for turning me into that image of me, a nymphomaniac, whom she has to satisfy.

She replies (although without much conviction) that it is not that she is turning me into that; rather, that is how it appears to be. And she does not know why I am so cold with her, and she perceives "sulking, tetchiness and bad vibes" in my gestures. In response to such a statement, I feel cornered, harassed, insulted ... and bewildered. And so all I can do is defend my reality. I tell her that the reality I can speak to her about, my own perception of myself, does not match up with the state of coldness she talks about me having. That's what makes me think that if she perceives me as cold and angry it is because at times she has that image of me as a nymphomaniac. She admits that perhaps she is feeling very sensitive today.

Comment s-424

In one sense, the corporal component persists as a route of evacuation of the painful element of this new mental state of having greater consciousness of her reality, which is so difficult for her to tolerate. This not being enough, she would tend to modify delusionally the analytic relation. First, with the experiences in which, upon reading a text of her own she is able to know the reactions that I experience, as if from within her I, too, was reading it, and then with the masturbatory fantasy that gives pleasure to the "nymphomaniac" analyst. If we remember the dream of some weeks ago, in which the analyst shows a feminine facet of himself while she watches him face to face, sitting on the couch, we understand that the term she applies to me should be one related to women. Needless to say, here she has erased the analyst who is behind her as a masculine figure who firmly upholds his method, and, of course, the analyst figure of the female–mother who does not reject, as she also mentioned some days before.

A few hours after yesterday's session, the patient calls me, in agreement with her father, to let me know that that night there would be a meeting with the doctors who are treating her (the internist and the psychiatrist) to review her state, and she wondered if it might be appropriate for me to be at this meeting. I tell her that she knows that, because of the nature of the analytic treatment, I would prefer to avoid other contacts outside the relationship between patient and analyst.

The following day, *Wednesday (s-425)*, she telephones to tell me that yesterday the doctors decided that if she continues to suffer from diarrhoea and menstrual losses (the first in over a month), they will consider it necessary to admit her for tests for ulcerative colitis. Today, she has woken up with acute diarrhoea, so they are injecting her with drugs to strengthen her, because of how weak she is feeling. She has spent the whole day in bed and she does not feel up to coming to the session. Depending on how she feels up until Monday, when she is being admitted to hospital, she will see if she can attend. I ask her if she is able to come to the sessions while they are running the tests for colitis, as this might be a factor that could also strengthen her. She complains that I am not taking into account the physical aspect, only the sessions. Just yesterday, she left the session deeply upset by the whole matter of the fantasies she told me about, and to deal with all of that she needs to be stronger. That is why she thinks that, first and foremost, she needs to get better physically, in order to continue the sessions in which there is so much to address.

Comment on s-425

The patient tries to throw me off my analytic position in every possible way. At times, with apparent sound judgement, such as in her phone call of the previous day supported by her father, with the therapeutic aim of exchanging opinions with other doctors. I think that the patient's unconscious aim, apart from getting me out of my setting, is primarily to get me on to ground where I focus attention on the body, and, in so doing, to involve me in that separation from the analytic work. She complains that I only consider her mind. In point of fact, yesterday we were discussing the problem of how she uses her body in her fantasies, as she recalls in the phone call to point out how difficult it is to discuss all of that. The trap is that, according to her, in order to deal with those emotional problems, she must strengthen her body, that is to say, I must also concede importance to the vicissitudes of her body, leaving aside the emotional ones.

Theoretical reflections on the material regarding the plurality of channels of expression: emotional, somatic, and delusional

I should like to add a theoretical reflection which shows the use of diverse channels of expression of the patient's emotional situation in the face of the painful reality: the somatic disorders (which she now wishes to bring to the fore), delusional thinking, dreams, and fantasies, together with the lucid thinking of the sane part.

Somatic disorders

I shall give some consideration to the symptom which emerges in this material, that of resistant colitis. In fact, her diarrhoea came on shortly after her discharge from the psychiatric hospital. Furthermore, at that point, her delusional activity had not yet ceased to any significant extent, although lacking the power of some weeks beforehand. By the way, it is curious that the day after the doctors meet to consider the possibility of a hospital admission to run tests for colitis, an "acute" diarrhoea reaction comes on, once again as if within her there is that wish to place the bodily illness at the forefront. We might consider: is there some relationship between the decrease in delusional activity and the presence of the colitis? Or, more precisely, between delusion, colitis, and the analytic relationship? To this should be added the experience of the previous session in which she describes sexual fantasies with the analyst, who is degraded to a voyeur who is excited by watching how she manipulates her own genitals.

Based on the concept of Bick's "second skin" (1968), David Rosenfeld (2006, p. 183) describes the primitive body image encountered in psychotic patients. This idea originates in primitive object relations with a bodily foundation; all psychic activity is based primarily on a biological function. The body is a reservoir of liquids, in particular, blood and urine, which are stored within the walls of the blood vessels and urinary tracts. In my patient, as we have seen, there is the worry that she will "deplete herself" if the losses of—mostly liquid—substances continue (blood, liquid stools, tears), emptying herself of mental contents along with it.

Moreover, it is worth recalling Britton's idea (2015) mentioned in the previous chapter, when he makes the distinction between the attacks on the link with the object, such as Bion describes it, and the severance with the link, which he suggests. For Britton, "Disconnection is a process, which in phantasy annihilates all phantasies based on introjection" (Britton, 2015, p. 93). He talks about the narcissistic function that rejects, or disconnects itself from, the object, because, in relation to it, there is "a psychic immune response to the ingestion (introjection) of objects that *are not identical with the self*" (Britton, 2015, p. 94, my italics). But, in my patient, the situation is somewhat different. A year ago, there was a denial (a disconnection/severance or attack) of the nourishing object through the denial of the patient's hunger, fuelled instead by delusion. Now, however, she does, in fact, feel hunger and she is managing to incorporate what the analyst provides her. The problem now lies elsewhere, in her difficulty in assimilating what the object that has been acknowledged gives her. Interestingly, the doctors diagnose her with a possible autoimmune illness, which was subsequently not confirmed, which gives us cause to think that this was bound up with the emotional situation of the time. As a result, the problem now is one of an immune reaction in response to the already incorporated content from the object, which is felt as a foreign body that must be expelled. So that, after overcoming the first phase of connecting with the object and recognising what it provides her, she cannot assimilate this because it is found not to be identical to the patient's self; as such, it is foreign and must be rejected.

Similarly we might consider other factors that hinder her "assimilation" of experience. I also believe that the acute diarrhoea my patient suffers is related to the feeling of guilt and corresponding persecution for having had those masturbatory fantasies with the analyst. In this instance, what she is unable to assimilate is not what is given to her; rather, it is what she makes of the source that gives her food, the analyst, by degrading him. That is to say, the problem of assimilation of the "food" given to her (diarrhoea) might be owing to several factors: first, her envy; she does not tolerate the object as source of nourishment which is able to feed her, after having recognised it as such; second, her guilt over the mistreatment of the analyst; third, because the quantity given to her (the aspects of reality which are painful) exceeds her poor capacity for assimilation, and, therefore, must be given to her by the "teaspoonful", in small doses so that she is able to tolerate it. The problem lies in how to go on increasing the patient's strength to assimilate what is said to her. This is likely to be connected with the following factor: fourth, the conflict between maintaining the image of a frail father (and his corresponding internal object) who does not provide her with experiences of assertiveness which she is able to introject, on the one hand, and the image of the analyst as a strong male figure in her dream of some weeks ago, on the other. The fact that the patient was able to recognise what she has learnt from the analysis: the experience of a maternal image who does not reject and a strong father, would count toward this strengthening of the patient; fifth, that she is not fed with genuine maternal care (her complaint of her mother is that she did not feed her willingly and with pleasure); sixth, the patient's difficulties in accepting an interlinked parental relationship; in the analytic situation, the analyst with his working method. It is likely that the descriptor "nymphomaniac" for the analyst not only reflects the projection of her voracious eroticisation of the analytic relation, but also the perverse distortion of the image of the analyst. In this distortion, the union between the masculine and feminine aspects is not so the analyst may better respond to the patient's needs (the analyst with his method, the analyst as a firm paternal figure with a maternal figure who does not reject), despite her knowing that these exist; rather, it would make him into a man with unsatisfied female desires which she would, moreover, attempt to satisfy.

By the way, the type of description the patient makes of the masturbatory fantasy has characteristics that lead us to think of a hallucinatory experience rather than a conscious fantasy. While it is true that the patient does not go so far as to say that I was present at the scene, nevertheless, as her fantasy progresses, it seems as though as her description ceases to be something which takes place only in her mind and becomes a more complete experience which would comprise the external reality as well, and, as such, would constitute a hallucinatory experience. If we review the sequence, we will see that in order to relieve the itching on her genitals she seeks a remedy by turning to the physical, the oil, but, upon application, it appears that sexual arousal ensues. As we know, sexuality is an area in which the body and mind unequivocally participate in tandem (hence, for example, Meltzer's well-known text, *Sexual States of Mind* (1973, my emphasis would be on "mind"), to distinguish them from bodily states). Ms B goes on to isay that the idea occurred to her—a thought she has had at times before—that the analyst might be a *nymphomaniac*. That is to say, her somatic discomfort arises in an area of her body (her genitals) that readily accesses its mental correlate. So, her manipulation of them with the aim of alleviating her physical discomfort stimulates in her mind another type of satisfaction that appeared to be underlying, the sexual, one that is, moreover, linked to the figure of the analyst. I could not remember her telling me this idea of the nymphomaniac analyst, which makes me think that her conviction that it has been something we have already shared must correspond to an instant of a fusional relationship where whatever she experiences I already know about. So, she specifies that she *imagined* that I must be aroused but the use of the verb is ambiguous. Does she imagine the scene? Or does she imagine, in the sense that she speculates that upon seeing the analyst while she is manipulating her genitals, the analyst, who is in some way present, would become aroused? The patient goes on to say, convinced of the analyst's state of arousal, that she is willing to satisfy him "by letting him watch her". Here, there would appear to be less doubt that Ms B is describing a "real" event which has occurred, in which she not only allows the analyst to continue to be present at the scene, but she will continue until he ejaculates.

We know, with Bion, that hallucinosis is an evacuatory psychic process. Consequently, here we encounter yet another form of expelling painful aspects which gnaw away at her mind with respect to an as yet unresolved analytic relation. For this reason, it is an evacuation that takes place into a very particular "recipient": the analyst, the projection into whom even makes it so that it is he who evacuates/ejaculates. However, in the same session that she explains this experience, Ms B says herself that I must think that she is absolutely mad because of the things she is telling me. In other words, there is a degree of consciousness of the psychotic functioning of all of this, observed by the non-psychotic part, which is able to bring this functioning to the session so that we can work through it, as painful as this might be to her.

In short, the matter of her intestinal evacuation should be considered from various perspectives. The patient is now able to incorporate the analytic experience through which she has come into contact with the possibility of being listened to, understood, and which brings her something that she accepts and acknowledges with gratitude. The problem is not that she cannot receive what is provided to her because her mental apparatus cannot digest it as these are "unsymbolised" elements. She has a good grasp of the meaning of what is said to her; she knows what is good and what is not, she recognises the need for differentiation of the object, and for separation from it in order to grow. Yet, in so far as this involves the psychic pain of having to recognise as her own something which does not belong to her self, then this becomes unbearable to her, that is to say, she cannot contain it and she must expel it. I think that this, rather than the problem of lack of capacity for symbolisation, might be one of the fundamental problems in psychotic patients. To put it another way, there are patients with the ability to symbolise experience, but who are unable to tolerate the mental pain that maintaining the experience symbolised entails. This would find its expression in the physical symptoms of diarrhoea, in which, as we have seen, other factors are also at play.

Hypochondriacal manifestations

In the clinical material that will follow in the second part of the book, we will find examples of this symptomatology. I would like to keep in mind the theoretical distinction established by David Rosenfeld regarding the hypochondrias. He speaks of three forms: (a) hypochondria based predominantly on autistic mechanisms, when there is a strong lack of differentiation with regard to the object; (b) hypochondria based predominantly on confusional anxieties and mechanisms (as described by Herbert Rosenfeld); (c) hypochondria based predominantly on the primitive body scheme which Rosenfeld himself suggests, and which has been mentioned above. This latter form is described thus: "the latter consists of the fantasy of a body image of a self that loses solidity, is disorganized and its contents are liquefied; hence the hypochondriac panic before any physical incident that could break the 'bag' that contains liquids and empty him mentally." (D. Rosenfeld, 1992, p. 136).

Delusional activity

On the one hand, we must consider the delusional activity related to her period of hospitalisation, which she is able to keep in her mind and not erase, as during previous episodes, although the possibility of these delusions being reactivated more powerfully continues to be a threat, for which reason there is no longer ego syntony. For example, in the session (s-424) when she explains "introjective reading", as she calls it, upon reading one of her texts she would not recognise the feelings awakened by this reading as her own, and she "deduced" that they must then be the analyst's feelings, whereby she was able to know what my reaction was to reading her texts (since she knows that reading them does not form part of my work, much less giving her my opinion on them), although, at the same time, she raised doubts about whether this was, in fact, a set up she herself had put in place. There is also a form of thinking, which we might call sub-delusional, if not strictly speaking delusional, when she interprets certain coincidences of reality as something that is more or less determined by somebody, perhaps through the messages, although she recognises that this is difficult to prove. The patient was absolutely convinced that her finding the door to the office closed was because I did not want to open it. Her homosexual feelings towards her friend or her mother also fall within this sphere of experience, feelings which she activates by drawing upon inferences that the other person has made an approach. In the latter sense, we should also include the homosexual relationship with the "nymphomaniac" analyst.

Psychotic transference

On the basis of her fantasies of massive projective identification in particular, as occurred in Tuesday's session (s-424), in which, after having projected the sexual voracity of a part of herself into her delusional masturbation, turning me into a "nymphomaniac", she is later convinced that she perceives "sulking, tetchiness, and bad vibes" in my gestures and in anything I say to her, with which she is projecting a persecutory internal object as a result of the maltreatment she has given it. In response to the intensity of that psychotic transference, we come across the problem of how to interpret it. Although we will discuss this at greater length in the chapter on technique, we have seen that my interpretations in this session are centred upon her fear of my vengeful hostile response to her degrading me by making me into a nymphomaniac. However, this intervention does not change her conviction: this is not about what she thinks, that is how it was, she replies. Faced with this delusional certainty, all one can do, and the only thing that occurred to me, was to safeguard at least the perception of my psychic reality, first for my own mental health, but for the patient's too. Indeed, the course of the session changed later, after this intervention.

Dreams and fantasies

Despite her fairly considerable somatic symptomatology by way of her stubborn diarrhoea, as well as the delusional activity (to some degree at that time), we are struck by the fact that she still has sufficient mental activity to dream. The dream reflected a dual conflictive transference situation (s-423), by relating to my feminine part in front and my masculine part behind. That is to say, that a splitting into two of the relationship takes place, a self–object splitting: she into heterosexual and homosexual, and the analyst into man and woman.

The masturbatory fantasy, by contrast, is seemingly connected to me as a man; however, she assigns me a term reserved for a woman, that of "nymphomaniac". With this, she once again brings together, in language, the dual masculine and feminine character of the analyst. However, this is a conjunction that does not correspond to what the analyst might be understood to fulfil in his dual masculine and feminine function, as she herself recognises above, rather in a kind of "combined" object (this might be one description, perhaps) of a male figure who acts like a woman, and, hence, the accurate expression "nymphomaniac".

What is surprising then, and what I would now like to underscore, is that the patient is able to maintain so many open fronts simultaneously, so to speak, to express her emotional experience: the somatic, the delusional, the fantasies, dreams, and lucid thinking, in such a short period of time. While it is true that the use of various channels generally speaking forms part of mental life, the striking thing here is the intensity with which all of these are manifested. Finally, I think that the indication for admission to a general hospital has constituted an iatrogenic measure. Although, on second thoughts, perhaps this is a lesser evil, as it might have contributed to avoiding further psychiatric internment.

CHAPTER FIVE

Symbolisation in the psychotic organisation of the personality

"Written on a lonely afternoon,
to conjugate the pain that would otherwise overwhelm me"

(Ms B, s-268)

I already mentioned that effects of PsOP dynamics on thought occur in two ways: by limiting the capacity for symbolisation, and through delusional thought. In this chapter, I address the former. I shall deal with the latter afterwards.

Limited symbolisation and concrete thought

There is a fairly generalised idea that the psychotic patient does not have the capacity for symbolisation, which is an argument used to draw certain technical conclusions, in the sense that such patients are not suitable for the standard psychoanalytic method, in particular for transference interpretation, requiring other forms of therapeutic approach. Or, in the best of cases, a first stage of psychotherapeutic treatment would always be desirable until the patient is in a suitable state for psychoanalytic treatment itself. The theoretical developments in the concept of symbolisation, on the one hand, and psychoanalytic work with psychotic patients, on the other hand, allow us to review this type of axiom.

With regard to theory, it is becoming more accepted that symbolisation is not an activity that one does or does not acquire. Instead, it is a process of learning during which many transitional states take place, from the more primitive forms of symbolisation to the most evolved and mature. In addition, there is fluctuation between one symbolic state and another, including in non-psychotic persons.

Symbolisation is a psychic process by which reality is represented in a such way that it is possible to remain in contact with it, without the concrete presence of that reality at all times. For example, it is possible to continue accepting object separation from an object as long as it is mentally represented. In this sense, the function of the symbol is to link to reality.

Klein described the importance of "symbol formation in the development of the ego" (Klein, 1992[1930]) by observing the inhibition of that process when there is an excess of anxiety, in particular with regard to the attack on the mother's body through an intense fantasy and the corresponding guilt. Besides, it is inevitable that to accept the representation of the object (the symbol), one must separate oneself from it and, as such, experiencing some level of mourning due to the loss of the object is inevitable. Since all mourning is also inexorably painful, acceptance of the representation of the object in its place does not happen immediately. A gradual process with some initial steps is needed. One of these steps consists of taking the representation as the object itself. Segal's (1981[1957]) example of the psychotic patient who could not play the violin in public because this was exactly the same as touching his penis is well known. This equating the representation with the object is what Segal called a "symbolic equation". This is different from the other patient that Segal cites, who could dream that he was playing the violin as a form of masturbation, which would indicate a capacity for symbolic representation. According to Segal, these two forms of symbolisation would correspond to the paranoid–schizoid and depressive positions, respectively. Given that it is necessary to tolerate object separation and differentiation to achieve the second form (otherwise symbolisation is not needed), when there is a prevalence of pathological projective identification in which parts of the subject are confused with the object, the process of symbolisation will remain hindered, with a predominance of the form of symbolic equation. This operation, as I said, appears to be a necessary first step in all individuals' development for acquiring the capacity for mature symbolic representation. Thus, it is something progressive and gradual, starting with the primitive forms.

Yet, at the same time, as Segal tells us, and whenever current psychoanalysis permits with other psychic processes, it does not evolve so that everything remains above the primitive. Instead, the old persists and, furthermore, as something that can always be activated. So, a continuous fluctuation between the primitive and the evolved is a part of all mental lives. Another thing that is necessary and which is also accepted today is that the primitive spurs the evolved, we could say, to continue evolving (another of the many paradoxes of psychic life that psychoanalysis demonstrates to us). Bion described this fluctuation within the realm of the paranoid–schizoid and depressive positions using the frequently cited Ps↔D graph. This fluctuation and interaction between the primitive and the evolved applies to any milestones in an individual's psychic development.

While Segal maintained that projective identification is at the root of the symbol formations (Segal, 1981[1957]), some time later (1997[1978]) she adds that this is not enough because one must know the nature of the relationship between what is projected and the object on which it is projected; that is, using Bion's container–contained model, if what is projected is adequately contained and returned. In this sense, it gives us an opportunity to help the patient: if the analyst operates as an object different from the projected internal objects, so that what is projected can be contained, a relationship of mutual communicative interaction opens up, and one can then re-establish the capacity to form symbols in a more evolved way than symbolic equation.

With respect to the initial proposal about the relationship between primitive symbolism and more evolved symbolism, Segal explained a few years later:

> I have presented two types of symbol formation in a very extreme way. There is a long transition between the one and the other mode and I do not think I have ever seen a patient the whole of whose function would be on a concrete level or whose concrete symbols would

ever be completely concrete; *only predominantly* so. (Segal, 1991, p. 43, my italics)

I am interested in highlighting the correction that Segal introduced, since the patient's entire personality does not always function at the concrete level of symbolisation, a very important consideration when evaluating the psychoanalytic approach for psychotic patients. Further on, Segal states that she does not even consider the symbolism of the depressive position to be free of concrete elements. To this, one must add that if we accept the existence of an ego from the beginning of life, with its functions, although precarious, we will also find depressive elements (some integration and tolerance of object separation) in the paranoid–schizoid position and, therefore, vestiges of symbolisation.

On the other hand, there is a note from Segal in which she warns that the fact that psychotic patients have been capable of abstract thought, for which acquiring the capacity for symbolisation was necessary, does not in itself constitute a sign of mental health because it might be the result of a splitting where abstract thought has remained devoid of emotional meaning (Segal, 1991, p. 48). This is what happened with my patient, in particular during a period of her life before analysis when she tended to write but did so with the involvement of certain delusional artefacts; the "little machine" as she called it, which, when manipulated by some alien beings, allowed her to produce. Years later, Segal continued to maintain that there are several forms of transition from concrete symbolism to mature symbolic representation, and that primitive forms of symbolism coexist with more evolved ones within a single individual (even in the non-psychotic), although in variable proportions (in Quinodoz, 2008).

The other argument to keep in mind, in order to consider the process of symbolisation as something that is not completely removed from the psychotic patient, is that analytical experience with such patients has allowed us to verify what has been one of the basic arguments of this work: the coexistence of the psychotic with the non-psychotic in all psychotic and even non-psychotic patients, although in different proportions, obviously. Therefore, if a non-psychotic part exists in a psychotic patient, there have been moments in his life when he has had experiences where an evolved form of symbolisation has been present. Another thing is that its presence does not last long, precisely because it entails psychic pain due to the inevitable mourning component in the process of symbolisation and, as we have maintained, and this is one of the pillars of this work, the psychotic patient has a limited ability to *suffer* the pain, because of which he will also be restricted in his capacity to maintain the symbolisation. However, one issue is the limitation for mature symbolic capacity, and the other is total incapacity, as if dealing with *asymbolia*, which sometimes appears to be deduced when one says, "The psychotic patient cannot symbolise, but merely has a concrete thought."

Keeping in mind these two factors, the current meaning of symbolisation as a process and clinical experience with psychotic patients with whom it has been possible to conduct analytic work, we should be more prudent when ruling out analysis for a psychotic patient due to the fact that he presents a clinical condition that we could formally categorise as schizophrenic, such as my patient did.

For example, H. Rosenfeld (1971) emphasises the importance of concrete thought in psychotic patients as another consequence of the lack of differentiation between the subject and the object, due to the pathological use of projective identification. He supports his argument with the aforementioned work of Segal (1981[1957]) on symbolic equation. However, Rosenfeld himself, like other Kleinian authors, emphasises the importance of transference interpretation, as well as the need for distinguishing between the patient's healthy part and psychotic part, given that the first makes transference interpretation possible by being capable of recognising an object relation.

As such, I insist that it appears necessary to clarify the affirmation that psychotic patients present primitive symbolisation, symbolic equation, and nothing more. Clinical experience shows us that this is not the case. The reason must be found in the frequently repeated fact that a non-psychotic part coexists even in psychotic patients. This part is capable of certain degrees of more evolved symbolisation.

I now wish to recall Resnik's (2016) interesting suggestion with respect to primitive symbolism, which has to do with what he calls protosymbolic thinking. This is part of Segal's symbolic equation idea, but it differentiates several types of this according to the prominent physical attribute, which is what establishes equity between the object and the "symbolised". Thus, he speaks of *phonetic* protosymbolic equation when a word has a phonetic meaning similar to another and, therefore, represents it; he cites the example of one of his patients who established the relationship between the French words *sourire* (to smile) and *souris* (mouse). *Textural* protosymbolic equation is indicating that the common element that allows the "equation" to be established is a material fabric, and he reminds us of Klein's Dick case, in which symbolic equation was established between the curtain fabric and the skirt that Mrs Klein was wearing. He even mentions *kinetic* protosymbolic equation, an example of which is Segal's case in which the patient's repetitive movements when playing the violin were equivalent to masturbatory movements.

Although the American analyst, Searles, starts from different theoretical assumptions (ego psychology) than the authors mentioned herein (mainly Kleinians), his experience with schizophrenic patients has led him to propose some ideas about symbolisation that do converge with some of them. This is the case with regard to concrete thinking in these patients. He says that when the patient talks about the body in metaphorical terms, he does not do so in the same figurative sense as a non-psychotic patient, who is relatively deprived of the concomitant somatic aspect, but, rather, it is felt as a predominantly somatic experience. He also proposes the interesting idea that, in the development of all individuals, the origin of metaphors is primarily supported by somatic sensations that later contribute to evolved metaphorical thinking (Searles, 1965, p. 582). This would coincide with what we have just discussed in Segal, who supports the coexistence of this primitive level of thinking alongside the more evolved level in mature symbolisation. Furthermore, Searles talks about the fact that, because of his illness, the schizophrenic patient suffers from a process of "de-symbolisation"; that is, the metaphorical meaning acquired at one point in his development loses its symbolic nature and only the literal meaning remains (Searles, 1965, p. 580). The author attributes this to a process of regression to infantile states, which is different from the idea that we have maintained here about pathology beginning at the start of development. Nevertheless, I am interested in the idea of recognising that if the capacity for symbolisation existed at one time, one can deduce that, despite "regression", it might persist in part, and with therapeutic intervention is recoverable and can be further developed. This corresponds to what we have been insisting upon here with regard to the existence of the non-psychotic part even if the psychotic part is predominant. In yet another quotation, to explain the fact that so many metaphors can entail a particularly moving beauty, Searles proposes the idea that perhaps it evokes in us the faint memory of the stage at which we lost touch with the external world; that is, when we first realise that the external world is outside of us and we are outside of it, and alone (Searles, 1965, p. 583). I do not believe in forcing the interpretation of the text too much if I associate it with Klein's idea of the depressive position in relation to acknowledging awareness of the loss of the primary objects (as the ultimate representative of this external world). Therefore, the metaphor, that is, the capacity for symbolisation, as we have said, is tied to the process of mourning this loss.

Below, I have transcribed a detailed session in which one can see the move from symbolic equation to evolved symbolisation.

Clinical material on symbolisation in psychosis: moving from symbolic equation to evolved symbolisation

The *session (s-369)* takes place toward the end of the third year of analysis, at five sessions per week. It is a moment in the analytical process in which delusional activity has slowed and, therefore, the experience of living in "absence" of delusional content in her psychic life was very intense.

I notice how poorly Ms B looks. It is as if she has been crying. She sits on the couch and lights a cigarette.

P: It's just that I'm stupid, I don't know how to do therapy, I don't know how to think ... [She begins to weep bitterly.] I'm not good for anything ...

A: Why do you *think* that?

P: Well, because yesterday I was with Mi [a friend]. She has been doing (or had done) psychoanalysis for fourteen years. And she asked me how I talk about these little things in here, about whether I have a bump in the bone on my hand, like I told you yesterday. That I have to work more, *think* more for myself, and deal with important things ... She does the type of psychoanalysis where the psychoanalyst never talks; I think it is called Lacanian.

A: In that case, today I would hope, like Mi, that you came here to talk about important things, not just any little thing that might be trivial; because if you don't, how could I be prepared for this psychoanalysis to last all the years necessary?

P: Yes, sometimes I *think* that you must regret having taken me on for psychoanalysis ... That I must your worst patient, the least co-operative, the stupidest ...

A: That is, you *think* that I would not accept everything that you talk about, including what you consider trivial, but, rather, that you would have to talk about very intelligent and important things ...

P: Well, I don't believe you *think* like Mi, but I don't *think* I have anything solid. I feel that I have neither a past nor a future. When you sometimes refer back to what we have talked about, what we have dealt with here, I don't remember these things ... It's like I'm stuck. And if I had the theory that aliens exist and that they send messages to people, then I had something ... [Troubled.] But now I don't have anything inside me ... I want to die [she stands, walks, while crying, distressed]. I want to throw myself out the window ... [It appears clear that the activity of thinking causes her pain, I think. She paces around the room. I do not move. I know that when she is like this, she cannot stop moving around. This is partly to calm her with the movement, and also so that I cannot see her, because when she feels so badly she says that she looks ugly.]

A: That is to say that your negative assessment of yourself makes it so intolerable that it would appear the only way out would be to eliminate these things, throw them out the window with all of your self ... We could not go on thinking about it.

P: [She returns to the couch and sits down] I don't know if what is happening is because the publisher has not answered me. Probably next week ... And this really stresses me out. And I have lost hope for the novel ... [Pause.] [At this time, in addition to having submitted an old text for possible publication, she has started another fiction work that was stimulating to her.]

A: You are probably looking for the solution to your life in the publisher's response. So there will be no partial solutions for each situation in your life, which each require thought, but instead it would solve all of them at once, or something like that.

P: But *what* am I? Nothing. I have nothing, neither a past nor a future. How will I be able to live without the messages, which is what Mi [her friend] told me to do? I would have to enter the real world, which is not the one of omnipotence and messages, but I don't know how to do this ... [She cries in despair.] And I need what they tell me. I need you to be frank with me. For you to speak to me without sugar-coating things ... I want you to be frank. If it's true that nothing I have experienced is worth anything, if everything has been madness and is not worth anything, then tell me so. [Pause.] Tell me something, please!

A: [The pressure that the patient is applying on me is evident.] Well, what I can tell you right now is that it is true that you need me to be frank with you, so you are even willing to hear the worst: that much of what you have experienced has been madness. But I believe [I try to take my time to think and avoid saying "trivial" things or reassuring platitudes] that you recognise this new world that I, like your friend, am talking to you about as valid, but it is difficult and painful for you so you don't believe you can enter into it, because it would mean recognising your feelings, wishes, fears, capacities, and incapacities; that is, that not everything is magical and fantastic. Although, on the other hand, the magical world of the messages is no longer very acceptable to you, because this would be going backwards, so you feel stuck...

P: [She listens to me attentively. She remains silent for a moment. She is somewhat calmer.] I was at home like this, without hope for my writing and feeling so stupid, so incapable, as if I didn't have anything in me, so I suddenly decided to go to L [a bar that she had visited some time before], as if I needed to find a handsome guy... And I was disappointed because people were talking about business. And I did find a handsome guy but he ended up behaving hysterically... [Pause.]

A: That is, you needed to find something handsome, beautiful, to neutralise the feeling inside of you that you were not this, because you felt stupid, ugly...

P: Later I received a *message* that Mi had apologised for having been harsh with me by talking to me about the new world... And I picked up a book that talked about the importance of words. The author wrote that when she was little she said: "soldier", and she went out on to the balcony and saw soldiers. As if she could summon those things into reality with words. This is what has always happened to me, as I have experienced it... Through words... So it is very hard for me now...

A: That is, when you realise that words are not things, that words are for communicating your thoughts and feelings to me, but that they don't have this magical quality of summoning them, as if words were the effect or the feeling they are trying to convey...

P: Yes, that's it, and it is very hard for me. And what am I going to do now? I also think that my writing lacks feeling, it is too sweet... And what do I do now to figure out where to go? Tell me.

A: It is true that it is hard. [I can't think of anything else to say to her that is not a platitude or something already known, although I end up stating the obvious.]

P: Don't sugar-coat things for me. Sometimes I think that I must be your favourite patient because I must be the most ill, the most needy, and so with me you feel more needed than with anyone else, and this is why I am the favourite. Although I don't think you will give me thorough explanations either, and this is why you tell me things are hard, that we must continue to see how it goes, and all that.

A: But that is because it's true, that I don't know where you need to go to find this other way of recognising and expressing what you are going through in words. Or, better said, I can't prevent you from experiencing what you are going through without magical intervention. I can, however, accompany you in this task.

P: [More calmly.] I brought the paper that yesterday I told you I had written. [She is not sure whether to read it.] But I don't want to. [She puts down the paper.] So that ... it doesn't matter [a tone of discouragement].

A: Maybe you don't know if it is worth the effort to communicate with words if it turns out that words are not exactly what they transmit, if they lose this quality of summoning things by turning into the things they name ...

Ultimately, she reads the short composition, which describes images of characters that make reference to the analyst as the *guide*, which is related to another composition from months ago when she spoke of the *lighthouse keeper*, also alluding to the analyst.

I tell her that she could now recognise me as someone who provides a certain light, certain guidance, by accompanying her on this difficult path of communicating with words without these being confused with what they represent.

She ends by saying that she needs to rebuild something solid, she was not sure what, but it would have to be something like building things; she did not know what things, but it has to do with this relationship, the relationship to her herself, and the relationship to the writing she is trying to do.

Comments on s-369

To analyse the session in detail, I will make sure to "zoom in" as much as possible. To that effect, I will differentiate between several movements from the patient–analyst interaction according to the patient's functional state and her reaction to my interventions, as well as my subsequent responses.

First movement

The patient arrives in a bad mood, hopeless, and the first reason that she gives is "I don't know how to *think*"; therefore she does not know how to do psychoanalysis and she feels stupid. From this moment on, I intentionally use the verb "to *think*" so and have italicised it. The patient also uses the word several times over the course of the session. With it, I intend to convey to her that this is precisely the fundamental task that we are in session for: to *think* about her. So, thereafter, I take her word as one way to emphasise this activity, and I try to explore why *she thinks* that she does not know how to think. Her response is the friend's criticism for not talking about important things here. I interpret the transference and point out her fear that I will not be with her for as long as she needs if she does not tell me interesting things. She confirms this to me by showing her preoccupation with the fact that I must regret having taken her on for analysis, although she calms down because, since she is so ill and needy, I will feel important. However, this is not enough, because she returns to the feeling that she does not have anything inside her, "neither a past nor a future", nor the delusions; she regrets that she cannot remember what we talk about here and becomes hopeless again, expressing her will to die by throwing herself out of the window. In as much as delusion has been discredited due to its false nature demonstrated in analysis, she cannot fall back on it. So she does not know how to proceed, because she has no future either, so it is very hard. She cries and she needs to walk around the room to calm herself down and to distance herself from my view so that I do not see her, because feeling badly equates to feeling ugly. I interpret from her how intolerable it must be to see herself in a negative light, so much so that only flinging herself out of the window could free her from such feelings. Thus, I neither deny nor trivialise her hopelessness, and I also offer my willingness to think alongside her.

Second movement

Following my intervention, the patient appears to feel contained and calms down. Then she is able to come near me again and sit on the couch. Indeed, she can think about another possible reason for her discomfort: the frustration of not having received a response from the publisher. The stress created by the uncertainty of waiting even causes her to lose hope for the writing that she has begun. I intervene to point out her magical expectation that the publication of the book is what will resolve every issue in her life.

Third movement

She responds by asking, "*What* am I?", not "*Who* am I?" because she is accustomed to identifying herself as a set of things within her, not as someone who "contains" these things, which make up an identity. Since these things are not present, she is nothing. If there is no delusion ("messages"), there is no past, because it was occupied by it, but it is not possible to build her future either. She desperately asks me whether it is true that nothing that she has experienced is worth anything because it was based on the lie of madness. It is one of the most difficult moments in the session for me. "Tell me something, please," she begs me. It seemed cruel to ratify her suspicion and tell her the truth that her life had, indeed, been based on madness, but also because it was not completely correct. At that moment, the patient was fighting to confront the hard immediate reality in a desire to find some way to enter into this new world of non-delusional reality, of which she had no knowledge either. It is the non-psychotic aspect trying to co-operate. So I limit myself to describing what she has said to me in different words, but with a wording that is not so absolute. It is true that there has been madness, although not only that. The problem is how difficult it is now to recognise her new world with her own feelings and experiences without resorting to magic and omnipotence.

Fourth movement

My intervention appears to have truly served as support for her, as demonstrated by the fact that she later brings up associations that contribute to the session's progress. The first is an attempt to seek relief in apparent beauty ("a handsome guy") but she ended up disappointed: she found the material and the superficial, which, on other occasions, had served to "fulfil" her. My intervention points to her need to find beauty to counteract what feels ugly inside her, and that it has to do with her negative feelings, and, of course, she did not find it in material and superficial beauty.

Fifth movement

Her answer is curious. Through "the message", she forgave her friend for having spoken to her so harshly. She cannot recognise the forgiveness as something of her own because it hurt her so much that she herself would not be able to give it. So, although she needs me to be frank with her, and she shouts this at me, when I do it, despite all the caution with which I try to express myself, it means so much pain for her that it is hard for her to forgive me. Nevertheless, the involvement of the messages remained limited to not assuming responsibility for this forgiveness (of the friend and, implicitly, of me) so that the session's progress can continue.

Sixth movement

She continues with another association: she picked up a book in which the author summoned things to reality by uttering the words that represent it. She goes a step further by being aware that this is precisely what has always happened to her throughout her life: "[Having] experienced it through words", it is painful to become aware that words are only a vehicle and not reality itself. This is why it is so difficult now, in this new world of reality. I intervene to reformulate this with my words and bring the insight that she had just conveyed to the session. Not only does she show that she agrees, but she can take it a step further by criticising her previous writings for "being too pretty, lacking feeling." We recall that she had talked about going out to look for a "handsome guy" to relieve her discomfort, but had found superficiality: the hard part is finding "real" beauty with its nuances and its disconcerting side. So, her hopelessness emerges again when she comes into contact with this hard reality, followed by the demand that I do something, but in the sense of a magical intervention. By limiting myself to indicating how hard the situation is, she complains that I sugar-coat things and asks for more. Again with ambivalence, she asks that I be frank with her, but she wanted me to give her magical solutions. My response, by telling her that I could not prevent her from experiencing what happens in her reality when magic is not involved, but that I can accompany her in this work that she is trying to do, does not provide anything new but insists upon the importance of recognising reality as a fundamental basis for this learning.

Seventh movement

The patient sits down again and is calmer, and she picks up a writing that she ends up reading, with some difficulty. While the text was written outside the session, she contributes it in this moment and I can take it as an association. The allusion to the analyst figure seems significant to me in the sense that it is someone who guides her, or the lighthouse keeper who lights the way.

So, the session starts with a state of hopelessness due to her becoming aware that she has lived all her life through words, to which she has given this magical connotation of summoning reality and not being the representation thereof, a process that involved delusional thinking, and that the result of this awareness is that she now feels she is nothing, that there is nothing inside her. Little by little, and despite the pressure applied to the analyst to enter into the magical realm, to use words that, like the messages, transform her internal world, the patient was able to continue thinking, associating, and using words in a metaphorical way. Thus, at the end, she herself ends up referring to the analyst using the metaphor of "guide" or "lighthouse keeper". That is, she has been able to use words to their fullest symbolic extent while connecting to what she is saying. Hence, the difficulty of bringing the text at this time, when other times she has had the opposite problem: the misuse of expecting to read her texts to me as a way to demonstrate a beauty that, as she says, "lacks feeling". The session I have presented is, therefore, a small sample of the painful transition from symbolic equation to a more evolved symbolisation. The patient's problem is based on her fragile ability to endure the pain that accompanies thinking, a necessary requirement for the process of symbolisation.

CHAPTER SIX

Delusional world, mental emptiness, and other clinical manifestations

> "With madness you don't realise you are suffering."
> "I would prefer to live with madness because I would suffer less than I do now, because I have to recognise the limits of reality"
>
> (Ms B, s-276)

This chapter studies the remaining clinical manifestations of the OPsP, giving special attention to delusional thinking and to the experience of psychic emptiness; although without neglecting the difficulties of communication in the analytic relationship.

Delusional thought: unconscious fantasy and delusion

Delusional thought is the other consequence of the limited capacity for containing psychic pain. If thought is the necessary detour for conceiving of the reality that we perceive when non-psychotic functioning is predominant, which implies tolerating the pain concomitant to this conception, in the case of PsOP the mind is structured with a predominant conception of reality other than the intolerable one. Thus, what is conceived is another separate reality; it is delusional thought. Obviously, what is thought—that is, fantasised—is superimposed over an unacceptable reality, although without completely negating it, as we shall see.

According to Freud, delusion is an attempt to recovery, a process of reconstruction, "like a patch over the place where originally a rent had appeared in the ego's relation to the external world" and "it is not much more noticeable is because . . . the manifestations of the pathogenic process are often overlaid by manifestations of an attempt at a cure or a reconstruction" (Freud, 1924b, p. 151). That is to say, a particular—subjective—reality is reconstructed to fill in the mental void following a loss of contact with reality by having attacked the very mind that senses it and gains an impression of it.

Generally, in order to balance our minds, we seem to need the persistence of omnipotent primitive elements underlying unconscious fantasies, which are similar to many of the psychotic patient's delusional ideas. The difference stems from the fact that the psychotic part resists proof of reality at all costs because of how unbearable it is, contradicting it and negating it when it is not enough to distort it. Ordinary thought is partially distorted when reality is painful, but there is enough capacity to tolerate the pain of apparent reality to prevent negating it. However, things are not always so clear, and any individual has moments when it is possible, and even necessary, to negate reality, even if only fleetingly. This is what happens in the first stage of working through mourning due to the loss of a loved one, for example.

In Segal's work "Phantasy and reality" (1997[1994]), she starts from Freud's statement that recognising external reality is necessary for the development of the psyche, adding that it is inextricably linked to the internal reality of one's own wishes and fantasies. Since the latter are not always satisfied immediately, there needs to be some way of filling this void. Freud (1911b) describes two ways of doing so: hallucinatory wish fulfilment, either according to the pleasure principle or the reality principle, which is what gives way to the development of thought. So, Freud considers thoughts to be an "experimental action" which, according to Segal, would also be present in a primitive way in preverbal unconscious fantasies. The author suggests that unconscious fantasy becomes a set of primitive hypotheses about the nature of the object and the world at the fantasy level, comparing different imaginary outcomes: "What would happen if . . ." This position is very different from delusional fantasy, which creates a world "as if" things were already as the individual imagined them: what I imagine *is* reality. Over the course of individual development and successful analysis, the old fantasy organisation that distorts perception and gives rise to compulsive actions changes into another type of mental organisation with a greater capacity for tolerating proof of reality. Segal concludes that this leads us to the basic conflict between omnipotent fantasy and acceptance of reality, and the gradual acceptance of the reality principle over the pleasure-pain principle (Segal, 1997[1994], pp. 38, 39).

Steiner maintains the idea that the delusional world may still be considered as a kind of psychic retreat (Steiner, 1993, p. 64), although it differs from other POs in the intensity and violence of fragmentation, which leads to the use of delusional omnipotent forces, to create order and provide relief (Steiner, 1993, p. 85); I would go even further to say to contain the psychotic anxieties.

However, I wonder whether the term "psychic retreat" would *always* be the most appropriate to describe the delusional world. The term "retreat" has the connotation of an area in which the individual takes refuge in order to find protection, security, and relief, as demonstrated by not openly psychotic patients, who speak of places as a desert island, or a cave. The organisation of the psychotic patient would be the only, or the least bad, resort available to the patient when facing the danger of a reality that is presented as catastrophic, but it also carries an emotional state of coercion and submission under threat, which is far from the state of placidity of the areas of the "refuge".

Reality and delusion. Binocular vision and bi-ocular vision

What happens to a reality that is feared, hated, repudiated, etc., when the psychotic organisation of the personality, which needs to create delusion, is predominant? What is this reality like for the psychotic patient? My patient, Ms B, defines it very well on one occasion when she tells me, "On the one hand, reality implies strength to achieve things, and then recognising that it is reality; that is, it is not fantasy [something she created], and also anonymity, because I am not the protagonist [the centre] ... And all of this implies being alone." And then she asks me, "But, Dr PS, how do you live with reality?" To answer *how*, I proceed to list a series of things that she mentioned during the session—things she saw that she should be undertaking and doing—as being necessary for dealing with reality. Therefore, when the patient creates a delusional universe, it is not because she is unaware of reality, but, rather, the problem lies in her limitations to tolerating it, so she must do everything possible to function *as if* it did not exist.

Thus, I think it is important to recognise that the psychotic patient also *knows* about (non-delusional) reality. Hence, we must speak of the coexistence of delusion and reality, of delusional "reality" and actual reality. This is in line with what we have been defending in this work: the psychotic part coexists with the non-psychotic part of the personality. We have already cited Freud in this regard, and we can also remember Bleuler, when he says, "the sense of reality is not totally absent in the schizophrenic patient ..." (Bleuler, 1960, p. 72, fn.), and, as a consequence, delusional ideas coexist with states of lucidity or full consciousness (Bleuler, 1960, p. 136). Among the current authors who point to this coexistence, we could cite Freeman (1999) and De Masi (2015). I will deal with the ideas of the latter.

According to De Masi (2015) the psychotic patient sees a double world, a delusional one and a psychic reality, without these contradicting one another and he refers to this coexistence as a form of *"biocular* vision", to distinguish it from Bion's *binocular* vision. De Masi says, "the two worlds are separate to each other and *do not communicate*; the patient can inhabit either at different times" (De Masi, 2015, p. 1205, my emphasis). As I have maintained and specifically indicated in Chapter Two, one of the primary issues in all pathological organisation of the personality, including psychotic organisation, is the *type* of communication and interaction taking place between the psychotic and non-psychotic parts; that is, I presume there is some mode of communication. Thus, I am not so sure that the delusional and the real constitute such clearly separated parallel worlds, at least for a patient who is receiving some kind of psychological help. On the contrary, I believe that there is an ongoing interaction that might result in an organisation of the personality further from reality when the psychotic part is dominant, or quite the opposite, an organisation with a greater acceptance of reality. This is where analytical intervention can tip the balance one way or another, or, as occurred with the patient that De Masi presents to us, delusion is circumscribed and the distance between the psychotic and the non-psychotic, between reality and delusion, does not grow.

To delve into this reflection, I wish to recall Bion's contribution of "binocular vision" in psychic life, an analogy that uses the dynamic of vision, in which both eyes must work together to achieve a more complete and harmonious perception of physical reality, and he indicates that the fundamental task of mental growth is based on this operation of joining two psychic "visions". He refers to this analogy at several points in his work. In *The Imaginary Twin*, he says that the fact that one of his patients values the advantages of the binocular microscope over the monocular one indicates a greater sense of reality, both with regard to the means used to establish contact with it and his confidence in his ability to explore the intrapsychic realm (Bion, 1993[1950], p. 19). In the same work, he indicates that the onset of vision in an individual's development implies a new capacity to explore the environment and, from this point of view, he believes that his patients experienced analysis as an expansion of their tools for psychic investigation, (1993[1950], p. 21) adding a new "vision". In a subsequent work, Bion specifies what this contribution to the patient's psychoanalysis consists of, according to this vision analogy: "The use in psychoanalysis of conscious and unconscious in viewing a psychoanalytic object is analogous to the use of two eyes in ocular observation of an object sensible to sight" (Bion, 1991[1962], p. 86).

Two years later he expands on the idea in the sense that a patient might change his attitude towards the object by changing the point of view from which he sees it; thus, it could be a perverse point of view or, on the contrary, a perspective similar to a surveyor who changes his position in order to better gauge the size of a distant object. This procedure implies the use of splitting (time and space), but the result will depend on the nature of the intention thereof (the split). That is, splitting can indeed help to resolve the issue of finding a substitute for "binocular vision" when this is not available, or it can obstruct the solution by destroying "binocular vision" when it is available. So, the issue lies in the use that one makes of splitting: whether it is a method of establishing correlation, in which case the mechanism implies rejoining the split components later, or, in the case of the personality whose split is caused by destructive impulses (the psychotic personality comes to mind, for example), one which tries to prevent correlation between the split components. The end of the sentence expressing this idea seems significant to me, stated in a clearly Bionian style, because it poses a question from the hidden viewpoint to the more evident one. Bion says, "The obstacle to correlation for a personality whose splitting is motivated by destructive impulses, is the need for two objects to be *brought together creatively*" (Bion, 1991[1965], pp. 66, 67, my italics).

Bion does not describe it the other way around, that the necessity of creatively bringing together two objects is obstructed by destructive splitting. As I understand it, while destructive splitting is predominant in the psychotic patient, the need to bring together two objects is inevitable. Therefore, the tendency to split the real world from the delusional world is met with resistance to *creatively* bring them together, and this implies the weakening of the delusional world with all the pain concomitant to its loss, as my patient expressed many times. In any case, I also wish to emphasise the inevitable conflict between the psychotic part (with destructive splitting) and the non-psychotic part (with the need to bring together two objects), precisely due to continuous interaction.

Another perspective on "binocular vision" is when Bion warns of the danger implied by the comfortable conditions in which psychoanalytical treatment takes place, although it is not as hazardous an affair as other activities in which danger is evident. In order to deal with this situation of "binocular" focus, he recommends that the analyst, on the one hand, be attentive to the patient's material and, on the other, his associations therewith (Bion, 1991[1965], p. 74).

Therefore, "binocular vision" is a function in which dual aspects are brought together which, according to my brief assessment of Bion's work, can include the following: conscious–unconscious; patient's perception–analyst's perception; the analyst's perception of what the patient says–the analyst's perception of his associations; the analyst's and patient's observations of the psychotic part–non-psychotic part; to which I would add, as I indicated in another work, the here and now aspects of the analytical reality, along with the perspective of other moments in the analytical process (Pérez-Sánchez, 2010). On the other hand, when dealing with bi-ocular vision (De Masi, 2015), the patient demands the same "reality" status for delusional reality as for non-delusional reality, which is logically impossible, so one can only propose parallel worlds that apparently do not affect one another. The problem, as I said, is that this coexistence is not possible without consequence to the parts involved. So, if there is a delusional world, the perception of the real world is inexorably affected, in the sense that the distance between them continues to grow, with the resulting decline of capacities to cope in the real world.

A summary of the delusional world of Ms B

I shall now describe the structure of my patient's delusional world, to bring understanding to the psycho(patho)logical role that it played in maintaining a certain balance in the psychotic organisation of her personality. With regard to the delusional object relationship, it was composed of two elements that existed both before and during analysis, although it continued to change over the course thereof. They are as follows: she receives messages from aliens who operate a little machine. This order of exposure corresponds to that of the priority in importance in her mental life.

Although the patient has never described the composition of the little machine, it seems to be a mechanical device capable of producing ideas, thoughts, or, as she called them, messages. It is notable that she always used the diminutive, which constitutes another element of concealment, giving the appearance of something small that one must treat with care, and not something malicious and destructive. The little machine is located nowhere and everywhere, but it tends to be operated by someone outside of her, and beyond this world: the aliens. The little machine reminds me of the mental device that Bion describes, which is the result of a hypertrophic use of projective identification; that is, "a device for evacuating". In this case, what is created moves not only outward, but also inward. To be precise, the patient can accept the content of the messages in as much as it originates outside of her. Rather, it could be said that she has evacuated her own apparatus of thinking, which has now turned into the little machine, as if it were something that does not belong to her.

Over the course of analysis, mention of the little machine began to disappear. I believe that this was possible in so far as the projection was situated in the analyst and was contained in the analytical relationship. Then this gave rise to two different experiences: the analyst responded with a "device for thinking", tolerating frustration and necessary pain, which the patient was able to connect with her non-psychotic part, and the other experience, the delusional one, was the psychotic part taking over the analyst's mind and using it to store her projections, treating it as part of her self.

The messages become her thoughts (those of a cognitive–emotional nature) that make reference to aspects of reality (internal and external), which she cannot tolerate. Above all, the message is a thought or idea that does not come from her, but passes through her. As analysis progressed, I was able to verify that the messages have always been present in her (mental) life, and not just during her psychotic breakdowns. The contents of the messages can vary greatly. During periods of her life when there is a pseudo-adaptation to reality, based on some elements in her relationships, such as a friend who treats her with fond affection, or feeling understood and contained by the analyst, the messages transform this experience into clear feelings of love for her. At first, it might go unnoticed to the patient, until she encounters frustrating responses from others, limited to a merely friendly relationship with her friend or the analytical relationship with her analyst. The messages might also make reference to the imminence of a positive event, such as being awarded a prize or winning the lottery. In episodes with a predominance of the psychotic world, that is, a greater attack on (or severance from) reality, both towards the objects on whom she depends (stripped of value) and towards her own self (impoverished in her capacities for perception of reality), and with intense annihilation anxieties, the messages inform her of the closeness of a world hecatomb. She experiences this with such delusional conviction that, for her, it has all of the characteristics of an incontrovertible and immediate reality.

Last, the aliens. It was a long time before she told me about the characteristics of this psychic device. They were simply the agents who created the messages, but she rarely·spoke of their characteristics. So she would say, "I received messages" or "I knew it through the messages" without specifying who sent them. She implied that they had been activated through the involvement of the aliens who operated the little machine. She only named them when reality became especially difficult to bear: "The aliens send me messages," she would say, and naming them means giving them a real, openly acknowledged existence. For a long time, Ms B told me that the function of aliens was to protect her from the psychic pain of reality. She had to go through analysis for a time in which her non-psychotic part was met with the analyst's support in order for her to be able to undo this deception and unmask the destructive and terrifying nature of these structures. She then provided another description of the aliens. They are beings from very far away, from another planet, who tend to do bad things, for which they take on human form, but they are not humans; even people close to her, including the analyst himself, at one time or another have been able to embody these beings. While she considered them to be omnipotent, they came to earth to take advantage of humans because their home planet had run out of resources for living. Later on, the aliens communicated their anguish about eternity to Ms B through the messages; that is, the fact that they are condemned to live forever. In this, one can observe a reduction in the omnipotent quality of the psychotic part, which causes it to weaken, in favour of predominantly recognising reality and its limitations. As such, even later on in analysis when the figure of the "aliens" appear, they do so in a dream in order to ask her to intercede for them before the kings, since she is the only human close to them, so that they can create a fairer world with a more equal distribution of wealth, or to save them from being condemned to eternity. When the omnipotent interventions of the psychotic part have been weakened and discredited through analytical work, it seeks the complicity of the non-psychotic part. The perverse element implicit in this alliance is clear, which is one of the most difficult elements of psychotic organisation of the personality to undo, because it is disguised as re-establishing equality and fairness, when in reality it is trying to conceal destructive activities in her mind and her relationships. One example is equality, which she defended on several occasions, between patient and analyst, in order to avoid a differentiation of duties and strip the analyst of his analytical function.

Throughout the work, we find various delusional manifestations. Now I shall point out the psychic structure that lies beneath, in a dual sense. On the one hand, as a delusion, which is the creation of a new world that saves the patient from the pain of contact with reality, but above all from any minimal responsibility for her psychic reality. On the other hand, the delusional world is a threat, when the psychotic part ceases to dominate her internal world. Instead, the non-psychotic part is able to denounce it with the help of the analyst. It is at times like these when she can give me this "negative" description of the aliens, or when the presence of messages is felt with concern.

As analysis with Ms B progressed, when the destructive nature of psychotic organisation was fully revealed to her, so she could not resort to it easily, this is felt with longing, causing her eventually to say that she "would give all the money in the world" to be delusional again because of how difficult her new reality without delusion is.

Bodily effects and manifestations

The intensity of catastrophic anxieties often makes it impossible for a patient with PsOP to contain them in the strictly mental sphere, so it is sometimes also necessary for the body to participate as a "container" into which mental overflow can be deposited. However, given the fact that in PsOP defensive domination against painful reality is the "modification" thereof, through delusion or its negation, when this defence weakens through analysis, it resorts to the body, as I illustrated in Chapter Four.

When reviewing Bion's statement on anxiety, along with feelings, which have no shape, colour, or odour, Resnik suggests that perhaps "feelings and thoughts have the colour, the form and the smell of the body" (Resnik, 2016, p. 15). In the case of the psychotic patient, the body acquires a special category as a way of expressing intense catastrophic anxieties; especially, I would add, when the delusional world has weakened.

In Ms B, the reference to the body as a "psychic" resource has been very variable and multi-faceted. At times, during moments of desperation, she wished that she had cancer so that her suffering would come to an end. This way she did not have to propose the idea of suicide, which was more problematic for her, because she would have to assume greater responsibility, especially since she had been in analysis. Other times, the idea of cancer comes up as a fear, an "anxiety about death" that she does not know how to control. Sometimes she is ambivalent; she wishes for it and fears it.

A frequent occurrence in the analytic process will be that as we progress with the collaboration of the non-psychotic part, some somatic discomfort usually tends to arise, to which the patient demands that I grant more importance than to the psychic. As delusional activity diminishes, the desire to suffer cancer resumes as a way to "have something" in her mental life, because, if not, she has nothing. Then she experiences a fatigue that she attributes to the analyst's intervention. However, it is not because of his analytical work, but, rather, because of the side effects of radiotherapy that he should be administering from a distance, as I mentioned earlier.

At these moments of progress, although the patient recognises that she feels better psychically, the small bodily discomforts that arise and that she magnifies are experienced as an effect of the insufficiency of the analytical treatment. Because, to be complete, the intimacy and depth of communication between patient and analyst achieved at the psychic level should also take place at the corporal one. Given this "lack", the patient tends to complain that, while the analyst has cured her of psychic issues, this has been at the expense of her bodily health, or, in more radical terms, she accuses me of being an "assassin that causes her physical illness . . ."

For Ms B, her body has also acted as a vehicle for pleasurable satisfaction, which can serve to neutralise, or even amplify, destructive experiences, when she attempts to reject object separation: masturbatory fantasies, for example, of hallucinatory character. She also experiences the perception of certain kinaesthetic sensations as feelings that are not her own, but, rather, belong to others, the analyst in particular; this is the case with her introjective "readings and visualisations" that I have already described.

Relational consequences: problems of internal and external communication

The patient's internal communication between the psychotic part and the non-psychotic part

One of the primary issues in treating psychotic patients is establishing an understandable communication between patient and analyst. The difficulty lies not in the lack of an object relationship, because of extreme narcissism, according to Freud's idea. On the contrary, the psychoanalytic framework shows not only the intensity of the relationship with the analyst, but also its fragility. The problem stems from the difficulty in communication between the psychotic and non-psychotic part of the patient. To achieve this communication, it is necessary to make a detour and detect each of the projected parts in the analyst.

Communication between both parts can take different courses, which is how different forms of pathological organisation are determined (see Chapter Two). In the case of PsOP, the conflict between the psychotic and non-psychotic parts reaches a point that makes it so unbearable for the patient that the former dominates in the personality's functioning. This happens with the collusion of the healthy parts attached to it, in the promise of a new "reality" as an alternative to the painful one. The result is a greater distancing from reality and a weakening of the healthy parts. Ultimately, a deepening rift forms between the psychotic part and the healthy part.

Communication with the analyst

For psychotic patients, communication with the analyst derives from the aforementioned type of internal communication, but it attempts to encompass the latter through intense projections. However, the exteriorised internal conflict in the relationship with the analyst is amplified because he is the representative of reality. As long as reality is associated with intense pain, from the perspective of the psychotic part, which implies a risk of entering into states of disintegration, the analyst's proposal to accompany the patient in his contact with, and discovery of, reality is discredited and rejected as a catastrophic threat. However, if the patient has made it to the analyst's office, it is because he, along with his non-psychotic part, also hopes that his intervention will be a valid alternative to psychotic organisation.

Therefore, it is essential, as all analysts who have worked with psychotic patients have emphasised, to find a way of accessing the non-psychotic or sane/infantile part, which is capable of establishing healthy dependence, in order to dismantle the lies of the psychotic part and distinguish it from the non-psychotic ones. Yet, when the psychotic part is predominant, we must "deal" with it, too. It is unavoidable if we wish to foster significant change. Hence, it appears very important not to respond to the psychotic part's provocation and arrogance, not by denying the psychotic reality, but defending the reality that the analyst perceives. In Chapter Two, I set forth the example of the failure of my intervention, in attempting to confront the delusional reality of my patient, and mine over indicating the conflict within her. It is impossible to directly contrast two realities, the delusional one and the analyst's, because they exist on different levels. Earlier, we discussed the "bi-ocular" coexistence of delusional reality and actual reality, apparently without contradiction. This is an appearance that it is wise to maintain temporarily with respect to the patient's convictions about herself, but not with respect to those that the analyst has of himself. The confrontation with the psychotic part directly intensifies psychotic defences and makes it more difficult for the non-psychotic part to hear us, if not now, then later.

Psychotic transference and countertransference

Transference, by definition, implies a certain distortion of reality: one has the experience that some type of relationship is taking place with the analyst that "is" a certain way, according to the individual characteristics of the two components of the relationship, and not that it is a relationship coloured by projections of internal objects and aspects of the self. That is, if the patient falls in love with the analyst, it is because these natural feelings between a woman and a man have arisen; if she gets angry with him, it is because the analyst has acted in an inappropriate way, which gives her reason to be upset, irritated, or offended. The patient does not think that the analyst is representing his old emotional ways of relating and this is why he experiences these emotions. The analyst's interpretation may redefine reality and help the patient to recognise this distortion according to the type of predominant internal object relationship. This happens, as we know, throughout the therapeutic process with any patient but it is much more difficult to demonstrate this "transferential" process in psychotic patients. Feelings come up in this relationship because this relationship promotes them, full stop. This involves the patient's limited capacity for symbolisation and his tendency to experience reality in a *concrete* way, when recognising reality is especially difficult for him. My patient said, "Psychiatrists are telling you that you have to be dependent, but later you have to be independent [on holidays]; they can give you affection, but not later on. You psychiatrists are like the aliens when you do these things." As such, there is not only the component of distortion in the analytical relationship, which is inherent to all transference, but we are witnessing a psychotic transference;

that is, a delusional one. Chapter Nine illustrates in detail different modalities of psychotic transference with my patient.

With regard to countertransference, as one can deduce from what I have said about transference, it is very intense and, as a result, extremely difficult to manage without losing analytical function too often. The best knowledge we have today about primitive levels of transference leads us to recognise inevitable countertransferential responses in the form of enactments, which are amplified considerably in patients with psychotic organisation of the personality. Thus, a large part of the analyst's work consists not only of understanding the patient, but also of frequent enactments by the analyst.

Forms of communication. Special verbal communication

Another problem that occurs in communicating with psychotic patients has to do with the use of words. On many occasions, words have different meanings for the patient and the analyst, both those uttered by the former and those used by the latter. The patient's verbal production "device" issues a discourse that is not on the same wavelength as the analyst's receptor "device" and *vice versa*. As such, it is absolutely essential to make note of the context in which each sentence and each word is spoken to reach a plausible understanding of what the patient is trying to communicate. This context includes several factors: the moment in the session when verbal production takes place, the patient's bodily involvement (gestural and psychosomatic), the moment in the analytical process, as well as whether or not a separation between patient and analyst is imminent.

Extraverbal communication

Given that verbal communication is restricted in the psychotic patient due to limitations of symbolisation, there will be attempts at other forms of communication. I include paraverbal communication here. That is, all bodily elements that directly accompany discourse: the way words are pronounced, the tone, rhythm, pauses, and also the bodily gestures with which he emphasises or, on the contrary, refutes what he is saying, and his bodily behaviour during the session. There is also preverbal communication; that is, the exteriorisation of unconscious levels that did not yet have access to verbal language.

The psychotic patient's anxiety comes from that force, due to its still formless nature, which means it is not sustained by any unconscious fantasy, that verbal language is sometimes an insufficient containment vehicle, so words do not suffice. All possible channels of expression are necessary for its release, or, perhaps it would be better to say, its communication. For example, in my patient's case, she often avoids lying down on the couch because she needs the analyst's visual support since the auditory aspect is not enough, and she needs to verify that the analyst sees her: she will see the body of the analyst who is speaking, and in the same way she will confirm that the analyst sees hers.

At times, certain gestures are so unique that they can be very expressive. As such, my patient tended to smoke a lot during the sessions. She would sit on the couch facing me to search for her packet of tobacco in her bag, and I could glimpse the host of objects that she would stir around. With this gesture she was indicating the state of her mind at that moment: it was full of things, without order or harmony, and she did not know where the things she really needed were. I generally avoided interpreting it, but I made note of it for myself as a first bit of information to keep in mind. When the clutter inside her bag appeared worse, the search for her pack of cigarettes became more arduous, creating greater unease until she found it. Every time she lit a cigarette with a match, when she put it out she would do so in a very peculiar way. She blew out the flame and closed her mouth at the same time. I was impressed by her ability to make such a complex gesture, condensing two opposing intentions into one movement: she closed her mouth in order to blow out the air. Since she repeated this gesture every time, I thought it must contain some meaning. Little by little, I began to realise that, in fact, one of the issues the patient continued to present was the feeling of emptiness, which I will discuss later on. So, I thought the gesture might address the fact that if she simply blew and displaced the air to put out the match it would be as if she were losing something important from inside her—her vital breath?—thus emptying herself; therefore, closing her mouth at the same time that she blew kept her from losing what was inside her, or to a lesser degree. If this could happen to the air that she exhaled, it could also happen to the words that left her mouth. When psychotic functioning predominated, speaking was actually "removing" words–things from inside her and placing them inside me. So, in addition to the feeling of emptiness, she developed a strong need to continue being part of the analyst. These were times when she could not lie down on the couch or when leaving the session constituted an authentic tearing apart.

Perceptive hypersensitivity

Another trait that tends to be found in many psychotic patients, and which I observed in Ms B, is hypersensitivity to, or hyperperception of, reality. In particular, this applied to everything that tied her to the analyst, his person, and his environment. No detail escaped her, whether in the external reality or the words said, as well as those not uttered but deduced from the analyst's expressions or gestures. That is, any information could be classified as a subject of utmost importance. Therefore (almost) nothing went unnoticed. So there is an indiscriminate perception of reality, in the sense that everything has the same status. It is probably a defence mechanism to keep from recognising the aspects of reality that are actually significant and painful, along with a form of control of the object. One consequence of this functioning is that the patient feels invaded by so much of the stimuli from reality that it causes an emotional and perceptive overload, which results in exhausting mental activity.

Obviously, the unconscious repercussions for the analyst from the interaction with the psychotic patient are often subtly expressed before he realises it: the promptness, or lack thereof, in responding to the patient, the tone and timbre of voice, the rhythm of speech, and cadence or irregularity thereof, are all signs of unconscious communication that the psychotic patient will notice precisely because of this hypersensitivity to which I refer. For patients with predominantly non-psychotic functioning, or at times when the latter is predominant in psychotic patients, these oscillations are overlooked. This is not so much because they do not perceive them, but, rather, because they do not take on the implied emotional repercussions for the psychotic patient. On the contrary, the psychotic patient becomes hung up on these movements and asks for explanations from the analyst, taking them as a sign of detachment, non-communication, or even rejection. To some degree, this could be true, but not to the degree the patient perceives it. So, the analyst continually feels controlled, even down to his smallest movements, which leads to a conflict between acting "freely" at his discretion and according to how he normally does things, and pressure from the patient, with his ongoing vigilance, which requires the analyst to exercise extraordinary self-control.

There are at least two reasons for this. One is the intense projective identification that the patient is exercising over the analyst, which implies a need to control the object into which he is projecting. The other reason, no less important, is to continually verify the analyst's mental state and, by extension, the state of everything attached to him which might be signs of his mental life, in order to know whether he is in a condition to tolerate these projections and help the patient.

Mental emptiness

This is another consequence of pathological projective identification and pathological splitting, when delusional thought does not work, or not enough, to alleviate the pain of reality. Ms B's references to the feeling of emptiness have been very present since she began analysis. Basically, the emptiness arises when she is alone, when she does not experience a relationship in person, and when delusional psychotic functioning is not active. In broad strokes, one must distinguish two ways of experiencing emptiness: a self-perception of feeling empty, which she expresses as, "I feel empty, I have nothing, only emptiness," implying that she recognises herself as a container with nothing inside of it; the other experience is feeling that she is *in* the void, which refers to catastrophic anxieties, something much more distressing because it implies neither possessing a container capable of harbouring her mental life, nor the expectation of an object that contains it.

I shall describe several instances in analysis that demonstrate the different meanings of her experience of emptiness. A few months after treatment began, Ms B feels that she is getting worse because the "little machine" is invading her. When a friend gives his opinion about her, she believes he has done so to control her through the little machine. She feels her excitement about looking for an apartment slipping away and this has converged with other things: her relationship with a close friend has been weakening, and when she went to meet her friends in the bar she felt rejected. The result is that she feels *empty*. It is clear here that insidious delusional activity is threatening to come into play when it "weakens" her fusional relationships with others, and especially if she feels rejected. However, when she is in a situation in which the delusion has not "invaded" her completely, but she feels excluded from her fusional relationships, she experiences a new psychic state (neither within the object nor possessed by delusion); that is, an intermediate state that she qualifies as *empty*.

Soon after (s-47), she comes into the session saying that she has many things to tell me and it is all very painful. For one, she went to visit a friend who was in a psychiatric hospital, which relieved her at first, but then she felt *empty* and it was painful. Here, emptiness is a defence against severe pain from feeling guilty, which seems worse, but the absence of this feeling is also painful because it means she has no emotional life. And this is this case in as much as Ms B retains some capacity experience pain, which is what has kept her in contact with her internal world and with analysis.

Later on (s-81), she insists during the first part of the session that she does not accept a relationship in which I am the doctor and she the patient because she wants another type of relationship in which I also talk to her about my feelings and my life. This is because, she says, "You know everything about me and I know almost nothing about you. You seem to have so much in your inner world, your books, your music . . . yourself . . . and this is not the case." I interpret her envy, gently: she wishes to have what I have. She prohibits me from interpreting because this is projecting my problems into her. She came into the session happy, she says, and now feels ugly, hostile, and *empty*, "because you project the emptiness of your loneliness into me. And I feel defeated, abnormal . . ." (After a pause, and looking at me intently, she continues.) "It's a good thing you have a good chair to support you, because the things I tell you would send you flying." I respond that it appears she can value my capacity to tolerate her attacks. Although she again forbids me to interpret, she goes on to talk about herself, about her insomnia and discomfort, and even recalls a dream.

To begin with, we see the patient's resistance to accepting the analytical doctor–patient relationship, although, in this case, it is not so much due to her intolerance of accepting object differentiation; it is demeaning to accept the object on which she depends; an object in which she recognises the values and internal richness that she lists. This is the source of the envy aspect that I indicate to her. When I maintain my position, despite her forbidding me to interpret, defending my freedom to interpret so that I can do my job, she feels rejected and *empty*. It is as if, by rejecting the relationship with the analyst who is trying to help her, she sees only the non-person to whom she would like to relate. It is curious that she says that I "project the emptiness of my loneliness into her". She cannot believe that I can contain my emotional life without needing to share it with her, despite all of the pressure she is putting on me. That is, she cannot believe that I can keep them to myself. I believe that when she judges the ability of my chair (and what this represents about my working method), she does so not only because I tolerate her attacks, but also because it allows me to contain my own inner world without unloading it into her, although she is asking this of me so that she can confuse herself with me. Right after this intervention the patient is able to talk about herself, about her discomfort, her insomnia, and even brings up a dream. That is, the complaint that I am projecting my emptiness into her now loses meaning, because she is able to find her own mental content.

With some frequency, Ms B began sessions by first bringing up the feeling of emptiness. Given my reaction of waiting for new associations, and not intending to fill this hole for her, she could show other feelings that were difficult for her to endure, so the emptiness constituted a defence. This defence implied not only separating her from painful feelings, but also inducing the analyst to express his internal world; that is, projecting into him her capacity for containing her emotional life, later reproaching him for projecting emptiness into her at the same time. If he speaks to her, he negates her—that is, everything constituting her emotional life is transferred into the analyst—and if he does not, his silence is taken as her projections falling into the void and she is left alone.

For several sessions, she comes in depressed, crying, with the feeling of *emptiness*, saying she has nothing and that it would be better to die. There are glimmers of the psychotic functioning that she now fears, because it feels persecutory, which she expresses as having felt "attacks" by the "little machine". She is afraid that it might be a prelude to a new psychotic breakdown. At the same time, she says that the analytical relationship is dead because it is not a fusional relationship. I indicate that perhaps the little machine's activities kill the analytical relationship because, if it is not a fusional relationship, it empties her of content, emptying her of what she has learnt here, although it is true that this implies tolerating the pain of absence from the relationship every time we separate between sessions.

In another session after that (s-241), she says she is tired, dizzy. She cannot lie down on the couch because if she cannot see me she loses herself. She says she is afraid of having cancer, although she would prefer this because then she would have something, not like how she feels as if she has nothing inside her now, just *emptiness*. Later, she adds that she has been eating better this last year, despite eating poorly all her life. I tell her that now she is making an effort to accept what happens to her, but perhaps the issue is that she has little experience with digesting, mentally assimilating what I give to her, so it is hard for her to know whether what happens here in our sessions is too little or too much. She answers that it is too little. I respond that perhaps this is why she has to sit up, because if she feels empty, she can at least assure herself that she can see me. "Yes, something like that," she responds and, after a pause, adds, "Just now I was thinking about your own fragility, which needs your method, how it is stuck inside you, defending itself." I tell her that now the dialogue has ended. She justifies this, saying that she is trying to be honest. I tell her that I believe a part of her views me as strong for being close to the situation she is going through and understanding her, and that was when another part of her ended the dialogue, because it does not want that. "I can tell you that I feel you are fragile because I view you as strong," she responds. In short, I believe that this session shows emptiness as a consequence of her psychotic part's activity, the part which does not tolerate the analyst's capacity to give her analytical "nourishment", and if she does not have him or is not a part of him, it rejects what it receives, it empties itself; then she tries to justify her attack, because she views me as strong. What she does not realise is that in doing so she is emptying herself.

Some time later (s-276), she explains that she has had a confrontation with her parents, that they stirred up many feelings in her—hatred, rage, revenge, fear of losing them—and then she says that she feels as if she is in outer space without any reference point to support herself. The matter of outer space brings up a memory of a delusion during one of her psychotic episodes in which she was an astronaut who had fallen into outer space, where she "would go on floating . . . forever. A terrible, very distressing feeling," she says. However, it is notable that she then adds that she would prefer to live with madness because she would suffer less than she does now that she must recognise the reality of her limits. I tell her that she is talking to me about the feeling of outer space, limitless, distressing, and terrible, but, on the other hand, she does not want reality to limit her either, she cannot bear it because it deprives her of "total" references, so she has to fill it with "madness". "But with madness you don't realise you are suffering," she responds. I tell her that then she is very limited in managing the reality of her feelings, of her life, of her relationships. She seems to understand this. The next day, she is grateful that we were able to talk about madness during the session. This material vividly expresses the devastating consequences of negating her feelings when they become intolerable because they turn her into a being without a point of reference, neither internal nor external, creating an "outer" space, where she goes on floating "forever". Moreover, she presents the difficulty of accepting the limits of reality, which she must sometimes attack until it leaves her in an endless space without a point of reference.

After that (s-361), the destructive activity of her psychotic functioning is unmasked again and continues to weaken, although, at the same time, Ms B feels this as a loss, and since it is something that has governed her life, dispensing of it is like having to erase her past when she still does not have sufficient tools to replace it in her handling of reality, which leads her to say that she is *empty* because she has neither a past nor a future. Nevertheless, at the end of the session, the patient says that while she initially came in with a feeling of emptiness, she is leaving with the pain of recognising all of this. Again, the emptiness is a defence for avoiding a painful reality because, as with all non-omnipotent reality, there are limits, and because of its painful contents.

Once analysis had progressed (s-431), she came in happy because she had signed a contract to publish a small book. Her family was also happy. However, at the same time, she is experiencing some fear. Her fear is that I will respond to her with an attitude of rejection because it is something that ties her very closely to me; that is, she is attempting a fusional relationship. She later adds that she fears that when I read the book (the patient knows that reading her writing is not part of my working method!) I would see that there is *emptiness* behind the writing. However, she clarifies that it is not a void in which there is nothing, but, rather, a void that can be filled with writing. Ms B states that what she wants to say now is difficult to put into words. I believe that her initial fear of my rejection has to do with the risk that the work she and I have done together, with all of the effort required and some success, such as the book—among others—will be transformed by the psychotic part into a heterosexual partnership with a baby-book, which she knows constitutes the type of relationship that there is no room for here. I believe that the idea that I would see emptiness in her writing has to do with the fact that I see it as an empty piece of writing, not as a response to creative activity, but, rather, the mere filling of a void; perhaps as a retaliation on my part for taking me out of my analytical function. In this session she also talks about "introjective reading", as she calls it: while she reads one of her texts, she suddenly experiences sensations that she does not recognise as her own until she realises that they must be the analyst's. Obviously, this is another way of filling the void that would arise defensively to avoid feelings of discomfort in the face of the fact that, according to his method of work, the analyst will not have read her texts.

Another time (s-445), when psychotic breakdown requiring hospitalisation occurred, Ms B says she felt empty, as well as claustrophobia and agoraphobia. She describes the feeling of *emptiness* as floating on a cloud. On the other hand, she had greatly feared that she could be catapulted into *outer space*. Thus, here we see at least two types of emptiness. One is represented by being in the emptiness of cloud, in an inconsistent state, without sufficient limits to allow her to differentiate inside from outside, so that there is a risk of feeling invaded or, on the contrary, cut loose, hence the coexistence of claustrophobia and agoraphobia at the same time. The other idea of emptiness is the vastness of outer space, the limitlessness of which transcends all, which would suppose a state connected to the more primitive catastrophic anxieties.

Curiously, at times of intense pain and unbearable suffering, the desperate solution she fantasised about was to "throw myself into the void". During one session when it seemed to me we had achieved a certain insight, even if a painful one, which implied recognising what she had to keep working on, where she made contributions and I gave interpretations that, while they did not coincide with hers, could supplement our understanding of what was happening, she felt that I was negating her and leaving her empty. It reached a point that suicidal impulses arose and the way of carrying it out was precisely to throw herself into the void, an idea that had already appeared before analysis started. It would come from a feeling of helplessness to close the gap between the psychotic and non-psychotic parts, between reality and delusion. So, the way out would be to throw all of herself into the void, as if death were the only thing that could close the gap. However, in Chapter Ten we shall see that the analytical process allowed her to discern other ways out.

CHAPTER SEVEN

Technical aspects of psychoanalysis in patients with psychotic organisation of the personality

> "It is difficult for you to be able to understand what I am referring to when I talk to you about pain, if you have not experienced it"
>
> (Ms B, s-459)

To study the treatment used with patients who have a psychotic organisation of the personality, I diverge from the idea that if we wish to develop a psychoanalytic process, only practising a psychoanalytic method will be valid. It is what I intend to demonstrate by showing the case in the second part of the book. I do not rule out that many psychotic patients, because of personal psychopathological traits and concomitant circumstances, might benefit from psychoanalytical psychotherapy, and it might even be the only possible therapeutic alternative. However, I wish to downplay what appears to have been taken as an inexorable principle, that the psychotic patient is not susceptible to the standard psychoanalytic method and needs modified versions thereof. The reasons given are the difficulties in tolerating the classical setting as well as accepting the transference interpretations. So, I will devote special attention to these two aspects, to support my idea of the feasibility of the psychoanalytic method in OPsP.

In my view, the therapeutic aim in psychosis is to help the patient to be able to establish links and bear their consequences. As such, the analyst's first task consists of the capacity to contain the patient's attacks on (Bion, 1993[1959]), or severance from (Britton, 2015), the therapeutic link, and from his containment the patient can learn to later link the different emotional experiences outside himself (with the analyst) and within himself.

There is an extensive bibliography on the treatment of psychosis from a psychoanalytic perspective, which I do not review. I shall just explain the technique that I use based on the experience of psychoanalysis with the patient to whom I have been referring. The appendix of Rosenfeld's work *Impasse and Interpretation* (1987) contains a rather complete revision of the theme from its origins through the date of publication. Later, I shall cite a few of the current authors.

The indication of psychoanalysis in patients with PsOP

The interest in psychoanalysis to treat psychotic patients began with Freud himself, and has continued through the present, with fluctuations in enthusiasm or pessimism with respect to therapeutic success. While Freud, as I mentioned, excluded them from psychoanalytic treatment due to their not being capable of transference, he left the door open to achieving it later based on two points. First, through gradual progress in the narcissism study (Freud, 1914c), and, later, in the fact that he observed that transference is not always completely absent in these patients, so analytical work would be possible when it is present (Freud, 1925d).

The optimism of the 1950s and 1960s about the therapeutic efficacy of psychoanalysis in such patients having faded, a more realistic attitude remains today. We are more aware of the enormous difficulty that it implies for everyone involved in psychoanalysis of this type (patient, analyst, family, and other professionals) when conducting similar work to achieve modest but important results, always evaluating whether the efforts of so many people justify the success achieved. Nevertheless, when conditions are favourable, some analysts accept the challenge of following the therapeutic line of investigation started by the pioneers: Segal (1981 [1950, 1956]; Bion (1993[1967]); H. Rosenfeld (1965, 1971, 1987, 1988[1971]); Searles (1965, 1979); Giovachini (1977[1974]), to name a few from different schools of thought, and continued to the present by others: D. Rosenfeld, 2006, Lucas, 2007, De Masi, 2010, Rosenbaum, 2010, Williams, 2010, to list a few of the most recent. The enormous effort required to perform this task not only results in some benefit to patients, but also has allowed for a deeper understanding of psychosis and, as a result, the development of both the psychoanalytical method being adequately applied to them and the techniques derived from it to enrich psychoanalytic therapy in the realm of psychosis care. In another very significant way, it has allowed us to delve into the human mind at its primitive and psychotic levels, with which we can move forward in our comprehension and psychoanalytic treatment of any other patient.

Nowadays, we know that the concept of "analysability" has lost momentum because many patients who would not be suitable, according to the criteria of a certain school of thought or analyst, may later enter into the analytic process with another analyst, or from another analytical perspective. So, it is difficult to establish the exclusion criteria. Therefore, according to the specific context of the school of thought to which the analyst belongs, and his scientific and personal interests, as well as minimal patient willingness—which I shall point out—and his environment, I think it is possible to consider conducting psychoanalysis on psychotic patients.

In another publication, I have described what I call "psychodynamic indicators" (Pérez-Sánchez, 2012) for assessing the indication of a patient for psychotherapy and psychoanalysis. Very briefly, I will say that the indicators are organised by polarities, based on two of Freud's ideas: ambivalence in psychic life, on the one hand, as well as the conflict between the tendency towards life and the tendency towards death, on the other. I distinguish the following as fundamental indicators: healthy aspects/diseased aspects; adult aspects/child aspects; sincerity/insincerity; love/hate for the psychic truth; tolerance of pain/pleasure; tolerance of link/separation anxieties; capacity for, and tolerance of, the feminine/masculine. I assume that both elements that constitute an indicator are always present, and that it is a question of elucidating the proportions in which they are at play. I use three sources of information as a basis for determining the indicators: the data provided in the diagnostic interviews themselves about the relationship that the patient establishes with the analyst, the biographical data that it provides to us, and the psychopathological data. I try to contrast the indicators in each of these areas in order to observe whether or not there is a convergence between them.

When dealing with psychotic patients, I have been able to verify, from the experience with my patient, that certain indicators become prevalent over others. As such, I would essentially highlight two: the curiosity to know one's own personality, which I include in the indicator "love/hate for the truth" and some capacity to endure the experience of psychic pain, included in the indicator called "tolerance for pleasure/pain (or pleasure/displeasure).

To put it another way, to form the basis of the decision to indicate analysis for a psychotic patient with the standard method, I wish to highlight the following: (a) a certain curiosity about one's own personality and a minimal tolerance of enduring the experience of pain, or, better said, the displeasure concomitant to this task, instead of just feeling it; (b) some tolerance of exploring the transference.

Other aspects to also consider for indicating analysis are, one, the need for conducting an assessment of the patient's whole personality and not just the pathological aspect, no matter how severe it is. Two, to consider the feasibility of applying the standard psychoanalytical method with these patients without needing to resort to special modifications; I refer to the "psychoanalytic method" as that which includes a specific setting and an analytical attitude of observation and interpretation. In my case, that is to say, a setting with a high frequency of sessions (four or five, and the use of the couch) and an analytical attitude of, essentially, listening and observing the patient's psychic reality as it unfolds in the relationship with the analyst, in the here and now of the session, and in the analytical process used.

The setting with the psychotic patient: the setting as an organisational element of the analytical experience

According to Bick, "It must be stressed that the containing aspect of the analytic situation resides specially in the setting and is therefore an area in which *firmness* of technique is crucial" (1968, p. 486, my italics). With the psychotic patient, it acquires special relevance and is more difficult because the functioning of the OPsP is resistant to accept anything implying the differentiation of the object, and, therefore, the setting, and attacks it.

Yet, what is a setting for? In a general sense, we refer to the conditions necessary so that therein a specific task can be completed, which consists of establishing communication between patient and analyst that promotes the manifestation of different psychic levels, in particular the unconscious ones. There are several possible routes of communication, but it is the analyst's job to transform them into significant verbal communication. That is, although we propose that the patient may *speak* of everything on his mind, we know that he will not only speak, but also *act*, including with words. Therefore, anything that threatens the conditions established in the initial contract must not so much be justified or prohibited, but understood. As we know, the latter is another way of communicating (including when it is a hostile acting-out against communication). From the moment the patient enters our office, the more he opposes communication, he also knows that we are committed to re-establishing it.

I have referred to the task to be performed "inside" the setting to indicate that I am alluding to a *space* in which an activity takes place; that is, a "container" in the Bionian sense. As we know, a container does not have life without its contents, and, depending on the nature of the relationship between container and contained, the result of the experience that is taking place contributes to the task that patient and analyst have proposed, or works against it.

Physical space and mental space

From the point of view of a psychotic patient, the idea of being inside or outside a space is fundamental. Either he is inside or outside of everything, in an absolute sense. My patient frequently speaks of psychic states of finding herself in the desert, or in the void. The latter, I already dealt with in the previous chapter. She also refers to being outdoors, or other images that give an idea of "limitless" spaces, such as outer space. Although we do not manage to experience precisely every dimension of how dreadfully painful the experience of finding oneself lost in cosmic space is, which is what my patient complained, we must force ourselves to get as close as possible. As such, the alternative for the patient is either being inside the object or remaining outside of it, that is, losing herself in a limitless vastness.

Having achieved these states implies that the patient has not constructed enough mental space to allow her to leave and enter the object, to the extent that this patient's space endures the containment of contact with the reality of object differentiation, and with reality in general. If her life has been mediated by the object within which she finds herself, through projective identification, she has not been able to develop an internal space that is sufficiently continent.

For example, these are some of the spaces where the inside and the outside are more opposite for my patient: the psychiatric hospital, her parental home, the analyst's office. Hospital commitment is, simultaneously for her, a cause of terror as well as a way to contain her madness. Being in the hospital is the alternative when the outside spaces where she lives are not sufficiently continent. Other spaces that present an alternative to the inside and outside are her parental home and the analyst's office.

With regard to her parental home. Within her, sometimes she needs the retreat of her bedroom, and this confinement can have psychotic or sane connotations. In the first case, she expels family members with whom she is openly aggressive from her life; other times the isolation could address an attempt to be with herself, through her writing, reading, or thinking; although this activity, in solitude, at times might have been determined by psychotic functioning. The importance of the parental home as a physical space became evident to me when, on one occasion (described in the s-396 material in Chapter Three), the patient told me that it constituted authentic psychological progress for her to have been able to walk from my office to her parents' home, which had happened for the first time and made her feel more free. She often went around in taxis or, with great effort, public transport. The area of the neighbourhood around the parental home was an extension of it that provided protection. As she said, she could tell when she had crossed the border of "her" neighbourhood. When she left it, she did so using a method of transportation that did not allow her to be aware that she was leaving this space. Her body did not participate in the task, so there was no proprioceptive awareness that would indicate that she was moving away from her parents' home. So, mentally, it was as if she remained within the sphere of the parental home because she did so packed inside a type of pseudo-pod (taxi or bus) that allowed her to explore other spaces. In fact, she did not tend to leave the city by herself. Only when analysis progressed was she able to travel alone out of the city.

With respect to the analyst's office, sometimes, for the patient, I think that being out of the office not only meant not sharing the same space with the analyst, but also not being inside him. So, one can understand her difficulty in lying down on the couch on several occasions, because not seeing me implied that she had lost me and it was as if she were completely alone, at least until she perceived my words, expecting that it often made it unbearable for her. I was surprised that, during the first months of analysis, she accepted the couch without protest. It was some time later that I found out this was possible because a psychotic dynamic had been at work: the "messages" could transmit my thoughts to her, and therefore be inside of me, even though she could not see me.

The problem worsened when her need to be inside me, and me inside her, increased to such an extent that the mere perception of the analyst was not enough to reach the degree of union she longed for. Hence, there was an increasing need for an incarnate relationship to be authentic. In retrospect, I believe that one of the fundamental issues of the analytic process with my patient was the battle between her psychotic part trying to achieve physical closeness at all costs, and the analyst defending the method necessary to sustain differentiation between the bodies, with their respective minds. Therein lies the transcendental importance of maintaining the setting.

How she moved within the office, depending on her state of mind, also turned out to be significant. For example, on several occasions when she felt that we were not understanding each other, or, rather, that I had not understood her or had responded in a way that did not meet her expectations, she became very angry, stood brusquely, and left the office. After a few minutes, or immediately after having slammed the door shut, she knocked again, entered, and her state of mind had changed; the aggression and hatred from moments before had been erased. Slamming the door had served to nullify them, both in her and, as she assumed had happened, in me, so that we could resume the session. Other times, she had to stand up from the couch to walk to the other side of the room as a physical way of distancing herself from what I was saying; sometimes she would remain there for a moment, and at other times she would return in order to move away again, coming and going, thus showing her ambivalence towards the analyst and what he says.

Over the course of analysis, material appears in which the patient clearly expresses her wish that my office were a room without "walls". All of her tenacity was used to knock down these walls, in order to be in the same space, more "free", according to the propaganda from her psychotic part, although in reality it was to nullify any differentiation between she and I. When this was not possible, despite her countless attempts to achieve it, because I had put the firmness of my faith in my method first, she despaired and I became a "stone wall". Curiously, she tended to refer to the walls of the asylum when she spoke of psychiatric hospitals in which she had been confined and to which she feared returning, although later she could understand that a wall also signified something that set limits and actually contains the destructive forces that threaten her.

The analyst's physical presence

While everything physical and material associated with the analyst are part of the setting for any patient, in the case of the psychotic, it takes on special relevance and requires meticulous care in order to control any slight modification. Both my manner of speaking and the appearance of my face, or the movements of my arms or legs allow her to deduce my mood, which would obviously refer exclusively to her: whether I am sad, aggressive, affectionate, cold, irritated, tired, suffering, etc. For example, if I exhibit a receptive attitude, with a serene state of mind showing in the slight movements of my facial expressions, or in how I cross my arms, or rest my head on my hand, or smile slightly, or tune into her suffering or the satisfaction that she brings in that day, the patient cannot experience it as a the analyst's interest in his patient, but rather as an indication of a "reciprocity" beyond the analytical relationship. Instead, if my attitude is serene, but perhaps somewhat serious, in an effort to try to understand what is happening, especially at difficult times when I have not yet formed an idea of what is happening, and I find myself in this state of unknowing, of uncertainty, she might feel that this attitude indicates coldness, distancing, callousness, and even rejection from me. Of course, these positions of mine sometimes increase due to countertransference reactions deriving from insufficient containment, giving rise to small enactments: a somewhat dry and blunt tone of voice, a longer silence than is proper, the use of an expression or word that is not very appropriate, etc.

In line with the foregoing, I have also observed the effect of possible changes in my clothing, my haircut, my external and physical appearance. In general, I try to have a, shall we say, cautious attitude in the sense of dressing as one would normally with all patients. But if there is any change on my part, the patient just looks at me and, after an immediate inspection, makes some comment, generally a positive one. This situation affected me to the point that, without being conscious of it, I made sure to avoid clothing that might stimulate her curiosity, so she became so present in my daily life that it was almost as if I were wearing a straightjacket.

Vicissitudes of the setting: firmness and flexibility

Earlier, I quoted Bick's recommendation on firmness in maintaining the setting as an important element of the containment factor in an analytical situation. Although Bick does not explicitly speak of flexibility, being a person who has developed the observation of babies in order to explore psychic life, one could infer the type of firmness to which she refers: the need for the baby to be contained. This task doubtless implies much tolerance and flexibility.

After the initial period of Ms B's efforts to co-operate, accepting the conditions of the proposed setting, it immediately became evident that she was not able to maintain them. Therefore, over the course of analysis, it was necessary to make some aspects of the setting flexible. By flexible, I do not just mean revising the contract and modifying the agreed-upon conditions, but, rather, temporarily accepting some changes due to the limitations imposed by patient's pathology, accompanied by the corresponding interpretative work in order to later, when it became possible, return to the conditions agreed upon at the beginning. This dynamic was repeated as many times as necessary, without assuming that the changes suggested as an exception would be established. For example, sometimes, many times, she sat on the couch or walked around the room (less often), while I remained in my chair next to the couch. When possible, I tried to frame this action in the context of the rest of the material and interpret it. So, I did not simply accept her remaining seated because it was difficult to lie down, but, rather, I analysed the difficulties and hoped that she could accept it and tolerate lying down again. It is also true that, on occasions, the acceptance of the couch was only possible by experiencing the situation with underlying psychotic meanings. Sometimes, lying on the couch meant not seeing me, since I represented the painful reality that she did not want to acknowledge; and sometimes, even in a radically psychotic sense, as the analyst disappeared from the room, being out of her field of vision. Other times, she would lie down as a way of pleasing me to the extent that I wanted but if it continued to be very painful, she would even resort to other types of psychotic communication: through the "messages" she knew what I thought or hoped she should think, so that, without seeing me, we were in perfect communication.

When psychotic transference was very intense, particularly before and during holiday separations, the patient needed other types of relationships in addition to those established during the sessions: telephone calls at any hour of the day and night on any day of the year, or asking for an extra session. Even here, my tolerance in accepting it was always accompanied by an interpretation and a minimum agreement with respect to the conditions of the extra contact necessary to later return to the usual setting.

The patient was presenting other ways of actings-out against the setting that I found much more difficult to deal with. I refer to the fact of bringing to the session her productions: writings, drawings, and cassette tapes on to which she had recorded her reflections. My responce was, first of all, to refer back to the commitment to the proposed and agreed upon working method: verbalising what happens to her in the sessions. At the same time, I could not reject these concrete materials because they constituted parts of her, and to do so, therefore, implied rejecting her, so I continued to accept them, although with caveats, according to the materials provided. For example, with regard to the writing, sometimes the patient followed my suggestion of reproducing the text from memory; other times she needed to read it to communicate to me exactly what it said. With respect to the drawings, of which there were fewer, I hoped that she would provide explanations for them, to use them as free associations, although without failing to indicate their defensive use, as with the writing. On one occasion, she brought me a drawing, and, leaving it to me, she asked me to take care of it because it was the original. This allowed me to interpret her tendency to bring me the "originals" of things she produced, like writing, drawings, and cassettes, as aspects of her self she would leave with me to take care of. Something similar happened with her ideas, thoughts, and feelings, I told her, the result of which was that she later felt empty.

Some sessions later, on a Friday, while a psychotic transference with massive projection persisted, she brought me a folder of drawings "so that they could accompany you, and who knows how they might feed you, and you could have a better weekend." I pointed out her fear that I will not sufficiently incorporate her and will not be able to reconnect with her when I return, so I would need her drawings to feed my mind with her, meanwhile they would keep me company; with that I would also remain the sole responsible party for keeping the analytical relationship alive during the weekend. With regard to the tapes, I did not facilitate playing them back during the session, so she left them with me, even without my promise to listen to them because my response was that over the course of the next sessions perhaps she could continue talking about their content.

What is the right ratio between firmness and flexibility with the psychotic patient?

The degree of firmness and flexibility with regard to maintaining not only the setting, but also the psychoanalytic method that we have decided to use is a question that, obviously, can only be answered with each patient. However, in the case of psychotic patients, given the serious difficulties they pose in accepting the analytical setting, it is relatively easy to conclude that a certain flexibility should be offered, either at the outset, or at the patient's request. My experience with Ms B raises doubts about this approach.

What I have just explained constituted my basic position during the first two or three years of analysis, based on the idea of combining firmness and flexibility as necessary to make the analysis of the patient feasible. When rereading it, I realise that I might have given the reader a false impression about the efficacy of this procedure. Yet, it was what I believed in until a moment came when the patient proposed stopping treatment. In her words, what made it unbearable for her to continue analysis was that *she saw me as depressed* when she was also depressed. That reasoning led me to ask myself what made it possible for the patient to have the impression that I could not tolerate the projection of her depression. It was then that I became more acutely aware of the importance of the quantitative factor for the psychotic patient, and also to tie it to the setting. I believe that the patient's interruption of treatment arose because it was already too late when I tried to re-establish the firmness of the method agreed upon. In a way, it was as if I had cheated the patient, because I did not assume my responsibility beforehand.

It is true that many times I showed an attitude of firmness, but more and more often the patient was taking a seated position without my being able to mention the fact under penalty of being branded as an insensitive and cruel person who did not understand how much she suffered if she could not see my face, owing to which, "for the time being", I overlooked it, demonstrating my capacity for "understanding" and the resulting flexibility. The other strategies for breaking through the limits of the analytical setting were also increasing, without me taking into account the number of materials that she had been leaving with me.

Therefore, the setting that creates conditions that make it possible for the patient to communicate with the analyst, but also, and in a very significant way for difficult patients like this, to protect the analyst, was being undermined at its foundations with perseverance of Ms B's psychotic part. The analyst, who, one assumes, should be the party with greater responsibility for maintaining the setting, did not appear to have enough strength to defend it, so the patient had managed to open gaps in the setting and, therefore, weakened my analytical strength.

In the case of the concrete objects (writing, cassettes, and drawings) that she brought to the session, the pressure was very intense in the sense that there was no option not to accept them because this implied a rejection of her person, and that was how she made me feel. That is where I think I lacked enough firmness to avoid falling into the trap of the psychotic part, which labelled me as inhumane, unsympathetic, or "alien" when I tried to show the attack on the setting concealed beneath this apparent attitude, which, according to her, was not only an expression of co-operation, but also of her profound affection for me.

After she interrupted treatment, I was able to review the number of these concrete objects, and, thus, I realised the power of the patient's invasive attitude. With regard to the cassettes, there were not a mere few, but, rather, fourteen, a number that I would never have guessed, such was my disassociation using the excuse of "being flexible". There were a significant number of thick folders containing her texts, along with those containing her drawings, although in a lesser quantity.

I began to perceive that the unstoppable increase of these objects, mainly her writings, was reaching a point that stripped the analysis of its specific meaning, despite my attempts to point out the defensive nature of the writings and even sometimes to interpret their content. So, I decided to take a firmer stance on my interpretation of each acting-out of this type, as opposed to a genuine communication between her and me. It became increasingly clear to the patient that giving me any of these objects constituted an act of violence against me, and my method of work.

From then on she stopped bringing me her writing and other work, which she experienced with pain, blaming and reproaching me for it. However, after a while, she began to describe what she called "introjective reading" or "introjective movie watching". The "introjective reading", which I have already mentioned consisted of unexpected experiences: "while reading a book or a piece of my writing, I suddenly begin to experience sensations and feelings that I do not recognise as my own until"—slightly smiling—"I realise that, in fact, they weren't mine, but yours, what you felt when you read those paragraphs." The same experience also came to her when watching a film; during a particular scene, certain feelings strike her that she cannot accept as her own, until she realises to whom they belong . . . the analyst. These would be a very unusual omnipotent introjection of the analyst, in which her mind was colonised by him in order to inform her of (the analyst's) emotional reactions to her writings. In fact, all this became clear to her when she began to experience menstruation with such intense pain that it could not be the result of the female physiological process itself, so she was absolutely convinced that it must be the consequence of an actual castration. "Obviously, I could not be the one being castrated, but a man could, and this man, it was very clear to me that it was you, the analyst." Shortly after, she stopped coming, claiming that I seemed depressed when she was. This material of the "analyst's menstruation", which she experiences through omnipotent projection/introjection, is also evident proof of the transformation of the analyst into someone "castrated" from his analytical function and, thus, unable to tolerate the patient's depression, or the projection of this into him. My hypothesis is that the idea of the castrated analyst arises from the fact that perhaps I did not defend with sufficient force, and at the right time, the work method that I had proposed, by "letting" her invade me with her material productions.

After a month without attending the sessions, she called me to tell me that she was going back to the psychiatric hospital, which she told me so that I was informed, and said that she would like to have an interview with me when she came out. Shortly after she was discharged, we decided to resume the analysis that had been going on for several years, making it clear that her "concrete" productions were not part of the type of communication in psychoanalytic treatment. She did not bring in any more cassettes, or drawings, and very rarely any writing. She did bring in some of her published books, as an inevitable thank you gift because they were largely a product of the psychoanalytic work.

Analyst's interventions and interpretations

As we have seen, given the patient's intense projections, one of the issues in obtaining interventions and interpretations appropriate for the patient is based on tolerating and resolving the strong countertransferential impact. Once these projections are contained or metabolised, another issue is knowing how to find the right moment and the best way to return them to the patient. It is not always possible to do it immediately because the latter is experienced as a rejection from the analyst. So, it is often necessary to resort to what Steiner described as analyst-centred interpretation, which is different from patient-centred interpretation. The latter tends to be the classic interpretation of showing what is happening in the patient, that is, "... is more concerned with *conveying understanding*, whereas analyst-centred interpretation is more like to give the patient a sense if *being understood*" (Steiner, 1993, p. 133, my italics). In another words, it is often necessary to direct the psychotic patient's attention towards his anxieties as to whether the analyst is resolving the impact of his projections, or metabolising it, in order to later, at the right time, focus attention on understanding what is happening in the patient's psychic life.

That said, analyst-centred interpretation can take on different nuances. I show some examples in my patient. On one occasion, after one of my patient-centred interventions, Ms B told me that I was the one who should know what was happening with me. I recognised Ms B's concern with whether I had looked inside myself enough to know how what was happening in that session had affected me. So, I did not tell her what was happening in me specifically, but, rather, about the mental process that must take place and that I was responsible for being in a better position to talk to her about what was happening in her. In another session, after a few days of absence from the session and the possible onset of a psychotic episode, when Ms B was sitting on the couch and looking at me intently, she scrutinised me and said, "You seem very concerned." I answered her: "Aren't you?" The patient smiled slightly and responded: "Yes, of course." In this case, I did not deny my concern for her, which was evident from the incidents that had been taking place which ran the risk of a new breakdown, but I introduced the question about whether she might be sharing that concern. So, the intervention was neither analyst-centred nor patient-centred: it was directed at both.

Another aspect that varies with respect to the attitude adopted for patients with non-psychotic functioning refers to the analyst's timing of the patient observation period prior to intervention. In a non-psychotic patient, the most important criterion, as I understand it, is to interpret when one has understood something from what the patient has said or expressed. For the psychotic patient, however, things tend to be different. In the first place, it can take a long time to understand anything in these patients, because the primitive pathological levels displayed in the therapeutic relationship need time to be detected, accepted, and understood. Second, it takes time to find a careful way to formulate the intervention so that it is tolerable for the patient.

So, according to the needs of each patient of this type, I try to learn how long he is capable of tolerating it without me intervening so that I can keep it in mind during each session. However, I try to keep my interventions from being trivial or merely soothing. Thus, I avoid long silences to ensure that my intervention helps to move us forward in the patient's associative process: for example, by highlighting a word or an idea that the patient has expressed. I am aware that this type of intervention can determine the course of free associations, but the issue is that, in these patients, the course thereof can be very unfocused and get lost in themselves, which is what they later accuse the analyst of. Furthermore, I can clarify an idea that the patient has expressed in a confusing manner, although sometimes, to the analyst's surprise, patients feel that it is an unnecessary clarification because they interpret it as us undervaluing their capacities. Regardless of the multiple risks of conducting these interventions, I believe it is better to intervene, not waiting to know what we really understand because, as I said, it can take longer than the patient can tolerate.

The limitations of symbolisation (see Chapter Five) should not constitute an absolute impediment for transference interpretation. Being that transference with psychotic patients is much more intense and present than with other patients, the question that arises is whether psychoanalytic treatment with them is possible without transference interpretation. The issue lies in how difficult it is for the analyst to formulate them with the tact and precision necessary to avoid encouraging more confusion between the analyst and the patient, but on the contrary, differentiating one from the other, but not so much that the patient experiences it as rejection. Then there is the patient's difficulty, if he accepts the transference interpretation at a more evolved symbolic level without transforming it into a "concrete" relationship. This means one has to repeat this work over and over.

Furthermore, the way I understand analytical work in general, I consider the most important thing is to pay attention to what is happening in the interaction between patient and analyst, but I also contrast this dimension of the here and now of the relationship with other moments in the analytical process evoked by the immediate situation, in which similar situations were presented that connect with the current ones. For a psychotic patient, this would be another slight modification in interpretation with respect to the one used on non-psychotic patients, in the sense that I think this alternation should be more regular. The actions of the patient's psychotic part tend to erase analytic work despite the non-psychotic part and, thus, the analyst must help the latter to establish continuity in the analytical process.

Moreover, although the relationship between patient and analyst is highly determined by the transference, it is not limited to it. It is necessary to take into account the elements of the reality of the analyst's personal characteristics, which, in the case of the psychotic patient, will be magnified. Searles affirms that the most strange and "crazy" manifestations of schizophrenia have a meaning and are related to reality, not only as transferential reactions, but as "delusional identifications", as he calls them, that go beyond transference, and arise from real aspects of the personality of the analyst (Searles, 1965, p. 716)

Interpretation of psychotic transference: clinical material

I shall refer to my schizophrenic patient to illustrate the evolution of psychotic transference through interpretative work. It is a period in which the psychotic part is accessible to interpretation.

It is a *Friday session (s-217)*. She sits on the couch. She is not able to lie down, just like yesterday, due to the persistence of a paranoid attitude with respect to me. Since she knows it is a point of conflict, she appreciates that I accept it. She explains a dream from last night.

> She is in session with me, outdoors, in a hilly countryside. There are children and aliens. She and I are seated face-to-face, like we are now—she clarifies—and the weather is nice. "You, who look much older, stand up and attempt to approach me sexually . . . and you give me a kiss. You are naked and you have an electrical net on your balls . . . I thought it was dangerous . . . But I woke up feeling fine."

Upon hearing her story, I am shocked by the images in the dream, in particular the one referring to me with electrical wires on my testicles, which also concerns me because it is a rude attack on the analytic relationship and indicative of a predominance of the psychotic. In spite of the openly psychotic nature of the dream, it seemed to me to cast a light on something; precisely by uncovering the psychotic so clearly. In the dream she feels restlessness, coming from the non-psychotic part, although the psychotic part later dissociates that insight, making the psychotic triumph predominate, through her waking up feeling fine.

So, I interpret it in two ways. First, the childlike aspects of her (non-psychotic) that need the analyst appear, alongside the alien (psychotic), in apparent non-conflictive coexistence. But then it seems that there is a clear predominance of the psychotic, by eroticising the function of the analyst; I cease to be the one who attends to her childish aspects. However, the electrical net on the analyst's testicles reveals that she is torturing him at the same time: I remain subject to her desires and my male analytical capacity is attacked.

After my intervention, the patient rises from the couch and walks to the opposite side of the room, telling me that she agrees. I tell her that then she has to get herself away from me, because I have become someone who can persecute her and tell her hard things, for denigrating me in the dream. She lingers for a moment, looking at the books on the shelf on the other side of the room, and, as if I had not said anything, responds that she would like to know what books I read and asks me if I have the one she told me about that she had read over the summer. I answer her with a question: to see whether I know the same things as you, and not something new, like what I just told you, and which you appear to have ignored?

I think that besides psychotic elements, the dream also has others that are perverse in nature, which act in the session to some degree. When she accepts my interpretation, she stands up because the guilt is unbearable for her and/or because she fears my persecution. Waking up feeling good, despite the intensity and vulgar attack of the dream, as well as her response to my interpretation, by trying to talk about books, she makes me think that she is very far away from the guilt she would be feeling, which would probably be unbearable for her; guilt that is mitigated, moreover, by some degree of perverse triumph.

Excerpt of the session from the *following Monday (s-218)*. The delusional psychotic transference persists, although it does not manifest itself. She stands up, walks around. She goes to the bookshelf on the other side of the couch. She criticises theories in books that are removed from practice. I tell her that she also seems to be removed from the practice of the relationship of being near me on the couch, to go over there to the theories in the books. She says she disagrees with the interpretation and that she is going to give me Susan Sontag's essay on the subject. I agree with her in not accepting intellectual interpretation that distances her from what she is experiencing at this very moment, but she distances herself because she might feel that I am a dangerous madman, as she said a moment ago about her father, who could decide to confine her in the psychiatric hospital or not do what is necessary to avoid it.

Two days later (s-221), on Thursday, a massive psychotic transference appears. She tells me that I must be suffering a lot and she worries about me. She explains a dream that disturbed her because of its openly psychotic nature.

> "It is as if there were something unstoppable on a train track. And I was supposed to save the world."

Later on she tells me that I must be "infected" and even must "have delusions". I tell her that if she thinks that I am infected by her ideas, and even having delusions, then she must be the one who has to save her internal world from danger.

The following day, Friday, she is somewhat calmer. She had a dream.

> She was outdoors with a young psychiatrist with whom she was in love. But he had a partner, and although she could have won if she had competed against the partner to win over the psychiatrist, things ultimately remained the same.

She says that this time it is her who appears to feel threatening and not the analyst, as occurred yesterday. She associates it with the dream from the other day in which the psychiatrist was older and had electrical wires on his testicles. And today she was able to look in the mirror and not feel so ugly. I told her that if the image of the psychiatrist–analyst improves, it makes me younger, and she accepts that everything is in its place, I am with my partner, then she can perceive a better image of herself. She responds that she envies one of her sisters (who is professionally successful). Perhaps she envies the analyst as well, I add. "Yes, it's because you would explain your pesonal things to me and I would be able to understand them." That is, when she is envious, she reversed the situation.

During the last session of this month that I am narrating, the patient tells me that the plant (located behind me) is sprouting new leaves (yesterday she also made reference to the plant, but to tell me that there were dry leaves, which reminded me that I needed to water it, which I did that day). I interpret that perhaps this also indicates to us that she is growing here in analysis, where new feelings are coming up in her. For some time now, the patient fairly frequently talks of feelings that she is recognising as her own for the first time in her life.

General comments on the interpreting psychotic transference

If, when talking about the setting, I referred to the need for balancing firmness with flexibility, I would say the same about interpretative work. Knowing the patient's limited capacity for hearing the truth of her psychic reality is easy in that the analyst feels that he must avoid telling it to her out of fear of hurting her. I believe that these excerpts show the contrary instead, the need to be firm in interpretation when necessary, and we sense that the patient can tolerate it minimally. In the first dream, she debases me by making me the victim of her erotic projections. Yet, at the same time, the perverse and sadistic nature of the scene is denounced: my testicles are connected to electrical wires. It was a scene that that did not offer much doubt about its destructive, perverse character. On other occasions, such psychotic and perverse destructive aspects are masked. The patient picks up my interpretation, but, as she cannot tolerate the guilt that it causes her, she needs to defend herself: first, physically distancing herself from my side, and then moving away from the subject when referring to the fact that she would like to know what books I read and whether I read the one she mentioned to me. When the dreams do not serve the psychotic part, but, rather, show the conflict of that part with the non-psychotic one, they become a great help in assisting the patient with understanding how destructive the delusional world is, and also to elucidate psychotic constructions (De Masi, 2010, pp. 139, 143).

Then comes the session in which she is "against interpretation", which I do not take as a confrontation, as the psychotic part intends, but, rather, I address the non-psychotic part who knows the importance of the experience and the deception of remaining among theories. Afterwards, she clearly becomes worried because the psychotic part is gathering strength and is unstoppable. In just few weeks, the psychotic has lost strength at the expense of triumphant perverse elements and now it appears clearly unmasked as an unstoppable destructive force. The serious problem is that the patient considers that the analyst has been deteriorated by her projections (infected by her delusions) to such an extent that he cannot come to her aid, so that she, maniacally, would be the only one capable of saving her internal world. My interpretation of it, showing signs that I am neither devaluated, resentful, nor vindictive, appears to calm her. The next day's dream with the young psychiatrist, whom she accepts has a partner, implies an internal change in her experience of the analytical relationship. This is well expressed by her perception of the newly sprouted leaves in the office plant. This means both her growth and the analyst's. So, I should need to recognise, first, that she observes that something in me is also growing in my understanding of her difficulties. In fact, her warning the day before about the dry leaves was correct. I learn from our experience if I take into account her warnings, what happens with her in each moment, whenever possible. So, it would have been preferable to interpret first by centring myself on the analyst, and then on her.

Therapeutic factors in non-interpretative interventions on psychotic patients

I consider that the interpretative work is the fundamental tool to generate changes in the patient, in particular the transference interpretation. However, I think the analyst's attitude is important, especially with psychotic patients, in two ways. First, sometimes the analyst should be able to tolerate the projections of the patient without verbally interpreting them, which, in itself, has a containment function, with which the patient can identify and learn; therefore, this becomes a therapeutic action. Besides, given the repeated alternatives that the patient usually poses in terms of absolute dilemmas, which he also finds unacceptable, such as the patient's delusional reality or the analyst's reality, it is important for the analyst to tolerate his countertransference, to understand it as much as possible, and then to convey to the patient an attitude that is coherent with himself (the analyst) and his method without attempting to impose his reality or to disregard the patient's.

PART II

CLINICAL (AND THEORY)

"Thus we discover that we must renounce the idea of trying our plan of cure upon psychotics–renounce it perhaps for ever or perhaps only for the time being, till we have found some other plan better adapted for them"

(Freud, 1940a[1938], p. 173)

"Walking through the pain becomes an endless motion"

Ms B (my patient)

CHAPTER EIGHT

The psychoanalytic method in a schizophrenic patient: indication and beginning of analytical process—psychic pain and transferential vertex

> "One of the things I find most difficult to bear is how hard I find it to tolerate pain"
>
> (Ms B, s-207)

Presentation of the case of Ms B

I heard about Ms B through several colleagues, who, although realising the gravity of the case, considered the possibility of psychological help, even though they did not agree on whether the immediate indication should be psychoanalytic psychotherapy or psychoanalysis itself. The patient had been confined to a psychiatric hospital for five months because of a psychotic episode characterised by delusional persecutory ideas (her food was being poisoned), high anxiety, and a state of certain confusion, according to the psychiatrist in charge. Her long stay at the hospital was due to a suicide attempt with an overdose of neuroleptics she had been prescribed, during one of her periods of release from the hospital. The patient herself informed her parents shortly after taking the pills so that they could help her. Previously, she had suffered other delusional psychotic episodes on various themes, but of a persecutory and manic nature, which had led to involuntary hospitalisation on four or five occasions. There had also been several attempts at suicide. The onset of her illness dated back twenty years. At this stage, I am informed that the patient is interested in, and even excited about, undergoing psychoanalysis, which she idealises and on which she hangs big expectations. Her family agree and get in touch with me.

Comments on first interviews

As, during my training, I learnt that, in theory, any psychiatric patient can receive psychoanalytic treatment as long as there are no signs to the contrary, the gradual emergence of the possibility of psychoanalysis for this patient did not seem too extravagant an idea despite the facts that the patient had been hospitalised on six occasions, had a psychiatric history going back twenty years, suffered from self-referrals and persecutory delusions, suicidal behaviour, was diagnosed with paranoid schizophrenia, and, as a consequence, had been taking neuroleptic medication for years. However, contact with the patient varied in the course of these first interviews, as did my decision as to whether or not to begin psychoanalytic treatment, starting with a very unfavourable initial attitude and ending with the indication of analysis.

In the first interview, no sooner has she entered the room than Ms B heads straight for the couch. Her desire to begin psychoanalysis is immediately automatic, without any previous thought as to what this will imply, or what she imagines will imply, or whether I consider it is indicated or not. She had decided that psychoanalytic treatment was what she needed, so she had come straight to do it before having uttered a single word to me about her life and psychopathology. Therefore, the first question is that the patient wishes to undergo a certain psychoanalysis that is in her head, not the treatment that might be indicated by the analyst, and without taking into account her own doubts, which later came up. She walks in and "gets into" the psychoanalysis that is in her head and that she has projected. Thus, patient and analyst are one and the same thing.

When she sees that I do not accept her proposal, because I show her to the other end of the room, where the armchairs for interviews are placed, Ms B immediately says that, even though she has come to "do psychoanalytic treatment", she is scared, because she has always criticised it. Therefore, if I do not allow her to "get" straight on to the couch, which is to say, into the psychoanalysis she has in her head, it must be because I am going to propose "another", the one I know, and which might be different from the one she has in her mind. In other words, I am not the analyst who practises the psychoanalysis she has in her head, but another, which produces her first frustration. So, I have become an external object, someone who is outside of her, who will be difficult, if not impossible, to control, and, therefore, dangerous. She shows this in her first paranoid reaction: "I'm scared", "because I am going to criticise and attack the psychoanalysis that you, the analyst, are trying to propose, and I will take it as an imposition because it is not '*my*' psychoanalysis, in which we should be merged as one. I am afraid you will then use 'your' psychoanalysis to attack me in turn, in revenge." These are ideas that could lie in the patient's unconscious fantasy.

Yet, at the same time, Ms B shows a *sincere* attitude. This is apparent when she clearly explains her fear of her hospital discharge being cancelled unless we begin treatment. She is also truthful when she immediately talks about the dependency and failures in her previous therapeutic relationships and when she expresses her ambivalence with regard to psychoanalysis: ambivalence because, on the one hand, she would like it to be what she has in her head, essentially a relationship in which she can experience all the affection and love she needs to find with a partner, but, on the other hand, she knows that this will not help her. Then, to accept another kind of psychoanalysis is what she finds hard, as she says in the first interview and repeats in the fifth: she cannot get into her head the idea that there should exist anyone, however professional they might be, who could give valid explanations when she herself has not been able to. So, here we have come up against the hard narcissistic core of any psychotic organisation.

After the *first two interviews*, bearing in mind all these questions, my attitude towards the indication of analysis is doubtful, or, rather, negative, although I left her in suspense until I saw for myself whether or not there was any possibility of putting it into practice. She seemed confused, depressed, and low in energy, though, at the same time, with an idealisation of psychoanalysis that did not correspond to her possible potential. That is why my first proposal is to begin with one or two weekly sessions of psychotherapeutic help, and after the summer (we were in March), when she has organised her external life and reduced medication, to consider the step to five weekly sessions, if the indication has then been confirmed. However, during the third interview, after discharge from hospital, I reconsider the plan again, admitting the feasibility of initiating psychoanalysis before expected, as her mental capacity and contact with me have clearly changed.

In the *fourth interview*, the patient puts herself to what she calls her little test, when she explains her stormy romantic relationships to find out if she could tolerate the pain in the experience of relating them. She agrees when I point out that this might also involve a test for me and, if she tests me in this way, I, on my part, do something similar with my interpretation as regards her. This is mutual sounding out, to identify the feasibility of psychoanalysis. There are other moments during the interview at which, when she talks about external issues that I consider as projections of herself, I also try to examine her reaction to my interpretations. This is what happens when she talks of the psychiatric hospital as a prison. Here, what is more, there was the countertransferential risk of an easy collusion on my part. Having worked years ago in a traditional psychiatric hospital at a time when progress in mental care had not yet arrived, I sympathised with the patient's criticism of the psychiatric hospital as a prison: even in hospitals nowadays, more modernised and in tune with patients' needs, it is not always easy; neither do the psychiatric staff always have the training and sensibility necessary to tolerate the suffering of psychotic patients and to act accordingly to deal with psychological needs other than with physical and pharmacological containment. Therefore, at this point of the interview, it was not easy for me to overcome a tendency towards colluding with the patient; I empathised with her idea of wanting to leave that "prison". Nevertheless, I was able to dissociate my role and my history as a psychiatrist in order to identify myself with the psychoanalyst who was listening to the patient so as to consider the possibility of carrying out psychoanalysis. After this slight dissociation, I was able to intervene to concentrate on her internal world and point out that the "prison" of which she was speaking could also mean something inside her. She replies that her problem is that her feelings are very intense, which she illustrates by recalling a delusional episode, which allows me to complete my interpretation: it is precisely because her feelings are so intense that she needs to imprison them, but the problem arises when she cannot control them, and whether she could communicate them here. My intervention is also designed to put to the test the patient's reaction to my reference to her relationship with me at the time of the interview.

It is not until the *fifth interview* that Ms B has really been able to feel sufficient trust in me to delve into her story and psychopathology. Her discharge from hospital and the beginning of the relationship with me had upset her too much to open up to me. It is now that she can explain the reasons proffered for the six suicide attempts and can talk a little more about her delusional world. Now she is also able to express again her ambivalence about analysis: forgetting the time of the fourth interview, but calling, and arriving fifteen minutes before the appointment when she consciously thought she was late, although within this ambivalence the positive side predominates. She can also talk about her childhood. It is striking that the first thing she mentions in her childhood memories are her parents, who do not take proper care of her, and that she needed to establish such a close and symbiotic relationship with a sister that she describes her as being "her other half" or "the air she breathed". So, when her sister fell into depression, the patient felt that part of herself was missing. The precise description of this relationship gives me a fairly clear idea of what the patient means, with regard to the intensity of dependent bonds she can establish, clarity which I consider as a favourable aspect, a collaborating attitude, for the indication of analysis because of her sincerity and capacity for self-observation.

I am struck by her comment that "when I speak I need to smoke". At the time, I told her I understood it as a resort to calm down when faced with stressful situations, such as the interview in progress might be. However, on another level, as I found out after the treatment, I can state that she needs to smoke because, if she talks, it is as if she is emptying, and she needs to incorporate something concrete and physical, the tobacco smoke, in order to fill this void.

During the fifth interview, I also try to interpret the dissociated transference, when she complains about the psychiatrist who did not provide what she had expected. She gives a frank answer, when she recognises her observational attitude towards me, to see if I will be a suitable interlocutor. Another positive feature regarding the consideration of the indication of psychoanalysis is a certain capacity to step back from what she is experiencing in order to observe from a distance. From this same sincere position, she insists on the question that she cannot get into her head the fact that someone outside would be able to tell her anything that she has not already explained to herself. My response is to offer her a work method: psychoanalysis, which, in my opinion, could provide her with some degree of help, even if limited to "as far as we can go".

As for her delusional world, the patient admits that this is something that is present in her episodes of psychic breakdown. That is to say, at no time does she deny, ridicule, or underestimate them. I also understand this as part of her sincerity. What is more, this makes me think that it is something that cannot be so far away, although now, with her medication, it carries far less weight.

Indication of analysis and proposed working method for Ms B

Although, as I said, my first impression was unfavourable, as I saw a very fragile patient with melancholic depressive elements, in the course of the interviews this image was modified. There were no active delusional ideas at this time. What is more, this depressive state could correspond partly to the absence of a delusional world. At the same time, she seems sincere and ready to deal with the source of her suffering, as far as she can. If it were not for the story she has recounted, my assessment from the contact established with me, particularly in the last interviews, would tend towards positive, except for this melancholic, depressive component. The delusional psychotic episodes were diagnosed as paranoid schizophrenia, which I could also confirm from what she related, with a twenty-year evolution, although subject to swings. All this should have led to deterioration in her personal capacities, both cognitive and emotional, which, to my surprise, was unnoticeable. However, she presented considerable difficulties, which is why, as I look back, I wonder what prompted me to embark on the adventure of psychoanalytic treatment with this patient. First of all, as in all adventures, there must have been some degree of unconsciousness (particularly with regard to the effort required from me) along with a certain curiosity and the acceptance of a challenge. Curiosity about the world of psychosis, which I had known for some years through my work as a psychiatrist, but in which I had not had the opportunity to delve deeper as I now had through a psychoanalytic treatment; a challenge because of the novelty of the situation. Then, and of great importance, I must have been encouraged by my confidence in a psychoanalytic method learnt in my professional group of reference, even for serious cases. Yet, all the same, I think there was something in the patient that was more influential in my decision to accept her for psychoanalysis.

On examining the first interviews, I see that I managed to distance myself from the information about her long psychiatric history and previous treatments in order to limit myself to what I observed in what she told me directly and to her relationship with me during those meetings. This allowed me to appreciate her suffering and interest, at least in part of her, in my doing something to try to modify it, so that she could also learn something different from what she had been doing until now. There existed an interest in aspiring to a more autonomous life, even if this would involve experiencing the pain necessary for achieving it, although, given her limited capacity to tolerate pain, she was desperately pleading for help in this, despite the psychotic part of herself. I think that there lies the key to my accepting her for psychoanalysis.

According to my proposal of "psychodynamic indicators" (Pérez-Sánchez, 2012) in Ms B's case, the account she gives me of her biographical data is both coherent and comprehensible and is in line with the type of relationship she establishes with me in the interviews, particularly the latter ones, where psychotic elements do not interfere with communication. Also, the biographical data that speaks of her tendency towards establishing a dependent relationship coincides with what she tells me of her difficulties in separating herself from her previous treatments, and from her sister. So, I think that all this gives consistency to the indicator sincerity–insincerity, with the former in predominance.

However, above all, I should like to mention two other indicators that turned out to be fundamental in establishing the indication for analysis. They are (a) some capacity for pain/pleasure, and (b) some capacity for love/hate in her search for psychic truth. Between the two indicators there exists an inverse correlation: the lower the capacity to tolerate pain/pleasure, the greater the hatred of reality. That is why it would seem paradoxical that, in a psychotic patient, we should talk of love of psychic truth—although only to a small extent—when one of the predominant characteristics is hatred of this truth. What surprised me even more was the persistence of Ms B's curiosity, despite the twenty-year evolution of her illness, to know what was causing her suffering, even though I had warned her of the enormous difficulties involved in a psychoanalytic treatment. I think this curiosity to learn about herself, about her pain, to be able to "suffer" it and not only "feel" it, was one of the principal reasons for which a deterioration, both cognitive and of her ego faculties, had not been produced and what finally decided me to accept her in analysis.

Proposal of setting

The treatment conditions I offered her were those I normally propose for psychoanalysis: high weekly frequency of sessions (five in this case), use of the couch, and her collaboration through free association. As for my task: to try to understand and explain what could help her, especially what I observed in the analytic relationship, in the transference. Given the patient's gravity, I considered it necessary to take into account other elements: the continuity of psychopharmacological treatment under guidance of a psychiatrist, and, bearing in mind her background of confinement, the acceptance of the possibility of resorting to brief hospitalisation, should the need become inevitable. This should be a joint decision between her and myself, along with the psychiatrist.

* * *

> "Now I am realising all the pain that I have had in my life, and it is impossible for me to endure"

(Ms B, s-63)

> "I have discovered a painful truth, that no matter how much I cry, it's still there: I am alone and I always will be"

(Ms B, s-87)

The beginning of the psychoanalytical process

I shall describe the early moments of the analytic process, in an approximately chronological order. I am using the predominant type of transference at a given moment, or, in Bionian terms, the priority transferential vertex, as reference for the evolution of the process, which I determine according to the concomitant pain.

Vertex of adult appearance and regressive transference

During the first months after she left the psychiatric hospital, the patient accepted the conditions of treatment: she came on time, lay down on the couch, and associated. This apparently adult attitude was accompanied by a desire to get her own apartment and become independent from her parents, with whom she still lived. During this period, Ms B made an effort to find signs in the analytical relationship that confirmed the certitude of her decision to embark on this experience. That same day she made the decision, after the interviews, she dreamed that she was freed from a prison. It appeared to her that this treatment was different from what she had had so far, which gave her some relief and hope, although at the same time it implied a more demanding process. She found the natural light of the office enjoyable and it reminded her of a calmly lit corner in her family home. (The subject of light would continue to arise throughout the course of treatment with very different meanings.)

This initial effort appeared to originate from two sources: denying the extreme need for the object (analyst), while trying to not burden him too much with her more intense needs. During the sessions, she contributes materials, associates, remembers dreams, and makes an effort to reflect on what the analyst tells her, while submissively accepting the frustration that, in some way, implied that the experience did not conform to the magical expectations that she had imagined. It was very difficult to recognise the most infantile levels of her mind, believing that experiencing them during transference would make the separation more difficult for her over the weekend and, moreover, during the longer forthcoming summer holidays. In the reality outside analysis, this translated into the urgent activity of seeking independence from her family.

It soon became clear that she still lacked the capacity to endure such efforts and that the goals that she had set overwhelmed her, so she began to complain and cry during almost every session, with tears that she herself categorised as "epidermic". She began to receive my interpretations with a predominance of paranoid anxiety, feeling that I was telling her that she was doing poorly at analysis; that is, that she was not doing everything right that she thought I was demanding. For example, she brought up a dream in which her family flogged her. Then I showed her that maybe this was how she sometimes received my interpretations. When the analyst did not explicitly approve of the effort that she was making, this was taken as an inadequate or erroneous effort. She appeared to be physically fatigued, and felt that she had failed in her life. She complained that she had not had a childhood. Combined with the idea that she was doing poorly at analysis, she felt like a "machine that didn't work", which depressed her. Little by little, this state of submission transformed into feelings of hatred towards analysis and the analyst who had placed her in this situation. Here, the patient found herself in a tremendous contradiction: by not having a childhood, she wished to experience it in the analytical relationship, but this would mean recognising that she is not adult yet, which was very humiliating for her.

So, the patient waited for me to encourage her to achieve success in the external reality, and for me to take complete charge of her psychic life. Having failed in this initial pseudo-adult attitude, a very primitive "regressive" infantile transference began to reveal itself, in which she was like a helpless child, incapable of making any effort because she had nothing in her personality but emptiness, having handed over all of her capacities to the analyst. I made an effort to help her understand what was happening in her relationship with me, particularly during weekend separations, which were especially hard for her. It was then that the feeling of emptiness was heightened as a resource for avoiding the pain because of the analyst's absence, an emptiness that caused her more pain because she felt it without internal points of reference. It was also then that her delusional ideas were at risk of reappearing in order to fill her mental life.

Although she was studying at university, she had merely been performing administrative tasks for some time, and with difficulty. However, she had always had some capacity for writing, although in an isolated and fragmented way, which she could no longer do. During the sessions, she complained of how difficult everything in her life was, and it seems that analysis only served as a container for evacuating into, which did not satisfy her either.

During one session from this period, she complains that her mother is so overprotective that "she devours me", and then she feels sleepy. I interpret this as a defence of her voracity, projected on the mother and the analyst: she does not need the analyst, but it is he who expects her to provide him with "analytical material". Later on, she is happy during one session because, the night before, she had been able to write a story. The story was about some mysterious characters who had been accused of murder, so they were the objects of a private detective's investigation. Here, we see that the patient, through her writing, can dramatise an internal situation that, at other times, would transform into delusion. The story is full of meaning: a detective (the analyst) investigates a murder committed by these characters that she created, perhaps the murderous aspects of her psychotic self. Her observant and creative ego had been able to look inside her and construct this piece of writing that reflected her internal situation. She was interested in the analyst solving this murder.

As the first long holiday approached, the patient continued to demonstrate that her attempts to function according to her pseudo-adult personality type failed because she had neither sufficient ego capacities nor the necessary strength to do so. Even though she made an effort in analysis, the reality of her ability to make changes in herself is slow and limited. Upon seeing the meagre results of her efforts, Ms B believes the analyst's own efforts to be completely insufficient. Her "machinery"-mind does not function when the psychotic part ("the little machine") is not at work because she does not have its omnipotence. Furthermore, the machinery-mind of the analyst, with the apparatus of the setting, only manages to provide limited and sometimes painful interpretations. By devaluing the analytical relationship, she feels even more lonely and desperate. This is expressed in her failure in the external reality in not finding an apartment so that she can have a place to live away from her family, autonomously, and this makes her feel badly, empty, alone. This is also an expression of not having been able to construct her own mental space separate from the analyst. She then begins to feel "without consistency, as if it were sand" and she "would cry twenty-four hours a day". Indeed, she appeared weak during the sessions, often crying, unable to maintain the level of co-operation that had existed up until then; she could only complain of her incapacity and helplessness and how badly she does everything. She had stopped looking for an apartment and had taken refuge with her parents to cry in their company. For this reason she felt guilty, and as if she did not deserve her parents or her analyst, recognising their help in supporting her and tolerating these moments of desperation. In such a scenario, signs of functioning of the psychotic part appear.

Indeed, during this period, after a couple of months of analysis, and when summer holidays were approaching, she brought up her concern about a dream "about the little machine":

> "The aliens, who did not appear in the dream, sent me messages that the end of the world could be coming. And they made me the leader. But everything was persecutory at the same time. I said: 'The egos have disappeared; that is, what makes you conscious of things.' And I appeared to be the saviour."

The patient was alarmed when she realised that these ideas had to do with the delusions of psychotic episodes, although now they were appearing in dreams, so she was afraid that a new breakdown was starting that would result in hospitalisation, which terrified her. I indicated that, given the very needy situation she was experiencing, the imminence of the holidays presented a great limitation in the reality of her relationship with the analyst, to such an extent that she could not longer expect anything here. Hence, she allied herself with "the aliens" in the dream; that is, with that part of her mental functioning that used "alien means" of communication, with promises of salvation, for which egos must disappear, precisely so that she would be unaware of the lie behind all of this. I add, "However, the egos have not all disappeared in the here and now with me, because one of them can communicate the dream in order to shed light on the deceptive functioning of the part of you that is in collusion with 'the little machine'."

There were also signs of psychotic functioning even while she was awake. So, when her father asked her if she was going to go out for a walk, "the little machine" interpreted the real meaning of those words: "Your father means to say that you have to leave." But this type of communication was not apparent in relation to me during sessions at that time. Or I was not able to capture it, then. In addition to these flashes of psychotic functioning, the patient began acting-out to change the setting and in this way transform the analytical relationship into another where there was no room for separation. Thus, problems in maintaining the setting were beginning to arise for the analyst, as I described in Chapter Six on technique.

So, we see that, given her failure to achieve rapid pseudo-adult evolution, she experiences tremendous disappointment when she encounters reality, which makes it very difficult to bear. Thus, psychotic functioning starts to emerge, gaining ground until it dominates the next phase, although in conflict with the non-psychotic part.

Psychotic transference vertex

During a *Wednesday session (s-22)*, she begins by saying that she feels empty. After a silence during which I do not intervene, she is able to contribute experiences that she has had: frustration because they had already rented the apartment that she was hoping for, a brother who talks to her about his affairs, a friend from whom she feels distant, and, above all, her mother, who explained a doctor's visit to her as if she were doing literature, which awakens in the patient a feeling of infatuation towards her. I tell her that it appears that when she feels empty, it is not because there is nothing inside her; on the contrary, everything she has told me implies different types of emotions, but they are perhaps difficult to take on, so she has to empty herself as a defence to dissipate the emotional impact of all of it.

One *month later (s-37)*, she talks about her relationship with her friend Mi, who she admires and envies, with whom she seeks a fusional relationship, but who has her own life, which causes the patient to complain. At one time, her friend told her that if she (the patient) liked poetry, it was because it (the poetry) had no limits, which made Ms B think of Mi as a psychoanalyst who was interpreting her, as if Mi could operate the "little machine" and control what happened to the patient, emotionally. I interpret that in a fusional relationship, which she is trying to have, the other person is the one who can decide, perhaps with the help of the "little machine", which feelings she has inside her, but if the other person, like the analyst, has his own life and does not make himself available to this fusion, she feels alone. She answers that this is correct, "I am not capable of being alone . . . or of being with someone either." Here, the patient shows a capacity for insight: she is aware that being with someone else, if there is no fusion, implies an element of solitude, which she cannot tolerate.

A few days later (s-41), she feels that things are getting worse because the issue of the "little machine" continues to invade her. When a friend gives his opinion about her, she thinks that this is to control her through the little machine. Her excitement about looking for an apartment is fading, she does it mechanically, and several things have converged: her relationship with her friend Mi has continued to weaken, in the bar where she went to meet friends, she felt rejected . . . and so she feels empty. Emptiness can serve different functions: to avoid experiencing the feelings that a relationship generates when fusion does not take place, or to avoid experiencing the feelings of losing that. She cannot tolerate the pain of such losses, but the feeling of emptiness that remains is even more painful. It is then that psychotic organisation begins to dominate, through the "invasion" of the machine's functioning: the messages tell her what she has to feel, which fills the void, avoiding her emotional life as her own, which then she can tolerate. However, her concern about feeling "invaded" indicates that her sane part can still see that it is dangerous, which distances her from reality and ultimately leads her to the psychiatric hospital.

Before the first summer holiday, she explains that she is worried because she has woken up several times feeling as if someone was telling her that a global crisis was going to occur. I talk to her about her fear of an internal crisis because of the approaching holiday from analysis. In order for her to feel more contained, we organised the external setting both with me and with the psychiatrist who controls her neuroleptic medication. While I was on holiday she called me on the telephone almost every other day, she said she felt powerless, had no memory, and had lost some of her vision. This interruption demonstrated the type of relationship she had with the analyst, with a predominance of omnipotent projective identification, so his absence implied the loss of her ego abilities such as memory and "vision", which she had handed over to me.

When we resume after this first long holiday from analysis, she is tired, she does not think she will be able to go on with the things in her life. She fears that she will have to be admitted to the psychiatric hospital. During this period, she has a dream in which the aliens ask her to try to convince people that they are not bad, even though they appear to be. That is, the patient's psychotic part is trying to gain the sane and dependent part's complicity. However, being in analysis allows her to communicate this internal situation to the analyst so that he can help her not to give in. The problem is that he cannot provide omnipotent answers, as I tell her, to help her to learn to better tolerate how painful the experience is. However, he has an ability, even if limited, to help her to put her feelings into words, to give her thoughts meaning, and to support her through this process, such as now, by indicating the risk of letting herself be seduced by psychotic functioning into thinking it is not harmful. During these sessions, she says that she is using me as an alibi; by her coming to analysis, her parents think that she is trying to stabilise herself and they will not hospitalise her. I agree with her that she certainly comes here so that we can prevent them from hospitalising her, not as an alibi, but rather so that we can really establish that it is not necessary.

She brings up a dream in which there appears a dim, gentle, very pleasant light while she is with a child, her nephew. I tell her that her dream indicates her need for me to show her things in a gentle way, so that she can bear them. She tells me that the light in the dream is much better than the one here, although she could recall what we talked about during the Friday session (today is Monday), which does not happen often, as she says, because she tends to erase it. This idea is similar to something we know about from the story of her childhood, that when she was little, she could only eat in small amounts, so things can only be introduced to her gently.

A week later, on Tuesday, she brings up a dream in which she is around people who accepted her despite her being dressed very casually in some jeans and a T-shirt. But she was still worried. During this session, she observes for the first time that next to me, behind the couch, there is a lamp that is always on. I understand, as I tell her, that maybe she is more confident in feeling accepted if she comes in wearing her "clothing", that is, her personality, as it is, without too much preparation or feigning, and she is also able to recognise the *light* in what I tell her without it being intolerable although, at the same time, there is some concern, perhaps because it is a new experience. Then she associates that she was with a friend who has suffered a lot, until she could not deal with it any more.

Afterwards, she felt very tired and as if she had gone blind, although she could see, of course. I interpret that perhaps her friend's suffering blinds her so that she is not able to see her own suffering, and coming here sheds light on it, so that she can see her suffering, which sometimes relieves her but at other times is intolerable. Then she says that she is still doing badly and complains that, since my holiday, I am more demanding of her. Sane depressive elements also appear in this session, when she says that the new experience of psychoanalysis shows her that she is the way she was fifteen or twenty years ago, that she has not made progress, which is very painful for her. So that is why she needed to tell me about her friend who suffers a lot, I say, to which she responds that she would prefer to be in her friend's place in order "to not see him suffer". That is, she would prefer to feel the pain, but not be aware of it, not experience it.

A few sessions later, she is doing badly and people think she is depressed. She continues to complain that since my holiday I am more demanding of her. I tell her I understand that it seems hard to tolerate the "light" of my words in order to see her suffering, so she would have to go blind. She protests that psychiatrists project on their patients. During a Friday session, she complains that the office is cold. She had felt a strange sensation coming to the session, because she has received treatments from psychiatrists for many years, but psychoanalysis is new. She also feels that she is the same as she was fifteen or twenty years ago when she began to feel badly, as if no time had passed. Now she is realising all of the pain that she has had in her life, and that it is impossible to endure; she cannot look backward or forward, she can only live in the present moment. The next day, she says she was able to get out of the pit of despair because of what I told her yesterday, that we could go looking at the painful things, not all in one go, but at the rate she can tolerate. She says that she should be happy because there is something new inside her and it is that she can relate to people more directly, according to what is happening in the relationship, and not what she thinks or hopes, which can be rewarding. However, she is in a bad mood. Perhaps, she affirms, because she feels that she cannot "project herself" into others, in the sense of sharing *everything* she feels and experiences with others. I think, I tell her, that her bad mood in response to this achievement of experiencing relationships with fewer prejudices and convictions about how they should be according to her expectations and wishes must have to do with seeing herself as separate from others, which implies that she cannot "project herself", as she says, and that she must understand it as giving up a fusional relationship with the other person. So, we can think she is aware that relating to others without psychotic functioning is very painful, just as realising that being dominated by this functioning has implied losing many years of her life. So, we find ourselves in a delicate situation, where psychotic organisation might become activated in response to how intolerable this pain is.

Then she begins to think that we are at a moment of stagnation, which she had known from the beginning, because all therapeutic relationships are limited: "You are not a machine, as you sometimes tell me, so if the things I tell you affect you, how can treatment continue without knowing how and to what extent they affect you?" Since I do not talk about it, she takes it as an expression of outright rejection of her, or that all that falls into the void.

On Saturday of this week, she calls to tell me that she wants to pay me for the sessions that she owes because she has decided to suspend treatment. I propose that she come in to continue talking about it. She comes in on *Monday (s-73)*, but maintains her decision to suspend treatment. When I show my willingness to continue talking with her, she pays me with a cheque corresponding to the previous month, but not for the sessions from this month. The following week, she does not come in or call. Her parents, who are worried, contact me by telephone. I tell them to ask the patient about treatment and to tell her that I am still willing to treat her.

On Monday (s-74) a week later, she comes in forty-five minutes into her session time to pay me for the month's sessions and permanently suspend treatment. She insists upon the fact that I am the one who has problems and that I need help, which she herself might be able to give me. Seated on the couch, looking at me intently, she says, half smiling, "Are you worried?" And I answer her, "Well, aren't you?" And, smiling, she says, "Yes, I am, but this is not where I need to solve the problems that I have. There is a power relationship here." She stops coming for the rest of the month.

Her father comes in the last day of the month to pay for the sessions. He justifies doing this for her because he thinks she is very tired and doing badly. When he asked her whether she wanted to tell me anything, she said to tell me that she loves Dr PS very much. I explain the patient's ambivalence to her father, and my decision to keep her session times open, and that I prefer that she be the one to pay me. The next day, the patient comes in while her father waits for her downstairs. She comes in to bring the cheque. She says that treatment has ended because she is cured; I have cured her. In a clearly manic tone, she says that she feels as though she has been touched by a divine grace. She talks about the office as an almost celestial space: how good she feels in this office, so warm, that it is the nicest office she has seen, and she has seen many. I tell her that this is also the first time she has undergone psychoanalysis. She says yes, and that is why she is cured. "This office is so nice. The first time that I saw it I thought I was *hallucinating*." She finds similarities between her idealised father and me, because of my appearance, my mannerisms, and my generosity. She indicates the books on my bookshelf, which cause her to say that I must know everything, and that this is why we have been able to finish treatment in such a short time . . . She tries to calculate the number of months. Since April . . . (about seven months). And that she has liked me since the first visit. However, the following weekend she is doing very badly and needed to contact me to talk about her anxiety, and her psychiatrist to prescribe her more medication. Over the next few weeks, she calms down and resumes treatment at five sessions weekly.

Vertex of eroticised psychotic transference

Her severe pain now arises from not accepting the reality that the analytical relationship, which she loves and appreciates, is neither more nor less than a relationship of professional help. Since it is very important in her life, she cannot accept that it is limited to the sessions. She is no longer the helpless child who wishes to fuse with the analyst-mother, or the adult who demands equal treatment through communication and not an unequal relationship, but, rather, an adult woman who hopes to have a complete adult relationship with the male analyst because that is what men and women do. The underlying reason for maintaining this cause is psychotic in nature, by confusing a relationship of closeness and gratitude for the help received with her belief in an erotic relationship. She is also convinced that I harbour feelings of affection towards her comparable to her own, but that I feel inhibited and not free to express them, due to which she is willing to help me so that, without fear, little by little, I can allow myself to communicate them. On one occasion, I tell her that she does not allow me the freedom to relate to her according to the commitment I have established with her to think about and understand what is happening to her and explain it to her.

On a Monday (s-81), she comes in happy. She insists during the first part of the session that she does not accept a relationship in which I am the doctor and she the patient, but, rather, a relationship in which I, too, can talk to her about my issues. Because "you know everything about me and I know almost nothing about you. You seem to have enough with your inner world, your books, your music . . . yourself . . . and this is not the case." I interpret her envy, gently, in the sense that I point out the possibility that it is hard for her to accept that I have my own inner world, my books, my music, that is, my life. She responds angrily that she forbids me to interpret because this is projecting my problems into her. She came into the session happy and now feels ugly, hostile, and empty, "because you project the emptiness of your loneliness into me . . . and I feel defeated, abnormal . . ." After a silent pause, she adds, "It's a good thing that you have a good chair to support you, because the things I tell you would shake you!" I respond that she can value someone who tolerates her attacks. She again forbids me to interpret, but then goes on to talk about herself. Last night she had insomnia and had to take a pill. And then she had a dream

> in which at first she was in bed, which her mother had moved, as if she were a child; but at the same time it was as if she were in the hospital because she was pregnant with a son she had conceived with X, a former therapist. The gynaecologist went to visit her but she was afraid that he wanted to make love to her.

I interpret her desire to feel cared for by the doctor–analyst at her most infantile levels, which she sometimes confuses with becoming his partner and having a child. She asks me whether I can recognise my own childish feelings. I tell her that it seems essential to her that I get in touch with the infantile levels of my mind in order to help her to recognise her own.

In this session, we see the patient's resistance to accepting the analytical doctor–patient relationship. However, here it does not have so much to do with intolerance of accepting object differentiation; if it feels demeaning, it is because she does not accept the object she depends on, an object in which she recognises the values and internal richness that she lists. Hence, the aspect of envy for everything the analyst has that she does not. Then, she tries to forbid me from interpreting. When I maintain my position, without entering into the type of relationship that she proposes, reclaiming my freedom to interpret in order to do my job, she feels rejected and empty. It is as if, by rejecting the relationship with the analyst who is trying to help her, she sees only the non-person with whom she would like to connect. It is curious that she says that I "project the emptiness of my loneliness into her". She is not able to think that I can contain my emotional life for myself, in solitude, without needing to tell her about it. Or, on the contrary, she can indeed see what I am doing, and her envy and the claim that I am the one projecting loneliness arise from there. I believe that when she judges the abilities of my chair (and what this represents about my working method), it is not so confused with the psychotic part. She values it, not only because I tolerate her attacks, but also because I contain my own inner world without unloading it into her, despite her pressure on me to do so and confuse myself with her. Right after this intervention, the patient can talk about herself, about her discomfort, her insomnia, and a dream. Of course, it is a dream in which she confuses a child needing care with actually having a child with the doctor, because the mother–analyst treats her like a child. So, it is difficult to address her childlike aspects because she thinks I am being like her mother, in that I infantilise her in order to sadistically dominate her better.

While, on the one hand, the solidness of my position (the solid chair) in not giving way to the pressure of eroticised transference calms her, on the other hand it makes her sad and fills her with pain. "Coming here," she said in another session, "I have discovered that, even though I cry, the painful truth is still there: that I am alone and that I always will be." Given my indication that it is possible to share this discomfort here, she tells me that she does not want a therapeutic relationship, that she will accept the rules of the game (of treatment) but that she will always resist accepting them. Here we see a new pain, derived from the recognition of a very sad reality: being alone means not being fused to the object (analyst), a first step in developing the depressive position, with the concomitant pain, although this pain is certainly magnified according to how much the psychotic part resists accepting therapeutic dependence and feeling the relief of this support, which makes her feel more alone.

Days later, on a *Monday (s-86)*, on the one hand she insists that she does not accept the therapeutic relationship, that she is only waiting for me to talk to her, because she will only be free if I feel free to talk to her about what I hide inside me, that which I do not allow her to see. On the other hand, she talks to me about situations that show her extreme need. Yesterday, during a television programme about

Angola, she saw a malnourished child in a hospital, full of tubes and with a swollen belly. At the beginning of the session, she said that she felt ugly and that her stomach is swollen, but when I interpret this aspect of her as a malnourished child, there is a lack of emotional understanding. She insists that this is my projection, and that it is not what she wants. She brings in a piece of writing about me that she did on Saturday and wants to know my opinion. She attempts to give it to me, but I suggest that she tells me what it is about. She reads it. The text talks about the absence of Mr Antonio, "and that his hands are not there to do the work [of taking care of her] . . . because his hands are busy taking care of children . . ." She let her parents read the text. She asks me what I think about it. I tell her that perhaps my absence on the weekend was not felt as loneliness, but, rather, as a stimulus for the dialogue within her. Maybe she felt warmth in the Friday session despite complaining that I was cold. She responds that when I say "you" I should say "I", in order not to project. She wanted me to show her my hidden side so that she could have it, and so that she was not always the only one giving by talking about her issues. She then recalls a song by Brassens that talks about a thirteen-year-old girl who asks him for kisses, and he tells her that he is too old and that he is married. She ends by saying that she wants to give me a Christmas present.

It is striking in this session the coexistence, on the one hand, of the needed childish aspect (malnourished and ugly), because of the predominance of madness that prevents the nutritional dependence of the analysis, and, on the other hand, the arrogance of the madness when pretending that it is she who feeds the analyst. And, since he does not accept it, he remains empty; a void that then he has to project into her, according to the "logic" of its madness.

The following day, *Tuesday (s-87)*, she comes in depressed, very sad because of yesterday's session. She insists on how much she gives me while I give her nothing. She woke up this morning full of pain. And she wrote a letter to her father, which she brings and reads to me, in which she talks about the distance between them, of her helplessness in spite of the shelter that he provides for her. She has been crying non-stop while writing the letter and now, when she came here, because, "I have discovered a painful truth, that no matter how much I cry, it's still there: I am alone and I always will be" She also says that, in spite of herself, she is becoming dependent on the analyst and it is as if she has given up, and while she accepts the rules of the game for a therapeutic relationship, she will always resist accepting them. She gives me some drawings that she has done. She thinks about giving me a cassette containing her voice and background music. Here, we see a type of pain linked to acknowledging a reality, which is different from psychotic pain. That is, rather like an expression of the psychotic patient's limitations for tolerating the pain of contact with reality, which is different from pain caused by psychotic functioning. The painful reality is recognising her need for the object and not possessing it.

The next day (s-88), she brings me a gift, a package. I interpret that perhaps it is an expression of her gratitude. She becomes angry and tells me no, that it is simply a gift that she wanted to give to me as a person, not as a therapist, because we had determined (?) that this was not a therapeutic relationship. She comes to the next session happy. She explains to me that the book she gave me is the collected letters between a writer and a philosopher. I would be the philosopher and she the writer.

Vertex of delusional psychotic transference

A few days later, she stops coming in for a few sessions, although she calls on the telephone. Her parents contact me, worried. I refer them to her psychiatrist, who monitors her medication. The patient returns with delusional thoughts. She is a clairvoyant, which is one of the several personalities that exist inside her. I first interpret that perhaps she is me, so she does not need Dr PS, and later I say that I understand that there are aspects within her personality that differ from one another. She responds that she has lost her identity, that her identity is inside me, and speaks in manic terms, identifying me with notable people. "You are Federico Garcia Lorca, Antonio Vivaldi . . . although more like St Francis of Assisi." I talk to her about the concern of her parents and those around her. "You also appear worried," she says. "Aren't you?" I answer. She smiles in response and agrees that she is, and that she herself asked her parents to take her to the psychiatric hospital. I tell her that it seems that coming here is not enough to stop the discomfort and suffering that she experiences.

On Saturday, I see her for an extra session. She comes in very anxious and reveals that she has lost vision. I tell her that on Thursday she felt clairvoyant and that today, on the contrary, she has lost vision.

Perhaps the weekend separation at this very difficult time renders this resource of considering herself clairvoyant useless. I offer her a session on Sunday as well. On Wednesday, she calls me to tell me that she will be admitted to the hospital, because "the only way to save world peace is by being obedient," and this is why she respects her father's decision to commit her to the hospital. He would later tell me that she was the one who asked to be hospitalised, this being the first time she was admitted willingly. Fortunately, the hospital accepted my collaboration and allowed us to schedule some sessions there, which we soon alternated with visits to my office, with someone accompanying her.

During one of the sessions at the hospital, she tells me two important things. One, that for the first time she can talk to me about her hatred for her father; such a kind man that it appears that all evil must be outside him, in his children, and especially in the patient because she is one of the most psychically vulnerable. The patient also acknowledges that the hostility that she unleashed inside the hospital was because "enemy forces" pushed her to do so, because of which they had to tie her down as the only way of stopping it. She felt omnipotent, although omnipotence has its limits, because even "God cannot prevent hostility and violence from existing in the world," she says. She does not remember that she was voluntarily admitted, as they told her, or that in any case, she did not consider these words to be her own. I tell her they must be mine. "Maybe so," she answers. I add that she was hostile toward her parents in order not to be hostile against me and to preserve this relationship. She feels that she must save the planet from so much suffering and wars, as the verses of a poet say: "And the voice of the maiden will save humanity".

During the next session, back in the office, while she is still hospitalised, she tells me that she made an effort to discuss her madness with me because she appreciated my work of going to the hospital to visit her and that she hoped to continue talking about her madness, but slowly, here in the office. "Every time I leave the hospital to come here it is like crossing a barrier that oppresses me and keeps me from getting here, a place of freedom." She reads me some pieces of writing in which she talks about loneliness and that "mothers do not abandon their children," which allows her to say that now she sees her parents differently, neither so good nor so bad. "In the text [she clarifies], when they realise that mothers do not abandon their children, they stop feeling alone . . . The loneliness fades when you can put it into words and explain what you feel . . . It is as if for the first time I could feel that I have a mother." She also says that she has learnt from me that love is never perfect. Nevertheless, in another moment, with some effort, she confesses to me that she still thinks that the "little machine" that sends her calming messages must be somewhat real. I talk to her about her fear of bringing up these ideas because she is afraid that I will reject her. She cries and says of course, that they are her defences, and that she cannot go without these defences. And if she brings it up I will destroy it, she laments.

During the *next session (s-105)* she is still in the hospital. She arrived more calm and apologised for having been hostile towards me (rather, contemptuous), but she recognises that the idea that others can influence her thoughts through the "little machine" is very ingrained in her and that this has been the case for twenty years. "And now it is as if I cannot imagine thinking 'normally'." She dreamed about me, she continues:

> "We were having a session, in a room that could be at the hospital or here, your office, and there was a very nice view."

We talked about integrating the hospital and my office as two aspects of the relationship with me that thus far have been disassociated from one another: the analyst who helps her and the one who does not prevent hospitalisation. Speaking of her parents, she says that it is hard not to see them in "absolute" terms, as with me, although she is learning from me how to see things in relative terms. She also says that, thus far, she has not been aware of the fact that she has been undergoing psychoanalysis. She does not know how that has been possible. She recognises that it is an important moment because she is touching on things in her that she has not dared to address with anyone.

Comments. The patient has needed hospitalisation, that is, her psychotic functioning has come to dominate in such a way that it becomes clear to me. It is as if until now there had been a silent pact between the psychotic part and the dependent parts of her to prevent the psychotic functioning from being revealed. Hence, she feels that she has not been conscious of undergoing psychoanalysis until now.

On Friday (s-106), she comes from the hospital. Her parents visited her and she complains that her mother speaks for her and does not leave any room for others. Later, she wrote some letters and, as she has recently tended to do, she brought them to me to read during the session. She says something about the big blue dam that contains and satisfies. I make reference to the containment that I have been able to practise during this time (my couch is blue), to limit the "enemy forces and the little machine", although it was not completely successful because she was hospitalised, but it might be useful now. She says that she has learnt from me to downplay the little machine due to the effect it has on the relationship. But then she is nostalgic for the lost magic. I interpret the lie that might lurk within this nostalgia. She complains that although I am right, it means she is naked, helpless, and defenceless. And she recognises that during the first period of psychoanalysis, the messages had functioned in relation to me, although she did not say so, perhaps because even she did not realise it. She also shows how painful it is to acknowledge what I say to her, because she feels that when I interpret it makes her feel inferior.

On Saturday (s-107), she comes in very sad because she has learnt about the death of an old friend whom she met in a psychiatric hospital, who had apparently been run over in the street, and whom she knew had lived a marginalised life. A few months ago, she encountered him on the street and he looked so bad that she offered to make love to him in order to give him something, but he did not want to. She asks me not to return to the hospital because she will not be able to handle it. She is supposed to be discharged next Thursday. I keep my commitment to her and the hospital and do not bend to her pressure.

On Monday (s-108), she explains to me that after the session she was able to return to the hospital. She also says that she has been reviewing her writing from years ago and she was surprised by the sense of self-glorification that it gave her, "about how I resorted to the messages from the aliens and the little machine", and she has thought about the possibility of revising them and publishing them. She does not want to remain on the margins and wants to be a part of her family. She tells me a story about the aliens that she experienced prior to hospitalisation, which she did not tell me about because she thought there was no need since I would know about it through telepathy. She explains it to me as a show of trust and so that I am aware in case anything similar happens again. She thanks me for having been able to keep in contact with her since the first day she was admitted to the hospital, for being able to call me and also have sessions during her stay there.

Comments. When she is about to be discharged, the death of a "friend" of hers occurs, a psychotic patient, who had become a beggar and who died as a result of being run over in the street like a dog, she said. It is as if this incident makes her sad and, at the same time, represents a wake-up call about how she herself could end up. But I believe that the fact that I remain firm by not interceding for her to be able to leave the hospital early (four days remained), might have contributed to the fact that she could contain the feeling of sadness without it overwhelming her and without resorting to psychotic functioning. Thus, she recognises and values the treatment and can feel more trusting in telling me her delusional stories about the aliens from before she was hospitalised, so that I am aware. Although this is possible, she also responds by thanking me for my efforts in not losing contact with her during her hospitalisation. I believe that this meant that she could remain in contact with the dependent, non-psychotic aspects of herself so that these had enough strength to reveal the disastrous consequences of psychotic functioning. Also, she has been able to reread her writing associated with periods of delusion in order to revise them so that they can become something publishable. At one time, several sessions ago, the patient said that she recognises that the issue of the aliens was like excessive imagination. Hence, it is possible that the delusion can become a literary text if she keeps the necessary distance and can also contain her death anxieties in other ways. She has been in the hospital for a little over a month. Her previous hospitalisations had tended to last between four and six months. Now she returns to the sessions worried about how she will function without the "little machine", without the energy that this provided.

To the extent that her attempts to eroticise the analytical relationship were unsuccessful and, not being able to give up an enjoyable fusional relationship, the patient resorts to psychotic functioning, which is the vertex of delusional psychotic transference, which we are analysing. However, a bodily repercussion was revealed to be alternating with it, with regard to hypochondria, in the sense of being convinced that she had developed cancer, for which at one time, after pressuring her family and doctors, she managed to get admitted to a clinic to undergo medical testing (which I described in previous chapters). To her dismay—she told me—the results ruled out any organic disease, particularly cancer, because of which she lost the magnificent opportunity to have, to possess, something, a cancer, so she remained empty by not having the delusional world whose deceit she had begun to see, and she did not have the complete affection of the analyst, in absolute terms, either. Complete affection meant that, following the analytical experience that had taken place, she had enough proof of the analyst's interest in helping her, but eroticised and embodied affection was missing for it to be complete. Since I did not offer it to her, it led to a paradoxical situation in which she came to conclude that while I was curing her mind, her body was becoming ill.

At a time when she was most in touch with reality, one day she told me that she felt bad with me, thinking that I judged her to be doing badly at analysis, and she was in despair, crying, and feared that it could destroy the analytical relationship. On Thursday, she was a little more cheerful and trusting. On Friday (s-115), she lies down on the couch, which is something she has not been able to do for a while, and brings up a dream in which the analyst appears and she feels like a bad person. She associates it with prior sessions. She recognises that, at times, when she was in despair here, she could use it to make me feel bad, like a form of hostility. She talks about the feeling of loss with regard to the little machine's functioning, because this allowed her to be the centre of everything, of the world. "And now I am just one more person." We can also differentiate the "bad" parts of her that might resort to the little machine from those that want to come to the session. A few days later, she came in feeling empty again. She was reading her writing from seven or eight years ago and it spoke of the feeling of emptiness. She brings one and begins to read about a girl, but is afraid of invading me with her writing and sets it aside to explain a dream to me.

> She was in the psychiatric hospital or in a classroom at the university she attended, and suddenly a metallic flying fish appeared and turned towards her to attack her. She ran towards a room with light and then the fish became smaller and then was harmless.

We see the metallic "fish" as a representation of psychotic functioning (of the machine), which is now felt as something persecutory, and when she takes refuge in the light of analysis, this threat shrinks. It is curious that the place is a mix of the psychiatric hospital, where she is confined, and the university where she is taught. I believe that this double image is valuable to analysis. So I did not inform her of the first aspect because it would certainly be more reassuring to me to only look at the second, in which the analysis–university provides "light"—knowledge. A short time later, when she was talking about a literary matter that made reference to the light needed to see, and she again related it to the light that analysis provides, she was surprised when she first realised that behind the couch, next to me, there was a lamp that had always been turned on since the beginning of treatment.

In these sessions, she demonstrates her gratitude for the help that I give her by tolerating her regressive moments and because she feels understood. "If only I had had these sessions twenty years ago. Because it has been twenty years of madness," she affirms. She is thankful that the analytical experience allows her psychotic functioning to be somewhat contained in different ways: in the form of dreams that she can retain, communicate, and share with the analyst instead of transforming into delusion; also through her writing, the literary content of which is formed by "metabolising" what has been delusion at other times, which she later verbalises during the session and shares with the analyst. The same thing occurs with the drawings that she sometimes brings. In Chapter Seven, we saw the problems arising from this. During this stage, the curious matter of her experiencing new feelings, which she has not previously recognised as her own, also appears with relative frequency. For example: suffering through being alone without needing to have to "do" something to neutralise that experience; that is, tolerating it, without resorting to psychotic functioning.

Vertex of "plural" conflictive transference

In this stage, the pain comes from several sources. One very important one continues to be the absence of predominantly psychotic functioning. She complains that she cannot lock herself in her room and have delusions, so a new type of mental functioning is emerging that is expressed in several ways. For example, she says that she can now experience a more "plural" attitude with respect to the relationship here, in the sense that, although it continues to be important, it does not invalidate other outside relationships. It also manifests in the different way she writes: before, it was enough to write whatever came to mind automatically (perhaps dictated by the "messages") and it was already valid, while now, once it is written, she reads it, rereads it, and corrects it; in particular, giving meaning to what she experiences is also new, recognising her feelings as her own. But all of this is so hard, she laments, because she would often wish to return to the "little machine" because it would allow her to have a fusional relationship with others, and this is revived in a dream in which she has my complicity. In the dream, the analyst appears, tells her that he is in love with her, and that she must resort to the little machine and the messages to save the world. The dream clearly reveals that the eroticisation of the analytical relationship, which had previously manifested itself at times when the psychotic part was predominant, is at the service of the latter. However, as she remembers, before hospitalisation the messages assured her that the analyst was in love with her; now, this wish takes on the form of a dream. During the session when we are able to see this, the patient ends up crying and says, "I did not plan on crying today. It's not just out of sadness but also out of gratitude from seeing the effort that you are making with me" (s-126). She laments not having these sessions twenty years ago, the length of time that she has been crazy, she says, and she again expresses her gratitude for the help and support that I give her (s-136).

The patient's depression during this period, then, has to do with several things. One is that she feels the most immediate sorrow for the loss of the little machine's psychotic functioning: "I don't know how to live without the little machine . . . I would give all the money in the world to be dead or have the messages," she says during this period; another is the sadness of seeing the years lost from having been subjected to the lie of madness. Renouncing psychotic functioning also involves the loss of the type of relationships that this provided to her, in particular with the analyst. Another consequence of that renunciation is seeing herself with "bad" feelings, and when she looks in the mirror she sees herself as ugly. Before, with "the little machine", she looked in the mirror and said to herself, "You are pretty." There is also pain in recognising the coexistence of the different types of transference with the analyst; this implies renouncing the exclusive relationship of eroticised libidinal transference, and admitting other maternal and paternal libidinal types of transference, as well as hate and rage. In addition, admitting the plurality of her relationships with her loved ones implies accepting that she is not the only one in each of these relationships.

"I feel pain when I remember the past. When I see that I have lived with the little machine for so many years, and that now all of it is false," she says a little later (s-150). And the next day, "I cannot tolerate relationships without fusion", which leads her to discredit the work of the session and turn it into me as an interpreting machine and she as an associating machine, because that is what I expect from her (s-151). She cries, she feels like a disaster, ugly. No one can love her; she does not deserve it. "Because I have lived with exaggerated infantile narcissism for many years: through the messages, everyone loved me, but it was actually a way of loving myself and no one else" (s-158). She is in somewhat of a state of desperation, with suicidal ideation. I am not helping her, she says, because I am not God, and then she explains a dream in which she led a revolution because she was omnipotent. Ideas, she says, that she had before while awake (s-163). While I support her through these sessions she tells me that she sees me as "the well cleaner of despair" (s-167).

Ms B insists again on the idea that she now has a more plural relationship with me, in the sense that it is compatible with her forming other relationships. But I think that she also refers to it being possible for her to see me as a polymorphous analyst object on which she can project different internal objects and aspects of herself. Throughout this period, she brought up a very revealing dream about this internal change in which the world of good and the world of evil come together, while the figure of a man is present. This is why I call this moment a "vertex of predominantly 'plural' transference", which is conflictive because it implies a tendency towards the integration of different aspects of her mental life, and a greater contact with reality. She recognises this "new method of mental functioning", which consists of the existence of new feelings "for the first time", she tends to add, as if she had never experienced them, such as sadness, envy, or hatred, which she can accept as her own and contain them, even if they are painful.

During one session from this period (s-181), she says that she would like to have a disease, a cancer, and to be hospitalised in a clinic, and then brings up the following dream:

> "There is a baby in a cot in a hospital nursery. Some men with knives threaten the baby and say: 'Let's go to make the test' or '(the baby) will have to pass the test."

Then, in the same dream, there is a gynaecologist with instruments associated with having assisted with a birth, and a baby who has just been born. I believe that the patient is experiencing having been born into a new mental life for herself in analysis, that she feels threatened, so she must pass a test. Perhaps the test of reality? Or the test of the temptation of madness, which attacks it? In situations when she should be happy because she is making progress in her external reality as well, with her writing and the work that she has been doing, anxiety about death still appears, that she might be suffering from cancer (here, it is no longer something syntonic that addresses a wish, but a fear) and she says, "It is as if by being more alive, the experience of death grows." This would show the acute conflict between the destructive psychotic part and the non-psychotic part that wants to live.

One can deduce a change in the perception of her internal, more plural world. Yesterday, she says, was a good session in which she felt alive. Today, on the other hand, she feels as if she has a small ego. It is difficult for her not to have the relationship from before in which the ego expands and is confused with her environment, or in which she related to others through the messages (s-195). It feels like a type of infatuation with her mother, because of her attributes. She immediately thought this was incest and associated the word incest with in-*cesta* (the Spanish word "incesto" allows the phonetic association with "in-cesta" (in-basket), being inside the basket), getting caught in the *cesta*. I tell her that this might be a desire to be inside her mother's body, as well as inside the analyst, since there is no longer a fusional relationship (s-197).

The wait after yesterday's session (in which I intervened very little) was long and over time she has had the sensation of having (grown) moved on from being a small, two-year-old child to being . . . three. These are sessions in which she feels older by assuming her responsibilities, but at the same time she wanted to be doing badly, because otherwise, if she does well, then she is just one more patient coming here, like any other of mine. Before, with the messages and the little machine, she wrote herself love letters as if they had been sent from other people (s-220 and s-221). The most important thing is that a new (child)-mental life came into this world of reality, a world where really almost everything has to be learnt. Therefore, her growth is very slow and it can be considered progress that the child has grown from two to three years old. But that is a process so slow that is hard for both, she and probably me, to accept.

The patient says, "Now I realise what it means to experience suffering, but in contact with reality." This is very different from the suffering of madness, without experiencing it, which is what she is accustomed to. Suffering from madness is linked to the delusional world, and, as a result, does not come from reality, whether the internal or inevitable external reality; she receives it from someone outside herself who intentionally created this reality and on whom she depends, whether good or bad: the persecutors, the aliens (good at times, bad other times), fathers, mothers, and the analyst (idealised or sadistic).

In a *later session (s-207),* when this plural and integrative vertex continues to be predominant, she speaks in such a low voice that I almost cannot hear her. I ask her if she can speak louder. Silence. I indicate that something has happened. She responds that she has pictured herself killing someone with a dagger. I tell her that it must be me because I interrupted the fusional relationship that we had where she almost did not need to speak to me. "I want to die," she responds. She is convinced that this means that I am rejecting her, I say. After a pause, she then talks about a friend who she goes out with (a somewhat marginalised person who she occasionally helps financially) and that he envies her for her better economic and social situation (I think about transference, about her envy towards the analyst, but I do not intervene. I wait.) Last night, while she was writing, the patient continues, she saw the photo of her grandmother on the table, a pleasant image that she associated with the analyst. But she felt mediocre. I tell her that perhaps we understand that if she stabs me it is because of envy, because she came in feeling badly and she sees me doing well. "I would like to have your capacity to endure other people's suffering," she answers. "One of the things that makes it more difficult for me to endure is that it is so hard to tolerate the pain. Because I see that life is also suffering." I tell her that by remembering her kindly grandmother being associated with me she has been able to tolerate the feeling of envy and has been able to recognise and express it. The session ends and, while putting on her coat to leave, she says, "What a shame, my pockets are torn."

Comments: At the beginning of this session, the patient tries to establish a fusional relationship with the analyst, which I interrupt by appealing to the differentiation between the two, implicit in my request for her to speak to me more loudly. It remains clear that her fantasy of stabbing someone is the analyst, whom she answers with her desire to die. Since she cannot endure the solitude of differentiation, she prefers to die, so it is I who rejects and abandons her and, in the latter instance, I am to blame for her desperation. By continuing to interpret that her wish for death must be because she felt my intervention as rejection, I am implicitly showing my interest in the patient even though I am not in a fusional relationship with her. Perhaps this allows her to calm down and continue associating. What she associates is the issue of her friend's envy. Although I think about transference, I wait. Then she brings up the pleasant image of her grandmother associated with the analyst, and that it took place precisely when she was writing (literary texts), which constitutes a creative activity, but, when comparing herself with her grandmother–analyst, she feels mediocre, and it is then that I interpret the feeling of envy in the transference, which confirms the final comment that she feels poor because her coat pockets are torn.

* * *

I have discussed different moments in this period of the analytical process, highlighting the predominant transferential vertexes along a line that implies a progression in which movement occurs from a regressive infantile situation, after a brief period of apparent pseudo-adulthood that she is not able to sustain for very long, then the attempt to overcome this tendency towards primitive infantile fusion using different methods of psychotic organisation: psychotic mechanisms, eroticisation of the analytical relationship to eliminate all differentiation, even the openly delusional activity, to arrive at a moment that I call plural transference in which she renounces the exclusive relationship, focusing on facing the complexity of relationships, with the analyst, with her family, with other people, and with herself, as well as the complexity of reality, which, when recognising and trying to integrate it, constitutes a painful process.

Such internal modifications are significantly reflected in the external order in her writings. She submitted some of her texts written before the beginning of analysis to publishers, and they objected that the content was too much about her inner life, being obscure for the reader; in addition, there was no continuity between the texts, which would result in a fragmented publication, so she would have to select the best, correct them, and connect them to give them unity. During the second year of analysis, she endeavoured to re-read the texts, with the consequent pain of recognising that some were unintelligible, since they were written through the "little machine"; she had to eliminate parts, which she felt as authentic mutilations of her self, title each of the remaining parts, and connect them to each other, with a more organised and unified result that allowed for publication. This task paralleled the analytic process, as she gained tolerance for pain by accepting differentiation from the analyst (and between the different parts of her self), as well as from the integration of her mental life. What about the implicit ability for more evolved symbolisation when writing creatively? This is what I anticipated in the chapter on symbolisation.

CHAPTER NINE

Emerging from psychotic organisation

"I feel pain when I remember the past. When I see that I have lived with madness for years and that now all of it is false"

(Ms B, s-150)

"We must continue our slow learning about existence ... exploring the small spaces of illumination ... the daily pleasures of generosity toward one another, so beautiful, so meaningful ..."

(Ms B, s-268)

In this chapter, I try to illustrate the permanent conflict between the pathological organisation of a predominantly psychotic personality and a pathological organisation with a predominantly non-psychotic functioning, that is, between tendencies towards life and tendencies towards death, but with a predominantly non-psychotic functioning. I have chosen a few moments in which the patient emerges from psychotic organisation and moves toward the depressive position, with difficulties enduring this and maintaining it long enough, needing to return to psychotic organisation, later to try again to leave. She has to repeat this process countless times. The material presented is not in chronological order, but comes from an advanced stage of analysis. With regard to the description of the interaction between the patient and the analyst, I have made sure to make alternating adjustments: as if zooming in, I sometimes get as close as possible to show the moment-by-moment of the interaction in a particular session, or during several consecutive ones; at other times, I distance myself somewhat and summarise what has been taking place in the relationship for several sessions. Last, I alternate between one and the other, when it appears to me that the process is better understood this way.

During moments of analytical progress, Ms B continues to accept that the therapeutic relationship is not one of "reciprocity", as she would like, or a fusional relationship. Sometimes, this new state creates severe pain due to the loss of psychotic functioning, with a subsequent feeling of emptiness and lack of identity; at other times, this loss is felt as a depressive state (Theme 1). On other occasions, the new situation shows her catastrophic anxieties that arise from confronting reality without her usual method of resorting to the psychotic organisation, "naked", which makes it very hard. Also, continuing to learn to recognise the analyst as a differentiated object allows for a more realistic introjection of him, which is accompanied by a perception of new feelings that she has never admitted to having before. This leads her to say that she can feel them "for the first time" (Theme 4); until now these feelings were projected, or, rather, induced in her by way of delusion. However, as that new emotional experience became unbearable, she had to freeze it, and project this defence into the analyst, branding him as cold as ice. At other moments, while she continued to accept her own psychic life, that is, having tendencies towards life in conflict against tendencies towards death, sometimes it was so unbearable that she needed to project the former into the analyst (Theme 2). These moments of progress, although fleeting, also create anxiety about a present that offers a limited, non-omnipotent reality, as well as anxiety about the component of uncertainty about the future: a reality removed from her conception of the future as something always known and controlled through delusion. The conflict between the psychotic part and the non-psychotic part, despite the analyst's mediation, sometimes leads Ms B to position herself in an experience between reality and madness (Theme 3).

Theme 1: Conflictive acceptance of the therapeutic analytical relationship

This material also includes emptiness due to the loss of psychotic functioning, anxiety about the uncertain future, and a non-omnipotent present. I will describe three consecutive sessions (s-360–s-362).

On Monday, the patient expresses her displeasure with feeling uncomfortable in her own skin, given the new reality of living without psychotic functioning and her fear of not being a container capable of tolerating her new feelings. *On Tuesday*, she says that she does not know whether to kill the mad sister in the story she is writing, although she would not do so violently but, rather, gently.

At the *Wednesday session (s-360)*, she explains that she has been anxious and crying at home, and her mother, who had been cheerful and content, tolerated it well at first. But as the patient continued to cry, her mother became angry with her and asked her to pull herself together a bit. The patient said that she felt lost, with no future, despite the effort made this morning to take care of her affairs by organising her wardrobe. Later, she began to calm down when she thought about the rough, difficult situation of Antonia (a lady who helps around the house, and my homonym).

The patient says that she feels in madness, that the state she is in *is* madness; she is lost because, she explained to her mother, she does not know how to continue writing her story. This is authentic madness: to have no future and, therefore, to be in the void. She also has to erase what already happened, the madness from before, which is her past. Thus, she sees herself as having no past or future. She cries in distress, seated on the couch.

I try to explain that she must surely feel that her doubts about how to continue the story are also based on how to continue our relationship here, since it is different from what she believed it to be. It appears that there is no future if the relationship is different from what she imagined. She responds that what I have just told her is like stabbing her with a knife.

I tell her that one part of her believes that if this type of fusional relationship does not exist, there is nothing. When I talk to her about how there is no future for a non-analytical relationship, as she experiences it, she believes I am affirming that there is no future for any type of relationship with me. She is not able to acknowledge the relationship that I can provide: the analytical one.

She says that I feel cold and distant and that I just talk about what I can contribute. She says I do not understand her because she is giving all of herself, her body, her soul, and her blood, while I only give her three quarters of an hour, and whatever I can contribute in that time. Also, it is as if I were the only one who knows anything, the one who contributes, as if she cannot give anything because she is the sick one. At one moment, she says she realises that trying to take me out of the therapeutic relationship causes the relationship to fail. She insists, while she cries inconsolably, that I am just fine in my armchair believing that I am the one who knows everything while she knows nothing, and she feels lost. And she does not know what to do. I tell her that the fact that I know something might, when joined with what she knows, allow for some part of her to admit how it validates this relationship.

She says, with greater despair, that all this type of relationship does is cause her more pain, which she can no longer endure. It is as if I do not realise it. If only, little by little, I could start expressing my thoughts and feelings without departing from the therapeutic relationship . . . During another moment in the session, she recalls that yesterday, in order to cheer her up, Antonia—a friend from the psychiatric hospital, who is also a patient—told her not to worry because Dr PS would marry her.

I tell her that there is a part of her that believes the only way of relating to me is for there to be mutual dedication, for us to get married (she smiles slightly). If that is not the case, the type of analytical relationship she needs is impossible, which makes her feel more devastated and helpless.

She iterates the idea that I might not realise how important I am to her. And she understands that there is inequality here, which she is trying to accept, but only if I am expressing my feelings. If I do not, she is nothing, she wants to die, because she has no past or future.

(The psychotic part is set on making me feel that I am a villain and cruel for putting her in such a painful situation and leaving her there.)

I tell her that, given how painful it is for her to envision the future of a different type of relationship, a part of her imposes itself, trying to take me out of the limits of the therapeutic relationship, while another part of her knows that this leads to the failure of the relationship in which I committed to helping her.

Thursday session (s-361). She arrives just over five minutes before her time. I open the door for her with the automatic buzzer, and when it is her appointment time I go to fetch her from the waiting room. She comes in and sits down on the couch. Yesterday, she left in tears. As I told her, she had been experiencing stark madness through her experience of emptiness (I do not remember this); it was later exchanged for the experience of pain and the need to cry. Her father kept her company. She told him that she was worried that he would become sad because of her. He answered that although it made him sad to see her like this, he knows that she will overcome the situation, which gives her hope.

Since she was so upset that she could not see a solution to our relationship here, she had been thinking about it and arrived at a plan that she wanted to propose to me. She is willing to accept that this relationship is a therapeutic relationship, that is, within the conditions that I propose, but she asks that I have a more dialectical relationship with her, so that we can enter and depart from this setting within the session itself, in order for me to be able to talk about my feelings sometimes. As I do not respond, she continues, recalling that, to cheer her up, her father read an article to her about art and science. She asks me if I know the author, about whom she has spoken to me on other occasions. I tell her that maybe the purpose of her question is to determine my interest in scientific matters, and so that she knows whether I remember what she talks about. The article stated that there are traditions to which one belongs in both science and art, but that one must go beyond them. Ms B thought that the scientific aspect had to do with me, and, at the same time, being part of that tradition, while the art aspect would have to do with her. However, she does not see herself as part of the social fabric. After her father read the article to her, she wanted to write another. She wrote a couple of pages that she let her mother read, who praised it, but the patient considered these to be very simple things. She had also been thinking about envy as a feeling that one has when one does things badly and sees others do it well, as she saw in the article.

(She explains all of this more calmly than I expected after yesterday's session.) After a pause, she says that while she was in the waiting room (for about three minutes) she had the experience of pain, that the entire room was filling with pain, and she remembered a horror film in which two sisters were in a room that was filling with blood. Afterwards, she recalled situations of madness during a period when she saw much suffering in my face and related it to the situation of madness that she was experiencing. "Yes, yes, you will see once I explain it . . .! (Smiling slightly.) (I was probably not able to avoid a small expression of surprise, which the patient immediately noticed.) "It turned out that I knew through the messages from the aliens that you were married to your sister, who was also blind. Imagine that! You made her work a lot at night and sometimes hit her because she didn't do things right. Also, your children were adopted. And when I came to the session I tried to help you, to cheer you up while you were suffering." She asks me if I remember when she talked to me about how she was willing to help me.

I tell her that while I was listening to her, I was thinking about her experience of the waiting room filling with pain, associated with the terrifying madness of a room filling with blood. And I wonder about the connection with the suffering and madness that she saw in me. I think it might have to do with the fact that she had to wait, although it was not time for her appointment. (She says her watch said it was.) So it is with good reason—I add—because she must have been convinced that I intentionally made her wait, perhaps as revenge; I leave her alone flooded with pain, maybe because she has sometimes treated me badly, such as when she turns me into this person who behaves cruelly and insanely. It is the madness of transgression in the form of incest and being someone who mistreats others. Maybe she would also prefer to see me as the analyst who suffers from madness, whom she must help, perhaps moved by envy of my scientific functioning, in a way that she can otherwise appreciate, although now she is able to make an effort towards sincerity by remembering those experiences in relation to me, in an attempt to achieve more understanding. She says that there was a moment when I was talking to her about envy in which she became angry with me again, but then it dissipated as I continued to talk to her . . . Then she again poses the question about whether I can enter and depart from the therapeutic setting.

I respond that she would need to reformulate this question, perhaps because of what we are talking about. Although a part of her recognises and values this relationship within a "scientific" setting, this awakens rage in her other part (the psychotic one), so she tries to believe in it and make me believe that I will be closer to her if I give in a little by departing from the therapeutic setting. Also, when she asks me to talk to her about my own thoughts and feelings, perhaps she is also reclaiming from me what I tell her I understand her to be, from what I think and feel about this experience that I am going through with her, and not on theories and interpretations that have already been made.

She says that she already knows that I talk to her through myself, although sometimes I tell her stupid things based on theories and things I have learnt (I must recognise her frankness and admit that, defensively at times, this has indeed been the case!), but in general I talk to her through myself. But what she is asking me for is a relationship of reciprocity. She does not understand how it can be any other way. We are just two people here, and if I only talk to her from a professional standpoint it ends up being a partial relationship, and a part of my own reality is mutilated. I tell her that it appears that if I demonstrate what I am able to do here, in the scientific sense, it is as if I am also denying her from participating "scientifically". It is as if I reject her assistance and will only view her as a patient.

The patient continues to harden, taking an increasingly aggressive and, I would say, almost cruel stance. She tells me that I have a heart of stone and that I am rigid, that what I am doing is impoverishing myself with my attitude. (A disparaging tone, which I feel to be very hurtful, while at the same time I believe a part of her finds it distasteful to attack me this way.) The session ends.

Comments on the Thursday session (s-361). During this session, the patient clearly explains the process that took place in the previous one. She came in with the stark experience of "madness" from the emptiness originating in the absence of psychotic functioning, not having a "past" or a "future", and she left in pain, crying. The decreasing of the predominance of her psychotic part constitutes a loss when she still does not have enough healthy tools to replace it when confronting reality. There being no present means that she does not want there to be one: the one the analyst is offering, the present of a therapeutic relationship, even if it implies the pain of a non-omnipotent new reality. However, the difficulty in accepting the analytical relationship, while painful to her, does not in any way prevent her from accepting it; acting-out or delusion is no longer needed. In contrast, on Tuesday she was able to accept the fact that her mother told her to pull herself together a bit after watching her cry so much, and she was able to be aware of how much the analyst–housekeeper is enduring. On Wednesday, when she left in pain after witnessing the analyst maintain the therapeutic relationship, this did not lead to any acting-out either, but, rather, she found support in her father. Nevertheless, the psychotic part insists on pressuring me to take me out of my role so that I will "depart and enter" without "departing" from the therapeutic setting, a clearly perverse proposal. I fixate on her perception of my "scientific" attitude in how I conduct analysis, although another part of herself does not like it and even brands me as cruel. Her subsequent association is significant when she recalls her delusion about the madness she saw in me, when she tried to invert the relationship, so that she would then be the one giving me support. She is able to explain it now because she is not identifying with the psychotic part. But the fantasy of the waiting room filling with pain–blood shows her fear of my retaliatory reaction to the destructive nature of that delusion. The difference with respect to when it occurred is that now it reveals the psychotic aspect and allows us to see its destructiveness. Nevertheless, more subtle psychotic activity persists in her qualifying as cruel rigidity my firmness in maintaining my analytical function, which is in conflict with the non-psychotic part that has just recognised the scientific validity of my method.

The next day, Friday (s-362), she is calmer. She takes a stance of having a good relationship with me to "dissolve" the bad atmosphere from the end of the last session. Last night, something new happened, and it was that she recognised that she has bad feelings, which she was able to see yesterday with everything that came out about envy. "But, well, that is reality . . ." She was also pleased yesterday that I remembered the name of the author from the article what she admired: "What a memory! What an ability to store and retain so many things!" She is active in her outside life, she says, so that she does not have to be so aware of the new status of her relationship with me, although, in reality, these are issues that interest her, too. For example, the procedures she has to go through to get financial help for her illness, or to call someone to explore the possibility of working part-time, and completing other tasks for her family. Later, she explained a story to me that she is writing. A child goes with her teacher to buy a feathered hat that she needed to seem bigger, but they did not have it in the store. She goes to the professor's house and is received by a woman, his wife, who is wearing a feathered hat. The woman offers it to the child to wear, and tells her that she can keep it because it is a gift, so that she can go out with him and be free, but she should not wear it to school.

Comments on the whole week. Each of the pieces (sessions) comprising the week highlights some particular aspect of the analytical relationship, and when we put them together a piece of the broader analytical process takes shape. Or, better said, if we zoom out to not only look at each session, but the entire week at once, we get a more complete picture. As such, on Monday, the patient sits down feeling uncomfortable in her own skin given the new reality of living without psychotic functioning, and her fear of not being a container capable of tolerating the new reality with its new feelings; on Tuesday, the idea comes up of radically eliminating the psychotic part, although in "a gentle way", because she sees no other way of coexisting with it; on Wednesday, the psychotic part reacts with propaganda that this discomfort of uncertainty and pain because of the new situation *is the* authentic madness, but to do so it has had to erase the past, attributing the discredit to the analyst, in addition to minimising the possibilities of the present by not having what the analyst does indeed offer, so that only emptiness remains, and as such, she pressures the analyst to step outside his analytical role to "take her out" of this "reality-madness". On Thursday, she insists on this tendency, but now the conflict between the psychotic and non-psychotic parts is uncovered and she communicates it to the analyst, even remembering her delusion from a while back of an analyst who was going mad, and the retaliatory consequences of it: leaving her in the waiting room full of pain. On Friday, the patient displays an attempt to reconcile with the analyst, and talks about the new feelings she is discovering, among them envy, and also that she has been able to continue writing, unlike days before when she did not know how to continue the story about whether to kill the psychotic part or not. Now she brings in another, very different one, and we see that the writing that she talks to me about is a way of replacing the delusion: the delusional idea of a psychotic oedipal situation (oedipal shipwrecks, as Bion calls them, when referring to the results of the oedipal conflicts in psychotic patients) projected into the analyst whom she, the child, would omnipotently help, transforms into a text with a story that expresses a more neurotic oedipal form, in which the analyst is recognised as the professor, married to a woman who has something (the hat) that she wants.

Therefore, the absence of psychotic functioning places Ms B in a difficult trance in which the conflict between the psychotic and non-psychotic parts fight to either avoid or accept analytical dependence, with the latter predominating in that moment. The analyst's firmness has been necessary in not giving in to her demand that if she is to renounce the psychotic part, it will be in exchange for the analyst agreeing to depart from, and enter, the therapeutic setting within the session itself. Throughout the week, she has been constructing a new oedipal form, also revealed in her external reality; after the session on Monday she went home crying because of the pain of the non-psychotic analytical relationship, and her mother responded with "you need to pull yourself together a bit," which the patient does not reject, but associates with what the other maternal figure, the housekeeper (associated with the analyst), is dealing with. Also in this sense, after the Wednesday session in which she felt she was experiencing pain from the new analytical relationship, she found solace in her father. That is, she could take to her external parents what internally she was beginning to experience in the analytical relationship, an analyst as a figure that is simultaneously firm and receptive.

Theme 2: Introjection of aspects of life of the analyst and later projection into him (s-490–s-491)

Weeks before the session that I will discuss, the patient complained that since she began analysis, she has made no attempts at suicide or had serious thoughts about doing it. Her link to treatment has not allowed this to happen, while at other times of desperation she was relieved just thinking that an end to her suffering existed. The patient has clearly expressed the double meaning behind death-related experiences many times: as something desired and feared at the same time. During the previous session, which I will discuss in detail, she explains that she had been seriously considering the possibility of suicide.

Friday (s-490). Shortly before her appointment, she calls on the telephone to tell me that she had had low blood pressure and had fainted, so she could not come in. I tell her that, considering yesterday's session when we talked about suicidal ideas, and the fact that the weekend was approaching, it seemed important to me to keep the appointment if she could make the effort to come in. She immediately accepts and answers that she will get dressed and take a taxi.

P: [She arrives on time. She makes a positive comment about the tie I am wearing.] Yesterday I left here feeling badly . . . Yes. And then I slept badly, superficially. [I ask her what she means.] Yes, I dreamed, although I don't really remember what about. Well, there was something about being outdoors with N [a friend]. He had a piece of paper with a drawing on it, which was also a musical score . . . I don't know. [She looks at me. The patient is seated on the couch.] This morning I didn't want to get up . . . It was hard for me to begin the day, and to live. And then I got the idea that I had a disease, that I was physically ill. When I smoked a cigarette, I fainted. It turned out my blood pressure was low. My mother got angry with me for smoking. Then she made an effort and was OK. We talked. She told me that if I was physically ill this would influence my mental state and that the inverse could also happen. And I thought: If you only knew! . . . And I got this idea that I have cancer because of this small sore in my nose. I made an appointment with the doctor. When I came here, my mother told me, "Tell Dr PS that your blood pressure was low. Even though he is a psychiatrist, you tell him . . ." (She looks at me intently). And with all of this discomfort I thought, well . . . I had the impression that I was undergoing chemotherapy to cure the cancer I have. [Some time before, this was the theme of a delusional conviction that it was I who, from a distance, controlled this chemotherapy.]

A: You yourself said, "If you only knew how the mental and physical can influence one another." So, your depression, your low mood yesterday, is less tolerable than low blood pressure, fainting. And the mental treatment, analysis, with its side effects, is more difficult to tolerate than the side effects if you were receiving chemotherapy for cancer, so you would prefer the latter treatment.

P: But don't talk to me about psychic matters [crying, and a little angry]. It's just that what also must be happening is that since I am making an effort to survive, all my negative feelings have focused on the disease, on the cancer, on the low blood pressure . . . [Pause.] This morning, the man who is teaching me how to use the computer called me and explained how to fix the problem that I had yesterday [she erased what she had been writing]. He taught me how to recover what I had lost, and then I wrote another page. So I had a positive attitude. And during lunch I was good with my family. I ate happily. I was hungry. We talked about giving my father a gift. He told me that it could be a tie. And I explained that I knew a place that had cheap ones ... That is, I was positive. [She stops, pauses for a moment, and begins to cry inconsolably.] But *I don't want to be fine, I don't want to be healthy, I want to be ill* ... I don't want to live ... [Interrupting herself with sobbing.] I don't know how to live. It is a life of mediocrity ...

A: If you explain to me that you have been positive but then, when you are here, you see yourself as incapable of living, it is as if this morning you could be positive if the negative thing, as you said, was a disease, cancer. But once you are here, the physical and the mental do not appear to be so separate; the negative and positive are joined together. This is why you called, preferring not to come in. But if I was willing to do the session, you immediately accepted, which would be positive for you, which would push you to make an effort to survive, which is what happens when you want to eat, to come to the session, to share the table with your family. But once you are here, it appears that everything positive about life only exists in the analyst, as if it disappears from you. And you are left with the negative, the disease.

P: But it's just, why live? What is the purpose if I don't have anything, not even these good moments like the meal? But they matter so little that they are nothing, because they are not connected; it's an isolated thing. Because then what? Then, just emptiness ... This morning I thought, why continue with the apartment matter, to be alone, with no one, with nothing in my head ...? I don't want that ... [She begins crying again more intensely.] I just don't want to go to my parents' home. I want to stay here ... I don't know how to live ...

A: It seems that there are times when you erase your abilities to live from your mind, as from the computer, but it appears that you can find the analyst who helps you to recover them. However, you would prefer that those abilities remain in me and you stay here, living with me.

P: [She cries, a little angry.] But I don't want to be OK. I don't want to live. [Pause, during which she starts to calm down, however. She gets a Kleenex to clean herself up. She comes back and sits down again. She is quiet for a few minutes. I also remain silent. There are only 10 minutes left in the session.] I am going to leave because I have nothing to say.

A: Maybe keeping today's session alive only depends on me speaking, since you feel that you have nothing positive in your life, because everything is inside me, and this is why you prefer to leave if I do not speak.

P: But I don't have anything [crying angrily], I don't have relationships, I don't have affection, I don't have friendships, I don't have relevance, I don't have writing, I don't have the absolute ... I don't want to live. The only thing I have is emptiness, or mediocrity, or all of this at once ... [Pause.]

A: So the issue is that if you do not have anything absolute, you have nothing. This desire to come to the session, to eat, to accept being with other people, and to feel that you contribute and co-operate, all of this is erased again if it is not in absolute terms ...

P: Yessss ... [Yelling with all her might.] I don't want the relativity of things, I don't want it, I don't want it ...I don't want it. [She continues yelling, as if to suppress and silence what I have just said, when I tried to support the sane part of her.]

[I remain silent. She also goes quiet. She looks at me. She looks at the clock. Calmer now, the violence has ended. With her look, she signals that the session has ended. I tell her as much. I say goodbye. She responds positively.]

Comments on the Friday session (s-490). I understand that the patient's initial refusal to come to the session is so that I will take on the aspect of living projected into me for the benefit of the session. She immediately responds positively when I show that I am interested in keeping the analytical relationship alive. Following the serious ideas of suicide when she had erased her tendencies towards life for a few moments, she has been able to recover them after yesterday's session, and to feel good with her family, to accept the meal, to share in it, to have "eaten" from the session yesterday, including having recovered part of her creative activity, writing. Days before, she had been very worried because she had lost her abilities, convinced that the analyst had nullified her and appropriated them with his interventions. Now, the analyst allowed her to repair her mind in order to recover her desire for life, she was hungry, ate happily, and was thankful to the analyst–father, to whom she wants to give a gift. It is significant that her first comment in the session is to praise the analyst's tie—precisely the gift she intended to give her father. Perhaps this is also an expression of her appreciation for the analyst.

However, at the same time, as she says, it appears that all the negative feelings have become focused on the cancer that she wants to have and which is currently located in a specific place on her body (her nose). But when she arrives at a point where she senses that she feels "positive" she bursts into tears and says that she does not want to be all right, she does not want to be healthy, she wants to be ill. I think that the session again requires her to put the negative—placed with the cancer—in contact with the positive, which had been dissociated; that is, joining the aspects of death with those of life, which is intolerable for her, so she needs to project the latter into the analyst. When she says that she does not want to live because she does not know how to live, at a deeper level she is referring to the fact that she does not know how to bridge this gap that has separated the aspects of life from the aspects of death all her life (or, worse, through fusions dominated by death-like aspects). She shows her powerlessness and incapacity for tolerating the pain of the threat that everything positive and associated with life can be affected by the anxieties of annihilation if both aspects are joined.

The patient's response is to ask why she should live, why she should have an apartment. The latter is an expression of why an apartment-mind, if "I don't have anything in my head." And there is nothing, because it is emptied of all the negative, which she has provisionally deposited in the cancer, along with the positive, which she has placed in the analyst. Having nothing is also an expression of this same idea of death.

During the session, one can see the patient's attempt to project the aspects of life into the analyst, when she affirms that she would like to remain here to live with him. Because how would it be if her capacities for life were placed into him? But then, when she remains here and sees that it is not an "absolute" relationship, that is, a fusional one, she wants nothing to do with this relationship, she wants to leave. And when the analyst talks about the fact that she has placed her aspects of life into him, the patient insists that there is nothing in her. When the analyst tries to recover the sane aspects of life in her, this gives way to the rage and violence of the psychotic part that hates life.

Her reaction is clear but impossible: she could only do the session if she were omnipotent, as if this were the only way to contain the negative along with the positive without the latter being destroyed. But it is precisely the analytical experience that has taught her that omnipotence is incompatible with reality, hence the psychotic part's momentary rage and hatred towards the end of the session. However, and to my surprise, her goodbye revealed the presence of the non-psychotic part that could understand the analyst and accept the limits of reality: she herself indicates that it is time to leave.

On Monday she notes that the office plant continues to grow. She remembers herself in love with the analyst and the pain of an impossible relationship. I say that the analytical relationship, like the plant, grows in a climate of work and not in love.

I shall now describe the next *Tuesday (s-491) session*.

P: I am disorientated and tired [she lies down on the couch after lighting a cigarette]. Yesterday I was at the doctor and he told me that the discomfort I had was due to something from here [she indicates her throat] up [indicating the top of her head]. He said I have pharyngitis due to congestion and I haven't recovered because I smoke. He asked me if I had symptoms of fatigue. Yesterday I didn't, but today I do feel it. He prescribed me some antibiotics and medications ... [A weary and tearful tone of voice.] Then I went home and explained it to my mother. She got angry because she thinks the problem is that I smoke a lot [a source of repeated confrontations with her mother]. I told her that the doctors have not told me that tobacco is the source of all this discomfort. She responded that they needed to be more frank with me. And yes, I also think they need to be more frank with me by telling me whether I have cancer [she starts crying again].

A: You said that you feel disorientated. Maybe it is because yesterday you had ruled out the idea of cancer since the lesion disappeared from your nose and you felt better after we talked. But now you again think that the doctors' comments indicate that you must have cancer but they are not telling you frankly.

P: No, I hadn't ruled out the whole idea of cancer. But yes, what I want is for them to tell me. [Crying.] And I can't do it any more [she pauses due to sobbing]. I can't stand the silence of not having the affection that I need. Not having the affection of my mother, who got angry with me ... I just remembered a telephone conversation that I heard my mother have with a doctor years ago, during which they talked about cancer for a moment, in reference to me.

A: Maybe you are asking me to talk to you more frankly, too. You are tired, you say, which might be related to being in a bad mood. I believe that the cancer you talk to me about might have to do with the fact that there is something in your mind that you feel functions the way a cancer would in your body. That is, something that takes up a lot of energy and activity to diminish life, what is alive inside you ... something against life. And it is important for us to know about it.

P: [Silently weeping, but paying attention while I speak. Uneasy. I think she sits up at this moment and remains seated on the couch.] I just can't take it any more, I can't take it any more. I don't have anything, I only have emptiness, silence, solitude ... I can't stand it any more ...

A: You talk about solitude, I believe this must be because, despite the effort that we are making here, you feel that it is not enough because you don't have my "absolute" support, which we talked about days ago.

P: Yes, but it's not enough. I have nothing, *I only have silence*, I don't have any affection, no one loves me ...

A: I am talking to you now, but you say that this is nothing, that there is no affection, but silence. This must be the cancerous aspect of your mind at work now, turning into silence everything that I am trying to contribute, to listen, to understand, to explain to you. The cancerous aspect is at work because you do not have absolutely all of this relationship.

P: But I cannot live with the affection that I receive here for three quarters of an hour. That is not enough ... [She stands up, pouting, whining, walks back and forth.] I can't do it any more, I can't live like this. [She stays on the other side of the room with her back to me.]

A: It seems you now prefer that I don't see you, because you don't know if I am going to tolerate you feeling badly, crying and rejecting what I say. [On other occasions, she has referred to how ugly she feels like this, crying and having an attitude of rejection.]

P: [She returns. She sits on the couch. She stops crying. In a whiny tone, she continues.] It's just that my mother got angry with me because I smoke, and she hates the fact that I smoke. [She lights a cigarette.] She can't stand it. And she doesn't understand that I cannot control my smoking.

A: So the desperate problem is that you realise that smoking is something that goes against your mother but that you cannot control this need.

P: So am I guilty of everything? [She is crying again.]

A: I am not saying that you are guilty of everything. I am talking to you about a reality that we can look at with what you are telling me, about not being able to control smoking, which is related to your mother at the same time; neither do you see yourself able to control the tendency to transform into silence what I bring to you.

P: You talk to me about the reality that we see, but I can't stand reality ... [She rises, walks around the room, crying again.] I can't do it any more ... [She sits. Pauses. Silence.] *I just can't stand the silence* ... I am leaving. [She stands and puts on her jacket.]

A: It is almost time to stop, but there's still some time left. [I remain seated. She sits, too. We are silent until the end. She is somewhat calmer. She says goodbye politely.]

Comments on the Tuesday session (s-491). Once again the patient insists on placing all of her negative feelings with the cancer, as we discussed two sessions ago. Not being diagnosed with cancer disappoints her at first, although it remains clear that the issue she has is from her throat up, that is, in her head, in her mind. But then she suspects that the doctor–analyst must know more than he is telling her, that there is a cancer in her, something destructive in her head–mind and she hopes that I will speak frankly to her.

First, I examine the subject of the fantasy of the somatic cancer with her, in order not to address her mental life directly, which she might feel as intrusive. But she herself responds in emotional terms, saying that she cannot stand the silence, which means the absence of affection from someone else: her mother and the analyst. During the Friday session, we saw that she could not unite her positive feelings, projected into the analyst, with the negative feelings that appeared to be projected into her cancerous body. Today, she cannot unite the object's affection with its hatred, so it must cause feelings of rejection in the former, which is very clear to her when she smokes in front of her mother, presenting it as an unsolvable dilemma, similar to what happens in the analytical situation: she needs, time and again, to turn what the analyst gives her into nothing, into smoke, into silence, and then he will feel angry, he will hate her, and he will withdraw his affection. So, the analyst will also remain the custodian of all of these bad feelings that she cannot tolerate or contain, if they are not placed in the cancer.

During the session, when I interpret that there is a mental cancer inside her, which is consuming her vitality, Ms B responds as she would to her mother with the smoking matter, that she cannot stand it any more, and that she cannot avoid it; that she has nothing, that she only has emptiness, silence, solitude. So, the cancer is not only the "container" of everything negative, but, with this disassociation, safeguards the positive projected into the analyst, as occurred in the Friday session. Now, cancer is the deadly force, the destructive force that she cannot contain and that manifests itself as an acting-out in the same session. Therefore, any of my attempts to help her that require some effort on her part are felt as impossible, because she cannot control the destructive activity. Moreover, the only way to get rid of the destructive activity is to negate what the analyst contributes, time and again, so that he remains empty and what he says turns into nothing. That is, it appears that she needs to project this intolerable deadly silence that she is experiencing into the analyst, because she could only neutralise it in her if she had *all* of the analyst's affection, such an absolute aspiration that she can only achieve it if she *is* the analyst or the analyst fuses with her.

When I indicate to her that she has moved to the other side of the room to separate herself from my view because she does not know if I will be able to put up with her feeling so badly, she responds by lighting a cigarette, while complaining of her mother's intolerance of her smoking. Thus, she activates a maternal transference, in an attempt to see if I can tolerate her. First, it would appear that she is testing me again to see if I tolerate her addiction to tobacco or not, like her mother. But she has evidence that I have never discussed it, despite the fact that she chain-smokes at each session. With me, the test to pass is her tendency to act out what is mentally harmful to her during the session and which, at the same time, has a hostile effect on me; in this case, by not accepting my interpretations, which she knows she needs, turning them into silence, into nothing, into smoke, she frees herself from the deadliness that she feels inside. My interpretation, points out the cancerous psychic aspect acting at that moment of the session.

As the session is ending, the patient complains of how intolerable the psychic reality that I am talking about is. There is a pause, as if she is waiting for some consoling words, that is, for me to do work that is her responsibility. I do not respond except with my presence, I do not say anything else, because it seems to me that if the analyst can help her it is precisely so that she can learn to continue tolerating the reality that we are uncovering, and I cannot do this for her. So, my response is a necessary silence, to which she responds by saying that now she cannot stand the silence, and tries to leave. Probably here she is trying to pervert reality and confuse me. She wants to equate the silence of this moment in which I am waiting, accompanying her, so that she can digest the reality that we are exploring, with the cancerous silence, the result of turning my words into nothingness

I only break my silence when she tries to leave, not to give her words of false solace (because the pain of the reality that we are discovering does not allow for sugar-coating things, as she told me on one occasion), but in order to protect the setting and indicate that it is not time yet, while at the same time maintaining my position. I think that the patient understands this and sits down again, until the few remaining minutes pass and she can take her leave more calmly. It is a very significant moment because it shows that introjecting the analyst's container function is possible for a psychotic patient, even when it appears that it is absolutely intolerable. Also, it is likely that her capacity for containment will require new experiences like today's to continue strengthening itself.

Theme 3: Between reality and madness. The failure of the logic of madness

We continue at a point of the analytic process in which there is the possibility of the patient coming out of the psychotic organisation. The material once again reflects the struggle between the resort to the psychotic, or to its avoidance, as it has now become a threat, because the fallacy of the "logic of madness" has already been unmasked. I shall describe three consecutive sessions, from Monday to Wednesday, prior to the Easter holidays.

On Saturday, Ms B telephones, highly distraught, as she feels as though she is being inundated with "messages". I tell her that I understand that she is going through a difficult time because of her sister's suicide attempt, causing her to lose the centre of the stage with the family. Nevertheless, she agrees to wait until Monday's session.

On Monday (s-477), she sits on the couch, with an anguished expression, while she searches in her bag and is disappointed because she has only one cigarette. She will repeatedly return to her bag throughout the session when she has already smoked it. She says that she is in a bad way, because of what she has done. This makes me think that she herself might have also made a suicide attempt by taking pills. She complains that her parents asked her to sign a lease for the apartment she will occupy, which she felt humiliating. As I say to her, it seems that she has felt expelled from her family house in which she felt the centre of attention, now also usurped by her sister. She feels bad about making a scene this morning . . . crying and screaming because they had made her sign the paper. After this, she went to meet some friends, among whom she hoped to take centre stage, but she found a relationship that seemed to her rather sadomasochistic; they first made her feel like the protagonist, as if they needed her, but then rejected her. Although she is not very convinced, she has the impression that the aliens have intervened in this. So she feels upset, disorientated, and "outside of myself". I remind her of Saturday's call when she felt expelled from home and tried to find shelter in the analyst. Then she explains she did not expect me to answer, which makes me think that she was trying to reproduce the sadomasochistic relationship with me, by running to me for help but not expecting to find me. As I answered her call, she is trying to act out this sadomasochistic relationship in the session: she appears willing to receive help from the analyst but then does not accept it when it is offered, as I tell her.

The next day, *Tuesday (s-478)*, she sits on the couch and looks for the cigarette pack she cannot find. She looks through her bag again and again, where there are several things but not her cigarettes. She looks at me in disappointment, uneasy, not knowing what to do. On some other similar occasions, she did not hesitate to go out to buy a packet. To my surprise, she remains seated and starts talking. From time to time, she will need to search again in her bag only to find, in disappointment, that reality has not changed: there is still no packet.

She has been talking with a friend regarding her worry about not taking centre stage, and about her feeling of being halfway between madness and reality. "It is as if I don't want to leave all the stuff about the messages, and I want to keep them around, even though I don't want to get overwhelmed by them. It's just that reality means the difficulty of making efforts to achieve things; accepting reality as such, in other words, as non-fantasy, but something that is outside of my mind and it still exists; and reality also means that I am anonymous, just another face in the crowd, rather than the protagonist . . ." At the same time, she woke up a little uneasy because she had the feeling that the messages were coming through. She has been quite worried, mulling over the stuff about the sadomasochistic relationship at the weekend with her friends, but it is something that comes and goes, which calms her down. It was just difficult for her to think that she had the whole day ahead of her. She found it really hard. After a while, she says that last night she had a bit of a row with her mother, and she had later shown her some old writings, which her mother did not like. They were stories about lullabies. She did not like them because she said they were very sad. She suddenly stops talking, staring straight ahead, rather concerned. "I just have this *feeling, like of unreality* . . . yes, yes, right now."

> A: Neither madness or reality, but unreality; it seems as though this is a state which, for the time being, is preventing you from feeling the pain of reality and the upset and all the worry over your madness . . .
>
> P: It's so painful to hear you say madness . . .
>
> A: It was your word . . .
>
> P: [Calmly.] Yes, yes, but it's just that when I hear it from you it is like a *rock*, like someone being hit by a *rock* . . . [She pauses.] And at the same time I hope that all of this stuff about the messages is true, that it isn't false, or madness . . . [She falls silent again.]
>
> A: [The patient knows that this is a vain hope, because it is impossible: to pretend that madness is "truth", and not a distortion of reality. So, I do not make any comment, but keep thinking about what she said regarding the lullaby text and her mother's rejection.] Before when you had that feeling of unreality, you also remembered your mother's rejection related to your writing . . .
>
> P: Yes, well, the writing dealt with the theme of a lullaby; it was nostalgic and sad and she didn't like them. Well, actually, it was an "un-lullaby" . . . Although afterwards, she did say some of my other writing was good . . . instead of feeling offended and attacked as a mother . . . The thing is I have real trouble with the whole reality thing . . . Like the effort of having to learn to use the computer, because it means learning, not being the protagonist, and I find it hard . . .
>
> A: Learning for you to cope with reality means waiting for those efforts to yield results... Such as now, the effort of being in the session, being able to tolerate being here even without smoking . . .
>
> P: But it's just that reality involves, in one sense, an effort to achieve things, then that recognition that it is reality, I mean, that it isn't fantasy, and then the anonymity, that I am not the protagonist . . . And all of that involves being alone . . . But, Dr PS, how come the effort to be with reality? [She pauses.]
>
> A: If you learn to use the computer, you can do translations on your own, going by what you have said. If you learn to accept your feelings and experiences as your own—for example, the pain that arose in relation to your mother's reaction to your writing about the "un-lullaby" song which you showed her and she rejected, you can feel somewhat more self-sufficient. I might tell you that . . .

P: Yes. At this point in time I feel as if I am in the position of reality that you are proposing, and I think that you're making points that convince me. But all of that stuff that I understand, it may be good for you, for your life, to do the session, but for me, I don't think I can do it, I feel utterly incapable, because it involves being very alone ...

A: If you cannot deal with reality as I do, then you are not capable of anything ...

P: But it's just that being in reality means being alone, utterly alone ... This morning I was brought another set of plans for the flat refurbishment, which was cheaper than the others. The person who delivered it is connected with the friends from the bar I spoke to you about, who tried to set up the sadomasochistic psychological game. So I saw this as a sign of reconciliation ... But then I wondered whether it might just be a ploy [she watches me, as if waiting for me to say something to her about it].

A: So, if there is an approach to help you, now me, here in the session, you put this down to a ploy ...

P: Well, the fact is, while I've been doing sessions with you I've been hospitalised in the psychiatric hospital ...

A: Especially taking into account that next week we will interrupt sessions for a few days for the Easter holiday, my approach to you now seems as though it could be a ploy to end up leaving you alone ...

There is a silence and she asks about the dates of the holidays that I had already given her long ago. I remember them. She agrees. It is the end of the session. Now, standing, she asks, "What do I do about the plans?" As I look at her as if I do not know what she means, she clarifies whether she should trust those people. I tell her that this is something we are looking at here.

Comments on s-477 and s-478. Although she has already begun to live it in the analytic relationship, the experience of being out of the object is something new. Therefore, it feels like a violent and humiliating expulsion to have to sign a contract to occupy the flat owned by her parents, when she has always lived in it as if it were her own; or she feels abandoned if she does not occupy the centre of family attention. But ceasing to be the protagonist and signing the "expulsion" from her parents' life brings, as a consequence, being in that state halfway between reality and madness. On the one hand, she does not want to give up madness, she wants to preserve it in case reality becomes intolerable; and, on the other hand, she woke up this morning upset precisely because of the presence of the messages. That is to say, she does not want to abandon madness, but she fears it could capture her, because through analysis she has learnt that madness is based on conceit. Reality involves facing the conflictive relationship with her mother, feelings of rejection by her mother, and of her hatred towards this mother who rejects her. Perhaps there is a part of the external reality, of a rather distant and cold mother, who had difficulty in accepting the patient's intense projective identifications. For this reason, Ms B needs, again and again, to act the projective identification in the analytic relationship to verify that the answer is not the negation of the same, but, on the contrary, their receptivity and return in the best condition. Hence, the enormous patience required with these patients.

It is at that moment of the session when the feeling of unreality arises, apparently as a defence against accepting either madness or reality, since coming into contact with a reality "naked"—as she once said, or, without delusional mediation—is something new, strange, and very hard.

It seems that the analyst's arguments for being in reality are convincing, as she acknowledges, but the problem is that she cannot bear the pain that comes with it. Although this limitation is real, she also tries to delegate all the pain into the analyst, despite showing, during the same session, a certain capacity to tolerate it by enduring the frustration of reality without tobacco.

Another point is her concrete use of words, which happens only when it comes to painful issues, such as when she complains that I say the word "madness", which she had just used. Clearly, at certain times, they do not symbolise the contents that are referred to. Rather, the word is the physical materialisation of what it refers to. I think that here I did not use the necessary tact to formulate my interpretation in other way.

Later, I attempt to bring to the transference this difficulty in walking the road of reality, in the sense that my approach to understanding her might be understood as a sadistic ploy to then leave her alone, which she confirms by recalling that even while she was in analysis, she was admitted to the psychiatric hospital. Here, she is perverting the reality of analysis as a situation of help by turning it into a sado-masochistic relationship rather than accept the pure, painful reality of separation along with my limitations and the analysis. However, after my response, in which I introduce the reality of the imminence of the holiday, the patient is also able to situate herself in that reality, accepting it and asking for my help to remind her of the specific dates of the holiday.

On Wednesday (s-479), the patient comes with feelings of strangeness and emptiness. Yesterday, she was happy to be coming out of the madness because the messages had decreased. Today, things have been different following a phone call from a person in regard to some doubts that have arisen about the presented budget for the flat refurbishment. As this person is connected with the people of the sadomasochistic psychological game, she once again saw signs that made her suspect that they might be initiating that type of relationship. Consequently, she has been as if "expectant, awaiting any new messages" which might clarify the situation. As these did not arrive, she has had the sense of a void. She is surprised, as the "logical" thing, as has always occurred in similar situations, would be for the messages to come through, and when she does not have this response she feels strange. At the same time, continues the patient, "I have the experience that every little gesture, every act I do now, is as if it is born from within me, and not as something that flows through me, coming from outside, from another, which is what I was accustomed to experiencing. But then, I have the feeling of loneliness."

I gather her feeling of solitude in the face of her own emotions, unmediated by the messages as usually occurs, as a difficult *new* experience, and, hence, the feeling of strangeness.

She associates that, coming by bus, she has received a "reference" from a book that a girl next to her had been reading, apparently on occult sciences, hermeticism, secrecy, and that all of that should be connected to the group of friends of the sadomasochistic game, regarding their secretive ways of imposing certain forms of relationship between people.

I tell her that, in so far as she finds it difficult to tolerate the solitude of feeling that her emotions and actions originate in her, then she would turn to the references; in particular, if we think of everything that I do not tell her about me, which remains hidden to her, then she would be able to know it by secret means, that is, the references, the messages.

She admits that it is so. After a pause, she talks about being in bed, half asleep and half awake, and having oneiric images. In one, she was making a great defecation, and in another she was taking steps to legalise her work situation (for a potential part-time job).

Then she explains that she has had erotic fantasies with a friend, because she needed physical contact with the other (!) and, thus, feel that her own body is alive. But it was as if the friend did not respond. And she continues thus:

> P: It's just that it's difficult for me to tolerate solitude. I must be stupid, because this is something very basic. It's something you learn when you're three or five years old ... But I just find it so hard!
> A: [I tell her that that is just it, that reality is also just that, moments of difficulty. Like the fact that we now have to stop because it is time.]
> P: [Half joking.] You were eager for the session to come to an end ... Because you know that I am going through a difficult and delicate time ...

I do not make any comment. I give a hint of a smile.

Comments on s-479. Yesterday, she was happy to be coming through the madness. Yet, in the face of a reality that generates uncertainty (the doubts about the budget for her flat), she must empty herself in order to rid herself of the anxiety of not knowing. To fill the void, suspicions arise—not yet conviction—of whether it has to do with the sadomasochistic relationship again, something that only the messages can confirm. So, she is waiting for them to arrive, as has always occurred. The surprising thing is that the messages do not arrive, "which would be the *logical* thing"; hence, her perplexity and strangeness.

At the same time, she has the experience that each small gesture, every action she makes, come from within her and are not ones that "pass through" her, originating in others (*via* "messages"). Something that is a new and difficult experience, because it implies the problematic issue of loneliness, which becomes unbearable, although it is hurtful for her to recognise that it is such an elementary lesson that a three- or five-year-old girl would have already learnt it. Therefore, she needs to believe in the secret pathways that other people use, including the analyst, as I say, to let her know what he conceals, so she will not be alone. (For a long time, the patient has complained that I do not talk about my feelings.) After the pain of my intervention, which she admits, what she associates with is the double reverie: the great defecation and making efforts to legalise her work situation. Probably, the former comes from the psychotic part, which attacks reality that it does not like, and the latter from the non-psychotic part, which wants to legalise its link with reality.

So, we see swings between accepting that new reality, from which she would try to escape by means of the feeling of "unreality" and the expectation of the "logic of madness" (Resnik, 2016), that at this moment begins to fail. Even the resort to other defences, such as masturbation, fantasised with the friend (rather than the analyst, which had occurred at certain intervals), is unsuccessful, because "he does not respond". That is to say, the fantasy no longer has that omnipotent character of literal substitute of the reality, in fact, of an authentic hallucination. Neither, now, does psychotic logic came to her aid.

Probably the feeling of unreality is a way we can talk about things that are very painful for her. It would be an intermediate state "between reality and madness": she is living something that she knows is "real", but without completely accepting it, leaving open the possibility that at any moment, through the intervention of the psychotic, it will become something more tolerable, a delusional "reality".

Theme 4: The "first time" experiences in the analytical process

Throughout the analytical process, I began to realise that the patient occasionally mentioned the existence of certain facts, perceptions, or feelings in her life that were happening "for the first time". So, I took these phenomena as psychic changes. Sometimes, they were fleeting, because, after a time, these same phenomena would reappear as if they were being experienced for the first time; that is, what she had experienced before had been erased. However, it is also likely that some of these experiences were actually new, because she had not had the opportunity to experience them thus far. Hence, the "first time" comes to represent her becoming aware of new aspects of her psychic life which, being painful for her to retain, she needed to erase, until the next time they arose as a new discovery, as another first time, having to repeat this process many times in order to accept that such experiences were already a part of her. Thus, she says that now that she is in analysis, she is realising all of the pain she has had in her life. The problem is that enduring this awareness is unbearable, so she must erase it. Alternatively, when she says that she should be happy because there is something new in her, which is relating to people more directly according to what is happening in the relationship, and not what she has thought and hoped will happen, while she considers this to be rewarding, at the same time she feels that it puts her in a bad mood.

I shall give other examples, some of which I have already mentioned in the clinical material in other chapters. However, I wish to bring them together now to emphasise their importance and bestow upon them the status of valuable psychic phenomena, which open up the possibility of departing from psychotic organisation of the personality.

Thus, after several months of treatment had gone by, one day she realised for the first time that, behind the couch next to my chair, there is a lamp that is always on. This was a very revealing insight to her, as she became aware that the analyst is behind her and not inside her. He provides her with "light", understanding of her mind (s-63). The curious thing is that this awareness of analysis being beam of light that illuminates her mind had appeared in a dream shortly before. It is as if, on an unconscious level, she anticipates perceiving certain realities that are difficult for her to become aware of because of how painful they are. In this case, it is that she is not inside me and that the analyst's "light" comes from him, not from her.

Around this time (s-101), Ms B is able to talk to me for the first time about her hatred towards her father, something she had never been able to acknowledge. At the same time, she admits that one of the things she is learning from analysis is how to accept her own hostility. Around this time she also says, "It is as if for the first time I could feel that I have a mother" (s-104). Precisely, her version of her parental figures had, thus far, been of a completely kind and generous father and a controlling and cold mother. Through transference, she could begin to experience the analyst as both a receptive maternal figure and a paternal figure with limits who does not always bend to her will.

After two years, she once came to her session wearing some earrings and at the end wanted to point them out to me, clarifying that it was the first time in her life that she had worn them (s-265). Here, her recognition and acceptance of her femininity, while indicating differentiation with respect to the analyst, opens up the problematic issue of eroticising the relationship to try to reunite the lost fusion; nevertheless, it is still a step towards accepting her feminine identity. Some sessions later, she evaluates the continuity of the analytical experience, which she expresses thus: "It is the first experience in my life in which I have achieved continuity." In fact, she had already been in psychotherapy for several years, although she went only once a week. However, it is important to emphasise this awareness of an "experience of continuity"; thus far, her relational experiences were isolated to a fleeting present with neither a past nor a future, which had to be renewed again and again. Now, she can recognise a continuous experience in as much as it is possible to accept what the entire relationship implies: differentiation and separation. That is, she accepts the experience of an analytical process.

She mentions affection among the feelings that are coming up "for the first time", but it is affection in a non-absolute sense because, Ms B says, she has learnt here in analysis that "love is never perfect". She is also able to express surprise at discovering that she has experienced the feeling of envy "for the first time", with respect to both the analyst and other people. When these feelings arise with any intensity, she then says she feels "uncomfortable in her own skin" and feels lost, given how difficult it is to recognise herself with such feelings being part of her personality (s-358).

Following a crisis in the analytical relationship during which she stopped coming for several days, although she was calling on the telephone, she comes to a session and tells me that she has arrived on foot from her home, "which is the first time that has happened!" she exclaims with admiration (s-328). A little later, after a difficult session during which I had to maintain my firmness against her attempts to try to take me out of my analytical function, the next day she tells me with no less admiration that "for the first time" she was able to return home on foot (s-396). She is also able to say that it is the first time that she has felt guilty for having responded with hostility to a relationship that she appreciates, having exhibited a hostile attitude towards the analyst the day before (s-246).

However, all of these first-time experiences are encompassed in the fact that the analytical experience implies a kind of birth. On one occasion (s-205), when she was doing poorly and recognised her great need for analysis, she says she feels claustrophobic and associates it with a fact that she had mentioned once, and which I had forgotten, if she ever mentioned it, which is that she was born prematurely. Although she was experiencing these feelings of claustrophobia and the need for analysis at the same time, the night before she also had an intense feeling that she was being born, in response to which suddenly arose the contrary feeling of not wanting to be born. In Chapter Eight (s-181), I describe her dream in which a baby is born and some men threaten its survival, which we were able to connect with the analytical process. As such, each fact, feeling, or perception of reality that she experiences "for the first time" would indicate this slow, arduous process of being born into a new life; that is, the process of emerging, not only from the maternal–analytical cloister, but also from the psychotic organisation.

CHAPTER TEN

General discussion and conclusions

The experience that I have tried to convey with my patient, Ms B, who is diagnosed with schizophrenic psychosis, and which we include in psychotic organisation of the personality, allows me to point out some conclusions. First, I am aware of the fact that a clinical study of a single case has limitations in establishing generalisations. On the other hand, it offers the advantage of a detailed description thereof, and allows for a deepening perspective that makes the arguments maintained more convincing.

As I understand it, the purpose of psychoanalysis in any patient is based on facilitating a therapeutic experience in which one is able to guarantee a mental space sufficiently containing for the complexity of his psychic life, which has been revealing itself and developing over the course of the analytical process. If this is the case, the objective for a patient with psychotic organisation of the personality consists of first helping him to create a minimally consistent mental space in which to tolerate part of the complexity of his psychic life. That is, I bring to the fore the need to create a psychic space with more or less defined limits in which some content resides (emotions, thought, etc.), which is compatible with reality and tolerable to the patient. Hence, I already anticipate the importance of being able to maintain the stability of the setting and the proposed working method.

We are already far from the Freudian conception of schizophrenia as an extreme type of narcissism; that is, unable to develop transference and, therefore, unable to access psychoanalytical treatment. That is the case precisely because of the theoretical contributions of Freud and the theory and clinical work from a host of subsequent authors, who tried to approach mental illness in general, and schizophrenia in particular, as susceptible to understandability. In this regard, I cited several times Freud alluding to the existence in the psychotic patient of sane aspects, capable of contact with reality, including in acute moments of illness. This coexistence of the ill with the sane has been one of the hypotheses on which I have based my theoretical proposal, following this psychoanalytical tradition, with its technical consequences for treating Ms B. I have used as a main reference Bion's idea about the psychotic personality, or, better said, the psychotic part of the personality, which implies the existence of a non-psychotic part. Yet, while Bion developed the study of this psychotic part, he left the interaction with the non-psychotic part open to interpretation. This is what later analysts have developed, in particular those who have studied narcissistic organisation of the personality, which has led to the concept of pathological organisation (Steiner, 1993). Here, I have attempted to continue this line of thinking with the psychotic organisation of the personality.

I have also tried to show that it is possible to offer the psychoanalytical method to psychotic patients, even if only in certain cases, without significant modifications to the classic technique. As a result, I believe that we must not rule out any patient as subsidiary to psychoanalytical treatment exclusively based on psychopathology if he meets some minimum conditions necessary to conduct it. Therefore, one must evaluate the patient's whole personality. Despite the long evolution of Ms B's disease, psychoanalysis with her was possible, thanks to her need not to complain only of the pain she feels, but to want to know, to some extent, the painful experience.

I wish to place psychic pain at the forefront because Ms B made me see its importance and, with Bion's help, I have been able to delve into it. The treatment experience with the former, along with the experience of reading of the latter, have allowed me to become aware of the nature and dimension of psychic pain, not only in the psychotic patient, but also as a basis of all psychopathology. As contact with reality and the progressive discovery of it bring pain, the capacity to manage it will depend on whether pathological organisation of the personality is more or less dominant in the individual's development. When faced with psychic pain, Bion tells us, an attitude of avoiding it or changing it is possible. If the patient chooses the second option, this means that he not only *feels* the pain, but he must also *experience* it. That requires some personal resources that, when precarious, need therapeutic intervention. So, what I have learnt in treating Ms B is that a necessary condition for that intervention to be possible, with any type of patient, is for there to be minimal tolerance of painful experiences. Thus, I now consider it a fundamental indicator when evaluating the possibilities of psychoanalytical help for a patient. In the case of the psychotic patient, given his scarce personal resources, the tendency towards avoiding pain predominates. But while pain remains present, as it does with Ms B, it is an expression of the fact that there continues to be internal conflict between the psychotic part and the non-psychotic part, and, as such, an emotional life ultimately persists. Obviously, I am referring to the presence of the inevitable and necessary pain when coming into contact with reality.

Thus, the nature of the psychotic patient's psychic pain has been the jumping off point. It is a pain that has a dimension of absoluteness, like something that overwhelms the entire personality, totally insurmountable in nature, but which also has strong death-related experiences whenever catastrophic and nihilistic anxieties have not been sufficiently "neutralised" by paranoid–schizoid mechanisms, or are only temporarily neutralised, the delusional world being activated thereafter. It is immense pain, both in space (it overwhelms the entire body) and time (experience of being an "eternal" pain).

We remember that one of my patient's delusions was the condemnation of living forever. On many occasions when she feels such unbearable pain, she actively wishes for death, which was one of the reasons for her suicide attempts, although, while she was in analysis, this was limited to expressing the desire. This desire sometimes transformed into a strong longing to develop cancer.

Because of its magnitude, psychic pain cannot be mentally contained because its dimensions are unbearable. Thus, both the delusion that "changes" a painful reality and the involvement of the body are needed. The bodily dimension of pain is not a metaphor in the way that neurotic patients sometimes describe mental pain. As such, my patient talks about deep pain that overwhelms her entire body and which corresponds to the words of the poet that she herself quoted on one occasion "that, because I am hurting, even my breath hurts", or when she says, "My soul hurts", or "I can't endure such pain any more." It appears that she is referring to the pain that occupies her whole person, and which almost nothing can soothe.

In moments when Ms B emerges from psychotic organisation, we have also seen that the pain is linked to the experience of the depressive position, which also makes it unbearable. In the first place, this is due to the loss of the delusional world present in her life for so many years; second, to the experience of recognising object differentiation (from the analyst) and, as a result, her own psychic life borne out of analysis, through the experiences of her feelings, which came up "for the first time" there, even the pain of integrating into her internal world what has been split and projected, and is now reintrojected.

Today, all psychoanalysts seem to accept the coexistence of a non-psychotic side along with a psychotic one in the psychotic patient. For many psychoanalysts, too, in every patient there is such a conflict. The problem lies in how to articulate one part with another, how they interact. The subsequent developments of many analysts on narcissistic "structures" or "defences", which culminate in the concept of "pathological organisation", appear to be a valid solution. Based on these premises, I have developed the concept of psychotic organisation of the personality. To do so, I have taken three elements of personality on which psychoanalysis focuses, according to Bion: psychic pain, the interaction of the positions (Ps$\leftrightarrow$D), and the interaction between the container and contained ($\female\leftrightarrow\male$). Then I propose that each of the parts of the personality, the psychotic and non-psychotic, handles the relationship of the three elements with each other and with reality differently, in such a way that it would be the interaction between the psychotic part of the personality (PsPP) and the non-psychotic part of the personality (NPsPP) that results in a more or less pathological organisation; that is, PsPP$\leftrightarrow$NPsPP.

I see the proposed schema as being valid for all pathological organisation of the personality, in both those I name as major (MPOP) and minor (mPOP), although here I am concerned with trying to establish the specific traits in the case of psychotic organisation. In addition, I would emphasise the following as fundamental characteristics thereof: pathological splitting, pathological projective identification, limitation of symbolisation, and the creation of an alternative reality (the delusional world).

One of the primary characteristics of schizophrenic mental organisation that I would like to highlight is based on splitting processes. The classics of clinical psychiatry already understood this. This is the case with Bleuler, who, at the beginning of his career, sympathised with Freud, but later diverged from him; perhaps this was due to the fact that psychoanalysis of that era has neither the conceptual tools nor techniques to account for the clinical treatment of the psychotic patient. However, I think that some of his ideas form the basis of what nowadays many psychoanalysts maintain with respect to psychosis. For example, Bleuler is known for creating the term "schizophrenia", the etymology of which indicates the characteristic that defines the disease, "the division of psychic functions" (Bleuler, 1960, p. 14). Bleuler also contributes with two basic concepts in his description of schizophrenia: ambivalence—a term used by Freud—and "autism", which he himself created. The latter refers to a tendency to distance oneself from the external world. This coincides more with the current idea of "splitting" and projection when he says, "Delusional ideas are often separated from the personality in such a way that they appear to the patient to be the product of, not of his own mental activity, but rather the other psyche" (Bleuler, 1960, p. 138).

Freud also studied it in the sense of splitting the ego as a defence (Freud, 1924c), in which one part rejects reality at the same time that another recognises it, which he described both for neurosis and psychosis (Freud, 1940e[1938]). Beginning with Klein (1992d), the fragmentation of reality tends to be described as specific to the pathological splitting of psychotic functioning—Bion added the multiple splitting of mental functions—as opposed to the binary splitting inherent to non-pathological development.

In the material about my patient, I have tried to reflect different forms of pathological splitting that can be observed at different levels of her personality, her psychic life, and in her relationships. So, I think that the kind of prominent splitting depends on the prevalence of a determined transference over others. While, for all patients, a particular form of transference tends to dominate at certain times in the analytical relationship, it is not unusual for other different ones to emerge, especially if the analyst helps to connect them. In patients with psychotic organisation of the personality, the dominance of one type of transference is so absolute and radical that any other modality is almost non-existent, and some time must elapse before it is possible to connect one with another, and, furthermore, for one transferential level to alternate with another after one or a few sessions. This is why, in Chapter Ten, I clearly describe different forms of transference as they manifest in different moments of the analytical process: regressive infantile, pseudo-adult, erotised, psychotic, delusional psychotic transference, and, last, what I call "plural" transference in the sense of pathological splitting between one transference and another to have decreased enough for alternation between them to be possible, indicating greater integration. As such, we could say that the specific aspect that lends a psychotic character to transference is the radical splitting that creates each type of transference when it predominates. So, talking to the patient about another disassociated transference is like talking about another person. Therefore, when the patient feels like a small child who can only cry, she neither accepts the slightest reference to the adult aspects of herself, nor its healthy dependents, which need to receive nourishment to grow. Coming to analysis as a child means being merged to the analyst, or living inside him. Therefore, the indication of her adult aspects at that time is felt by her to be asking her to assume responsibilities that she cannot, and so this means the analyst is not accepting her, but, rather, rejecting her. In contrast, when she comes in as a pseudo-adult, she does not use the couch so that she can remain face-to-face with the analyst, like one adult to another, and any reference to needy aspects is felt as a humiliation that the sadistic analyst wishes to inflict, a relationship in which she must reveal herself violently.

Other manifestations of radical splitting have taken place in the spatial realm. For example, when, during one session, she experienced a moment that was painful and difficult to endure, she needed to leave the session, close the door, and then ring the bell again after a few minutes to resume the session, as if leaving the space of the office erased the immediate reality of what had happened thus far. Whereas, before, she had confronted the analyst with rage, now she returns like a child or a very needy and wounded patient who hopes that the analyst will take care of her. As such, closing the door left the previous relationship outside for her and she returned with another. Also, she tended to close the door violently, which expresses the destructive nature of splitting.

It is also worth recalling the splitting in the material about the twin siblings in its different varieties. This sometimes occurred with respect to the object (the analyst), and other times with respect to herself. With regard to splitting the analyst: there must have been two identical Drs PS, one who is helpful, and the other, the alien Dr PS, who was cold, sadistic, and abandons her at the weekends and during holidays. Or, even within the analyst himself, there is one, the renowned psychoanalyst whom she values and admires (he is married, has children, and practises his profession well), and another devalued one who is dependent on the former (he is not married, lives with the former, and depends on him, and he is the one who needs the patient's help). Yet another type of twin Drs PS could exist: one who has helped with her psychic illness as a psychoanalyst, but who cannot do so with her "bodily illness", since it consists of the lack of physical love, which is only curable by satisfying it, which is not compatible with the psychoanalytical method, and another twin Dr PS exists who is not a psychoanalyst and, as such, would be free to operate outside of that method and could aid her in her bodily affliction by consummating the physical union. Another form of twin splitting is the relationship between the patient and the analyst. The latter is Ms B's twin, which allows for both to experience the same feelings, even though they inhabit different bodies.

Now, from another, more global, perspective, I believe that one of the most significant pathological types of splitting is the one that takes place between the psychotic part and the non-psychotic part, where the main objective is to keep delusional reality and non-delusional reality separate in order to perpetuate the former, with the subsequent distancing and weakening of the latter. Though precisely, as this began to occur less radically in my patient, it allowed her to avoid a more marked mental deterioration despite her long psychiatric history, to come to analysis, and for certain analytical work to be possible.

With regard to pathological projective identification, I have devoted less space to it, as it has been studied more and because it is clear that the current conception of the pathological splitting processes that I have just reviewed implies the concept of projective identification, as we have seen in the examples of my patient. The split part does not become negated and disappear, but is, rather, destined to some external object, where it is lodged, or to one of the patient's internal objects.

Another aspect I wish to emphasise now is the discussion about what has come to constitute a type of axiom: the psychotic patient's incapacity for mature symbolisation due to the predominance of concrete thought. The discussion arising is not purely academic because it has clinical and technical consequences. Psychoanalytical work entails the participation of evolved forms of symbolisation to understand an interpretation and to produce significant communicative material (associations and dreams); as such, this would immediately rule out any psychoanalytical help for psychotic patients. However, as I said, both the current conception of symbolisation and the experience of psychoanalytical treatment with these patients, to which this work is trying to add, allow for this statement to be revised. Thus, the best knowledge about the primitive states of individual development, also partly from work with psychotic patients and children, allows for symbolisation to be presented not as a capacity that one does or does not have, or that everyone acquires once and for all, but, rather, as a progressive type of learning that requires a process and, therefore, different levels of development; levels that, once surpassed, do not disappear, but coexist with other, more evolved ones. If we agree with the psychoanalytical principle defended since Freud of the coexistence of ill and sane aspects in all individuals, including psychotic patients, or, to be more precise, of psychotic parts and non-psychotic parts of the personality, we expect that the latter have been able to reach certain levels of mature symbolisation. Another thing is the limited capacity for consolidation given the precarious tolerance for psychic pain and, as a result, for the pain concomitant to the symbolisation process. Therefore, instead of talking about the incapacity for symbolisation, I prefer to talk about "limitation", hence the title of Chapter Five, which is devoted to it. I hope that the description of my experience with Ms B has convincingly shown authentic moments of insight and understanding of transferential interpretations. Moreover, I believe that the patient's literary production that occurred over the course of analysis is another indicator of her having reached these evolved levels of symbolisation.

Certainly, this limitation in the capacity for symbolisation hinders psychoanalytical work, because the successes achieved are inconsistent and need to be renewed countless times. This requires an enormous amount of patience on the part of the analyst. From there arise the technical issues that are difficult to resolve if one wishes to use the psychoanalytical method, which I have attempted to reflect, both in the chapter devoted to "technical aspects" and in the description of Ms B's clinical material. I would like to underline a few of these technical issues: analytical attitude, the setting, and interpretation.

Analytical attitude about the psychotic patient

The delusional patient presents the technical issue of how to re-establish the truth of psychic reality. To interpret the delusional content in terms of another internal reality different from the one the patient is defending is to indicate that there are only lies and falsehood inside him, which is tremendously painful and also, to some degree, inaccurate. There is always a speck of truth in delusional thought, no matter how negligible, and the patient needs this to be recognised. For example, when the patient talks about the messages that the analyst sent her, beyond what he verbalised during the sessions, it is certain that there is something he has not verbalised which has been "unconsciously" transmitted in non-verbal communication. But what does appear significant to me is that the analyst is able to maintain an attitude in which, at all times, he prioritises safeguarding the consistency and authenticity of his position, which implies preserving his psychic reality, and from there trying to use his treatment method. We have seen that, at several moments, when the patient defends a delusional reality, I do not question it, but I do defend my reality in relation to her. In this way, I ensure that I avoid entering into the false dilemmas into which the patient tries to drag me: either the absolute acceptance of her reality or her demands, or, on the contrary, rejection and abandonment. Another way of showing the analyst's consistency is by defending his working method to which he has committed himself in order to help the patient.

Setting

This is an essential factor for containing all the emotional turbulence that calls for work with patients with PsOP. As such, firmness is necessary for maintaining the proposed setting. While, as we have seen, it is impossible to expect these patients to accept this proposal in the same way as a non-psychotic patient would, what is one to do then? I have tried to answer this in the chapter on technique, which is largely devoted to the difficult task of combining firmness with some flexibility. The general principle would be that the proposed method is the frame of reference always to have in mind, and any change is made temporarily and with the corresponding interpretative work in order to return to the previous state as soon as possible. We already saw that the patient's immense pressure to change the setting led me to continue yielding under the pretext of flexibility, until such a point when the patient decided to interrupt treatment because she felt depressed and was convinced that I could not tolerate her, and that I would become depressed with her. So, it is a very difficult task to combine firmness with flexibility and to know the ratio between them at any given moment.

Interpretation

Within the standard psychoanalytical method, I believe transferential interpretation to be important. As I said, my way of conceiving symbolisation in a psychotic patient allows me to keep this interpretative work in mind. Like many analysts who have worked with psychotic patients, the issue is finding the time when it is possible to access the patient's non-psychotic part. It also seems important to me that transferential interpretation should "focus" the field of observation by limiting it to the analytical relationship, in contrast with psychotic functioning, which tends to establish two unique alternatives: fusion with the object or diversification and fragmentation of relationships. In this sense, transferential interpretation constitutes one of the foundations for containing psychic pain. Also, the intensity of psychotic transference makes reference to it inevitable.

Another issue arises precisely because of this transferential intensity, which I observed with my patient, which is that the patient cannot accept that the deep relationship established with the analyst, which is necessary for unconscious communication to be possible, in which she shows her internal world and intimacy, cannot be reciprocated through communication of the analyst's intimacy. Furthermore, if this psychic intimacy to which she surrenders occurs, as she said on more than one occasion, on a purely psychic level she does not understand why it is not accompanied by equally deep physical intimacy. There is a double frustration: the analyst does not match the intimacy that the patient offers through "reciprocity" and, furthermore, this degree of intimacy is partial because it is only limited to the psychic aspect. The difficult work of differentiation with the patient takes place on different levels: between subject and object, fantasy and reality, external and internal, and also between body and psyche. With regard to the difficulty between the latter two, this is what makes the psychotic patient unable to understand that psychological intimacy (emotional and cognitive) is established between the patient and analyst without this entailing physical intimacy.

Last, I indicate how essential the task of countertransference is, as the attentive reader will be able to deduce if he has had the patience to accompany me on the lengthy description of my experience with Ms B so far. This is because of the intensity of the projections of patients with this type of pathology, besides the patient's precarious capacity for psychically working through the analyst's interpretations, leading the former to new projections into the latter, so that the analyst can tackle this work, which will require a new interpretation, and this process will take place repeatedly. Nowadays, we recognise that inadequate responses from the analyst, or enactments, are inevitable with any patient and are part of our task of recognising them and understanding them to extract information that complements the patient's understanding. As a result, in the case of the psychotic patient, it is easy to suppose that enactments will take place more often and be more difficult to understand because they call on the very primitive levels of the analyst's mind, from which arises the extreme difficulty of analysis with these patients.

Finally, in addition to symbolisation, it is believed that the psychotic patient will have difficulty in dreaming. This is not the case with my patient, and a theory rejected by other analysts with respect to their psychotic patients (De Masi, 2015; D. Rosenfeld, 2006).

Other technical consequences

As I said before, in psychotic patients psychotic and non psychotic parts are so split off, and there is such a gulf between them, that any attempt by the therapist to bring the patient closer to reality is felt as an act of violence. The primary task of the psychotic patient—when the psychotic organisation is predominant—consists of tragically perpetuating that internal rift which opens up between the psychotic and non-psychotic self. Whenever, in a therapeutic process, there is growth in the non-psychotic self, there is an exacerbation of violent reactions against it in order to quash it. This means renewing the attacks against one's own ego capacities, and, hence, the progressive deterioration of the personality which we find in long-term psychotic patients.

Bearing these points in mind, we can draw some conclusions in terms of therapeutic strategies for these patients. In the first instance, it is evident that any attempt to tackle the psychotic part head-on, in the sense of confronting it with "reality", will end dismally, as this is felt as something violent, as demonstrated by my patient (see Chapter Two). I have already described the dilemma in which the analyst finds himself, between colluding with the patient by accepting his delusional "reality" or openly calling it into question, which is felt as an attack. It is here where patience and skill are required to attempt to connect with the non-psychotic part. The problem is exacerbated because the patient's suffering creates magical, omnipotent expectations regarding what might "make him better", while the tools at the analyst's disposal are limited. If the therapist tolerates the attack on his limitations by the patient's psychotic part, and defends with strength and conviction the validity of his work, as limited as this might be, I think he will create the foundations for a link of trust in the non-psychotic part.

In the case of the non-psychotic patients (see Chapter Two), the problem consists in laying bare the psychotic functioning, which may be disguised or concealed by the non-psychotic part—but not contained—and, as a result, is operative. In my opinion, arguably, many of the stagnations of psychotherapeutic and psychoanalytic processes happen on the grounds that this psychotic part has not been detected, or has not been detected adequately enough for the forms of acting-out and influence on the non-psychotic part to be understood.

Consequently, I think that the study of the links between the psychotic and the non-psychotic part of the personality is vitally important to our understanding of the patient in the first instance. Above all, because it provides us with the opportunity to intervene appropriately, to generate some change in the psychotic patient, as well as to limit the consequences of impairment upon his mental life. With regard to other non-psychotic pathological organisations, this opens the way towards resolving moments of impasse in the therapeutic process by accessing psychotic levels of the mind, the integration of which into the rest of the personality might provide greater personal development and richness.

We were saying before, in agreement with Bion, that the conflict between the psychotic part of the personality and the neurotic part is a constant in any personality organisation. I would now add that the pathological development of the personality organisation depends upon the ability of the neurotic part to contain the psychotic part. The smaller the capacity of the non-psychotic part, the greater is the tendency for it to be distanced from contact with reality and for the gulf with the psychotic part to be widened, as well as increasingly narrow links with it to be established, in the service of the psychotic self, with consequent mental deterioration. For this reason, the intervention of the analyst seeking to forge an allegiance with the non-psychotic part cannot confront the psychotic part until this part, or the link with the therapist, has been strengthened. If the patient does not have the capacity, or, in other words, sufficient strength, to tolerate psychic pain, alliance of the non-psychotic part with the psychotic part is inevitable, and co-operation with the therapist becomes very difficult.

Finally, I have discussed elsewhere (Pérez Sánchez, 1996b) the treatment of psychotic patients within the institutional framework of a hospital or healthcare team, so I shall not deal with this question in detail here. Suffice to say that, given the particular features of psychotic functioning (pathological splitting and pathological projective identification in particular), the consequences of the acting-out of these mechanisms on the members of the team treating the patient should be taken into account.

Corollaries

I do not believe that any patient should be ruled out as suitable for psychoanalytical treatment merely because of their psychopathology if they meet some minimum conditions necessary for conducting it. Therefore, one must evaluate the patient's entire personality, in addition to the psychopathology, and an important issue is whether the patient, to some extent, not only feels pain, but is also able of experiencing it, to some extent. Another corollary is that if the psychotic part and the non-psychotic part constitute the personality, as I maintain here, the understanding of the interaction between the two parts not only allows a greater access to the psychotic patient, but will also be useful for any patient.

REFERENCES

Abraham, K. (1927). A particular form of neurosis resistance against the psychoanalytic method. In: *Selected Papers of Karl Abraham* (pp. 302–311). London: Hogarth Press.

Bassols, R., & Beá, J. (1981). *Relació entre estats perversos i psicotics*. III Symposium Internacional sobre Psicosis, Martorell.

Bick, E. (1968). The experience of the skin in the early object relations. *International Journal of Psychoanalysis, 49*: 484–486.

Bick, E. (1986). Further considerations on the function of the skin in early object relations. *British Journal of Psychotherapy, 2*: 292–299.

Bion, W. R. (1989)[1963]. *Elements of Psychoanalysis*. London: Karnac.

Bion, W. R. (1991)[1962]. *Learning from Experience*. London: Karnac.

Bion, W. R. (1991)[1965]. *Transformations*. London: Karnac.

Bion, W. R. (1993)[1950]. The imaginary twin. In: *Second Thoughts* (pp. 3–22). London: Karnac.

Bion, W. R. (1993)[1956]. Development of schizophrenic thought. In: *Second Thoughts* (pp. 36–42). London: Karnac.

Bion, W. R. (1993)[1957]. Differentation of the psychotic from the non-psychotic personalities. In: *Second Thoughts* (pp. 43–63). London: Karnac, 1984.

Bion, W. R. (1993)[1959] Attacks on linking. In: *Second Thoughts* (pp. 93–109). London: Karnac.

Bion, W. R. (1993)[1962]. A theory of thinking. In: *Second Thoughts* (pp. 110–119). London: Karnac.

Bion, W. R. (1993)[1967]. *Second Thoughts*. London: Karnac.

Bion, W. R. (1993)[1970]. *Attention and Interpretation* (3rd edn). London: Karnac.

Bleuler, E. (1960). *Demencia Precoz. El grupo de las esquizofrenias*. Buenos Aires: Paidós.

Britton, R. (1997). Making the private public. In: I. Ward (Ed.), *The Presentation of Case Material in Clinical Discourse* (pp. 11–28). London: Freud Museum.

Britton, R. (1998). *Belief and Imagination*. London: Routledge.

Britton, R. (2015). *Between Mind and Brain*. London: Karnac.

Caper, R. (1998). Psychopathology and primitive mental states. *International Journal of Psychoanalysis, 79*: 539–551.

De Masi, F. (2010). Some considerations about the psychoanalytic conceptualization and treatment of psychotic disorders. In: P. Williams (Ed.), *The Psychoanalytic Therapy of Severe Disturbance* (pp. 137–150). London: Karnac.

De Masi, F. (2015). Delusion and binocular vision. *International Journal Psychoanalysis, 96*: 1189–1211.

Federn, P. (1952). *Ego Psychology and the Psychosis*. New York: Basic Books.

Freeman, T. (1999). The delusions of the non-remitting schizophrenias: parallels with childhood phantasies. In: P. Williams (Ed.), *Psychosis* (pp. 55–64). London: Institution of Psychoanalysis.

Freud, S. (1894a). The neuro-psychoses of defence. *S. E., 3*: 43–61. London: Hogarth.

Freud, S. (1895d). *Studies On Hysteria* (with J. Breuer). *S. E., 2*: 19–312. London: Hogarth.

Freud, S. (1896b). Further remarks on the neuro-psychoses of defence. *S. E., 3*: 162–186. London: Hogarth.

Freud, S. (1910c). *Leonardo da Vinci and a Memory of his Childhood. S. E., 11*: 59–137. London: Hogarth.

Freud, S. (1911b). Formulations on the two principles of mental functioning. *S. E., 12*: 215–226. London: Hogarth.

Freud, S. (1911c). *Psycho-Analytic Notes on An Autobiographical Account of a Case of Paranoia. S. E., 12*: 3–82. London: Hogarth.

Freud, S. (1914c). On narcissism: an introduction. *S. E., 14*: 69–102. London: Hogarth.

Freud, S. (1924b). Neurosis and psychosis. *S. E., 19*: 149–154. London: Hogarth.

Freud, S. (1924c). The loss of reality in neurosis and psychosis. *S. E.*, *19*: 183–190. London: Hogarth.
Freud, S. (1925d). An autobiographical study. *S. E.*, *20*: 3–70. London: Hogarth.
Freud, S. (1937d). Constructions in analysis. *S. E.*, *23*: 257–269. London: Hogarth.
Freud, S. (1940a)[1938]. *An Outline of Psycho-Analysis*. *S. E.*, *23*: 141–207. London: Hogarth.
Freud, S. (1940e)[1938]. Splitting of the ego in the process of defence. *S. E.*, *23*: 273–278. London: Hogarth.
Giovachini, P. L. (1977)[1974]. Impacto del delirio y delirio del impacto. In: L. Grinberg (Ed.), *Prácticas Psicoanalíticas Comparadas en las Psicosis* (pp. 84–108). Buenos Aires: Paidós.
Green, A. (1990)[1986]. *De locuras privadas*. Buenos Aires: Amorrortu.
Hernández, M. (2001). *The Selected Papers of Miguel Hernández: A Bilingual Edition*, T. Genoways (Ed. & Trans.). Chicago, IL: University of Chicago Press.
Isaacs, S. (1948). The nature and function of phantasy. *International Journal of Psychoanalysis*, *29*: 73–97.
Joseph, B. (1989)[1976]. Towards the experiencing of psychic pain. In: M. Feldman & E. B. Spillius (Eds.), *Psychic Equilibrium and Psychic Change*: *Selected Papers of Betty Joseph* (pp. 88–100). London: Routledge.
Klein, M. (1987)[1946]. Notes on some shizoid mechanisms. In: *The Writings of Melanie Klein. Volume 3* (pp. 1–24) (4th edn). London: Hogarth.
Klein, M. (1987)[1952]. The origins of transference. In: The Writings of Melanie Klein. Volume 3 (pp. 48–56). London. Hogarth.
Klein, M. (1992)[1930]. The importance of symbol-formation in the development of the ego. In: *The Writings of Melanie Klein. Volume 1* (pp. 219–232). London: Karnac.
Klein, M. (1992)[1935]. A contribution to the psychogenesis of manic-depressive states. In: *The Writings of Melanie Klein. Volume 1* (pp. 262–269). London: Karnac.
Klein, M. (1992)[1940]. Mourning and its relation to manic-depressive states. In: *The Writings of Melanie Klein. Volume 1* (pp. 344–369). London: Karnac.
Lucas, R. (2007). Psychotic process and psychotic disorders. Paper presented to the Spanish Psychoanalytical Society.
Meltzer, D. (1973). *Sexual States of Mind*. Perth: Clunie Press.
Meltzer, D. (1974). *Terror, persecución y temor. En Estados Sexuales de la Mente*. Buenos Aires: Paidós.

Meltzer, D. (1978). The clinical significance of the work of Bion. In: *The Kleinian Developments. Part III* (pp. 1–126). Strathtay, Perthshire: Clunie Press.

Mitrani, J. L. (2015). Taking the transference: some technical implications from three papers by Wilfred Bion. In: *Psychoanalytic Technique and Theory. Taking the Transference* (pp. 59–80). London: Karnac.

O'Shaughnessy, E. (1981). A clinical study of defensive organization. *International Journal of Psychoanalysis, 62*: 359–369.

Pérez-Sánchez, A. (1991). Estructura perversa de la personalidad y componentes adictivos. *Revista de Psicoanálisis de Madrid, 14*: 35–60.

Pérez-Sánchez, A. (1996a). Perspectiva psicoanalítica de los trastornos de la personalidad: organización patológica de la personalidad. *Temas de Psicoanálisis, I*: 145–170.

Pérez-Sánchez, A. (1996b). *Prácticas Psicoterapéuticas. Psicoanálisis aplicado a la asistencia pública*. Barcelona: Paidós.

Pérez-Sánchez, A. (1997). *Análisis terminable. Estudio de la terminación del proceso analítico*. Valencia: Prmolibro.

Pérez-Sánchez, A. (2003–2004). Comunicación con la parte psicótica de la personalidad. *Temas de Psicoanálisis, VIII–IX*: 89–119.

Pérez-Sánchez, A. (2010). Transferencia y temporalidad en el proceso analítico. Paper presented to the FEPAL Conference, Bogotá, September.

Pérez-Sánchez, A. (2012). *Interview and Indicators in Psychoanalysis and Psychotherapy*. London: Karnac.

Quinodoz, J-M. (2008). *Listening to Hanna Segal. Her Contribution to Psychoanalysis*. London: Routledge.

Reich, W. (1933). *Character Analysis*. New York: Farrar, Strauss, Giroux.

Resnik, S. (2005). *Glacial Times. A Journey Through the World of Madness*. London. Routledge.

Resnik, S. (2016). *The Logics of Madness*. London. Karnac.

Riviere, J. (1991). A contribution to the analysis of the negative therapeutic reaction. In: A. Hughes (Ed.), *The Inner World and Joan Riviere. Collected Papers 1920–1958* (pp. 134–153). London: Karnac.

Rosenbaum, B. (2010). First you were an eyebrow and "How do I know that my thoughts are my thoughts? In: P. Williams (Ed.), *The Psychoanalytic Therapy of Severe Disturbance* (pp. 49–68). London. Karnac.

Rosenfeld, D. (1992). *The Psychotic Aspects of the Personality*. London: Karnac.

Rosenfeld, D. (2006). *The Soul and the Mind and the Psychoanalyst*. London: Karnac.

Rosenfeld, H. (1965). *Psychotic States*. London: Hogarth.
Rosenfeld, H. (1965)[1964]. On the psychopathology of narcissm: a clinical approach. In: *Psychotic States* (pp. 169–179). London: Hogarth.
Rosenfeld, H. (1971). A clinical approach to the psychoanalytic theory of the life and death instincts: an investigation into the aggressive aspects of narcissism. *International Journal of Psychoanalysis*, 52: 169–178.
Rosenfeld, H. (1987). *Impasse and Interpretation*. London: Tavistock.
Rosenfeld, H. (1988)[1971]. Contributions to the psychopathology of the psychotic patients: the importance of projective identification in the ego structure and object relations of the psychotic patient. In: E. B. Spillius (Ed.), *Melanie Klein Today. Volume 1* (pp. 117–137). London: Routledge.
Searles, H. (1965). *Collected Papers on Schizophrenia and Related Subjects*. New York: International Universities Press.
Searles, H. (1979). The function of the patient's realistic perceptions of the analyst in delusional transference. In: *Countertransference and Related Subjects* (pp. 196–227). New York: International Universities Press.
Segal, H. (1981). *The Work of Hanna Segal*. New York: Jason Aronson.
Segal, H. (1981)[1950]. Some aspects of the analysis of a schizophrenic. In: *The Work of Hanna Segal* (pp: 49–68). New York: Jason Aronson.
Segal, H. (1981)[1956]. Depression in the schizophrenic. In: *The Work of Hanna Segal* (pp: 49–68). New York: Jason Aronson.
Segal, H. (1981)[1957]. Notes on symbol formation. In: *The Work of Hanna Segal* (pp: 49–68) New York: Jason Aronson.
Segal, H. (1991). *Dreams, Phantasy and Art*. London: Tavistock/Routledge.
Segal, H. (1997). On symbolism. In: J. Steiner (Ed.), *Psychoanalysis, Literature and War. Papers 1973–1995* (pp. 41–48). London: Routledge.
Segal, H. (1997)[1972] A delusional system as a defence against the re-emergence of a catastrophic situation. In: J. Steiner (Ed.), *Psychoanalysis, Literature and War. Papers 1973–1995* (pp. 49–63). London: Routledge.
Segal, H. (1997)[1993]. On the clinical usefulness of the concept of death instinct. In: J. Steiner (Ed.), *Psychoanalysis, Literature and War. Papers 1973–1995* (pp. 17–26). London: Routledge.
Segal, H. (1997)[1994]. Phantasy and reality. In: J. Steiner (Ed.), *Psychoanalysis, Literature and War. Papers 1973–1995* (pp. 27–40). London. Routledge.
Spence, D. (1997). Case reports and the reality they represent: the many faces of Nachträglichkeit. In: I. Ward (Ed.), *The Presentation of Case Material in Clinical Discourse* (pp. 77–93). London: Freud Museum.
Spilllius, E. B. (1988). *Melanie Klein Today. Developments in Theory and Practice. Volume 1: Mainly Theory*. London: Routledge.

Spillius, E. B., Milton, J., Garvey, P., Couve, C., & Steiner, D. (2011). *The New Dictionary of Kleinian Thought*. London: Routledge.

Steiner, J. (1993). *Psychic Retreats. Pathological Organizations in Psychotic, Neurotic and Borderline Patients*. London: Routledge.

Steiner, J. (Ed.) (2008). *Rosenfeld in Retrospect*. London: Routledge.

Tizón, J. (2013). *Entender las psicosis*. Barcelona: Herder.

Tuckett, D. (1993). Some thoughts on the presentation and discussion of the clinical material of psychoanalysis. *International Journal of Psycho-Analysis*, 74: 1175–1189.

Ward, I. (Ed.) (1997). *The Presentation of Case Material in Clinical Discourse*. London: Freud Museum.

Williams, P. (2010). *The Psychoanalytic Therapy of Severe Disturbance*, P. Williams (Ed). London: Karnac.

Winnicott, D. W. (1974). Fear of breakdown. *International Review of Psycho-Analysis*, 1: 103–107.

INDEX

Abraham, K., xiii–xiv, 20
aggression, xx, 65, 67, 95, 109,
    164–166, 223
  motivation, 59
  object, xx
  tendencies, 27
anger, xxv, 65, 110–111, 147, 165, 204,
    219, 222, 227–228, 231–233
anxiety, 5, 9–10, 12, 22, 38, 42, 45, 53,
    57, 61, 63, 144, 149, 172, 200, 204,
    213, 218–219, 241
  annihilation, 5, 13, 17, 142, 230, 249
  basic, xxi
  catastrophic, 7, 13, 22, 53, 82, 85,
    144, 151, 156, 218
  confusional, 117
  death, 41, 144, 208
  depressive, 21
  excess of, 122
  extreme, 82
  fragmentation, 7
  great, 12
  high, 183
  intense, 7, 39, 41, 44
  minor, 13
  paranoid, xxi, 191
  persecutory, 98
  predominant, xxii
  psychotic, 7, 52–53, 137
  separation, 161
  severe, 13
  signal, 13
  state, 90–91

Bassols, R., 37
Beá, J., 37
behaviour, xviii, xxii, 46, 85, 129, 148,
    184
Bick, E., 13, 113, 162, 167
Bion, W. R. (*passim*)
  cited works, xix–xx, xxii, xxv, 4, 6,
    8–11, 13–14, 16–18, 23, 25, 30,
    34, 56–58, 84, 139–140, 160–161
Bleuler, E., xiii, 20, 138, 251
Britton, R., xxiv, xxviii, 25, 33, 58–59,
    76, 113, 160

Caper, R., 56
case studies
   Ms B, xvii, xxvii, 1, 59–61, 63, 79, 89–92, 98–99, 103–104, 108, 115–116, 121, 127, 135, 137, 141, 143–145, 150–153, 155–156, 159, 167, 169–170, 173, 181, 183–185, 187–191, 193, 195, 198, 212, 217–218, 221, 226, 233, 235, 239, 243–244, 247–250, 253–255, 257
   non-psychotic patient, 46–53
   schizophrenic patient, 38–45, 175–179
conscious(ness), xxviii, 17, 30, 32, 104, 107–108, 111, 116, 139–140, 167, 187, 194, 206 see also: unconscious
   fantasy, 115
   full, 138
container–contained, xv, xviii, xxi, xxv, 9, 23, 32, 53, 123, 250 see also: mental
countertransference, 148, 179, 257 see also: transference, transferential
   reactions, 166
Couve, C., 21–22

De Masi, F., 138–140, 161, 178, 257
delusional, 12, 41, 91, 100, 104, 111, 117, 119, 138, 142, 144, 147 see also: fantasy, transference, world
   activity, 113, 117–118, 127, 145, 151, 215
   artefacts, 124
   aspect, 22
   certainty, 118
   content, 127, 255
   conviction, 68, 142, 227
   dimension, 35
   episode, 107, 186
   experiences, 82, 103–104
   ideas, xiv, 59, 85, 95, 136, 138, 188, 192, 225, 251
      persecutory, 183
   identifications, 175

manifestations, 143
masturbation, 118
mediation, 239
nature, 85
object relationship, 141
omnipotent forces, 137
part, 106
patient, 40, 255
psychotic
   episode, 38, 183–184, 188
   functioning, 151
   transference, 176, 204, 208, 252
reality, 42, 45, 132, 138, 141, 146–148, 179, 242, 253, 255, 258
   non-, 138, 141, 253
states, 83
stories, 208
structure, 12
sub-, 117
thinking, 88–89, 104, 112, 121, 134–136, 151, 204, 255
universe, 138
withdrawal, 7
depression, xiv, xxv, 40, 45, 64, 68, 77–78, 81, 90, 93, 96, 98, 105–107, 109, 153, 169–172, 185, 187, 192, 198, 203, 211, 227, 256 see also: anxiety
   cyclical, 19
   component, 188
   elements, 124, 188, 197
   manic, xiii–xiv
   pain, 7
   position, xxii–xxiv, 7, 13, 18, 22, 29, 59, 122–124, 127, 202, 217, 250
      infantile, 6
   state, 90, 96, 188, 218
development(al), xi, xiv, xvii, xxi, xxiii, xxiv, 6, 16–17, 19, 21–23, 27–28, 56–57, 84, 122–123, 126, 136–137, 139, 161, 249–250, 254, 259
   mental, xxiii
   normal, 9
   pathological, 251, 259
   personality, 26

psychic, xxiii–xxiv, 17, 56, 123
stage, 21

ego, xxiii, 15–16, 19, 21, 27, 29, 58, 68, 122, 124, 136, 194, 213, 251
abilities, 196
apparatus, 8
boundaries, 15, 27
capacities, 36, 38, 52, 193, 258
creative, 193
faculties, 190
functions, 28
libidinal, 7
psychology, 15, 126
small, 213
syntony, 117
envy, xx, xxiv, 8, 51, 58, 76–77, 100, 114, 152, 177, 195, 201–202, 212, 214–215, 221–222, 224–225, 244

fantasy, xxii, 8, 17, 22, 62, 84–85, 94, 112, 115, 117–119, 136–137, 156, 215, 224, 233, 237, 242, 257
see also: conscious, unconscious
delusional, 137
erotic, 241
intense, 122
masturbatory, 62, 111, 114–115, 119, 145
non-, 236
omnipotent, 56, 85, 137
omniscience, 85
organisation, 137
sexual, 113
splitting, 8
Federn, P., 15–16
free association, 89, 168, 173, 190
Freeman, T., 138
Freud, S., xix, xxiii, 5–6, 13, 15–17, 19–21, 29, 31, 55–56, 136, 138, 145, 160–161, 248, 251, 254
cited works, xiii–xix, 5, 19–20, 29, 136, 160, 181, 251

Garvey, P., 21–22
Giovachini, P. L., 161

Green, A., 34
guilt, xxii–xxiii, 5, 9–10, 22, 36, 114, 122, 152, 176, 178, 193, 232, 244

hate, xx–xxii, xxv, 59, 137, 161–162, 189, 211, 230, 232–233
Hernández, M., 3

instinct
death, 6–7, 15
theory of, 15
intervention, 25, 31, 34, 40–41, 44, 46, 49, 52, 62, 71–72, 80, 83, 99, 118, 130–133, 146, 153, 172–174, 176, 186–187, 195, 202, 213–215, 229, 236, 241–242, 249, 258–259
analytical, 139, 145
brief, 107
interpretative, 179
magical, 130, 133
object, 10
omnipotent, 143
therapeutic, 126, 249
introjection, 18, 27, 35, 59–60, 69–70, 73, 76–77, 113–114, 171, 226, 235
see also: projection
balanced, 17
movie watching, 171
omnipotent, 77, 171
pathological, 35
re-, 9, 102, 250
reading, 117, 145, 156, 171
realistic, 218
Isaacs, S., 14

Joseph, B., 7

Klein, M., xiii–xiv, xviii, xx–xxi, xxiii, 6, 13, 21, 29, 56, 84, 122, 125–127, 251

Lucas, R., 31, 161

Meltzer, D., 13, 20, 30–31, 115
mental see also: development
activities, xxiv–xxv, 29, 118, 150, 251

annihilation, 8
apparatus, 116
balance, 23
cancer, 233
capacity, 78, 186
care, 186
change, 81
container, 87, 104, 249
contents, 113, 153
correlate, 115
depletion, 27
deterioration, 253, 259
device, 141
digestion, 51
discomfort, 52
disorders, xiii
disturbance, 17
emptiness, 151
functioning, xviii, 25, 29–30, 69, 83, 194, 210, 212, 251
growth, xxiii–xxiv, 30, 139
health, xix–xx, 118, 124
illness, 248
images, 18
impairment, 4
integration, 6
life, xxiii, xxv, 3, 5, 12, 35, 37, 56, 81–82, 85, 119, 123, 141–142, 145, 151, 192, 212–213, 216, 233, 258
organisation, 137, 251
overflow, 144
pain, 3, 8, 15, 18, 27, 116, 249
pathology, xvii–xix
patients, 19
position, xxi
process, xx, 173
representation, 14
resources, 83
shock, 11
space, 10–12, 18, 56, 69, 163–164, 193, 247
sphere, 144
states, xiv, xxi, xxiii–xxiv, 4, 11, 21, 46–47, 49, 56, 76, 111, 151, 227

structure, 9
sustenance, 27
treatment, 227
void, 89, 104, 136
work, xix
Milton, J., 21–22
Mitrani, J. L., 16
mourning, xxiii, 5–6, 88, 122, 125, 127, 136

narcissism, xix–xx, xxii, 13, 19–22, 31, 58, 82, 113, 145, 160, 185, 212, 248, 250 *see also*: object
neurosis, 15, 20, 22, 28, 251
   adult, xiv
   childhood, xiv
   psycho-, 20

object (*passim*) *see also*: aggression, delusional, intervention
   afflicting, 15
   bad, 5, 10
   concrete, 70, 170
   dead, 13
   differentiation, 152, 163–164, 201, 218, 250
   external, xxii, 28, 185, 253
   good, xxii, 10, 21
   hated, xxii
   hostility to, xiv
   ideal, xxii
   independence, xxii
   internal, 17, 114, 118, 123, 147, 212, 253
   -less, 21
   loss, 5, 7
   maternal, 102
   narcissistic, 19, 31
   needed, xix, 204
   no-, 5
   nourishing, 83, 102, 113
   part, 27
   primary, 22, 103, 127
   psychoanalytic, 139
   real, xxii
   receptive, 102

relations, xiii, xix–xxii, xxiv, 5, 17, 21, 53, 58, 113, 125, 141, 145
self–, 118
separation, 122, 124, 145
stable, 18
subject–, 59
substitute, 82
tridimensional, 11
oedipal
conflict, 31, 225
form, 226
neurotic, 225
pre-, 31
shipwrecks, 225
situation, 225
O'Shaughnessy, E., 20

pain(ful) (*passim*) *see also*: depression, mental
avoidance of, 4
concomitant, 191, 202, 254
emotions, 10, 108
experience, 12, 15, 103, 162, 221, 248, 249
healthy, 5
immense, 249
intense, 146, 156, 171
pathological, 5
physical, 5
pleasure–, 15, 57, 137, 162
profound, 4
psychic, xix–xx, xxvi, 3–4, 6–7, 12, 14–15, 23, 26–27, 32, 36, 53, 87–88, 109, 116, 125, 135, 143, 162, 248–250, 254, 256, 259
psychotic, xii, 3, 12–13, 41, 59, 204
reality, 37, 94, 112, 144, 151, 155, 168, 204, 234, 237, 239, 249
severe, 152, 200, 218
somatic, 3
unbearable, 12, 249
unnecessary, 14
unspeakable, 4
paranoid–schizoid, xiv, xxiii–xxv, 13, 22, 89, 184, 188 *see also*: anxiety, schizophrenia

defences, xxiv
mechanisms, 249
mode, xxiii
position, xxi–xxiii, 17–18, 29, 122–124
state, xxiii, 5
Pérez-Sánchez, A., xiii–xv, xxiii, 25, 31, 33, 37, 140, 161, 189, 259
phantasy, xv, 21, 113 *see also*: unconscious
infantile, xiv
omnipotent, 58–59
psychotic, xiv
projection, xxi–xxii, 8–10, 17, 22, 27–28, 30, 35, 38, 44, 82, 85, 94, 109, 114, 116, 118, 141–142, 147, 151–153, 170, 172, 178–179, 186, 201–203, 226, 251, 257
erotic, 178
explosive, 10, 18
intense, 146, 172
–introjection, 27
massive, 42, 45, 169
omnipotent, 171
projective identification, xiv, xx–xxii, 7–8, 27–28, 30, 35, 37, 57, 72–73, 84–85, 102, 123, 125, 141, 164, 239, 253
communicative, 72, 84
evacuative, 72, 84
excessive, 18, 28
intensive, 22, 151, 239
massive, 118
omnipotent, 35, 196
pathological, 10, 17–18, 26–27, 35, 56, 60, 84, 122, 151, 250, 253, 259
psychic *see also*: development, pain
activity, 4, 113
apparatus, 17
aspect, 234, 257
breakdown, 188
change, 82, 242
device, 142
dynamic, 59
emptiness, 135

equilibrium, 21
experience, 5
functioning, 32, 251
illness, 253
immune response, 113
intimacy, 256
intra-, 139
investigation, 139
issues, 145
level, 59, 145, 163, 256
life, xviii, xx, 4, 58–59, 69, 84, 104, 107, 123, 127, 139, 161, 167, 172, 218, 242, 247, 250–251
pathology, xxvi
phenomenon, 84, 243
process, 57, 84, 116, 122–123
reality, xx, xxii, 36, 38, 88, 108, 118, 138, 143, 162, 178, 234, 255
representation, 58
resource, 144
retreats, xv, 137
space, 247
state, 152
status, xv
structure, 143
truth, 40, 161, 189
vision, 139
work, xxiii, 109

Quinodoz, J-M., 30–31, 124

rage, 91, 154, 211, 222, 230, 252
Reich, W., 20
Resnik, S., 4, 125, 144, 242
Riviere, J., 20
Rosenbaum, B., 161
Rosenfeld, D., xiv, 13, 20–22, 84–85, 104, 117, 125, 160–161, 257

sadism, 17, 99, 178, 202, 214, 239, 252–253
sadomasochistic, 21, 236, 238–241
schizophrenia, xiii–xiv, xvii, xix, xxvi, 3–4, 7, 26, 38, 40, 56, 59, 125–126, 138, 174–175, 184, 248, 251
equilibrium, 8

paranoid, 89, 188
partial, 19
psychosis, 247
psychotic, xvii
Searles, H., 126–127, 161, 174–175
Segal, H., xiv, 6–8, 18, 20–21, 30–31, 122–126, 136–137, 161
self (*passim*) see also: object
-boundaries, 27
-control, 150
corporal, 73
destructive, 22, 104
disintegration of the, 7
entire, 12
fragmentations of the, 8
-fulfilling, 46
-glorification, 207
infantile, 51
libidinal, 22
not-, 58
-observation, 187
-perception, 151
psychotic, 193, 257–259
-sufficiency, 22, 237
sexual(ity), 115, 175 see also: fantasy
arousal, 106, 109, 115
hetero-, 118, 115
homo-, 61, 103, 118
psycho-, xxiii
voracity, 118
Spence, D., xxvii
Spillius, E. B., 7, 21–22
splitting, xxii–xxiii, xxvi, 8, 17, 26–28, 30, 35, 37, 59–60, 70, 73, 84, 99, 118, 124, 139–140, 250–251, 253, 257 see also: fantasy
binary, 57, 251
destructive, 140, 252
dynamics, xii
fragmentary, 17, 59
multiple, 28, 58, 251
pathological, 26, 28, 56–57, 59–60, 70, 73, 99, 151, 250–253, 259
physical, 70
processes, 251
prominent, 251

radical, 41, 59, 99, 252
of reality, xxiv, 57
twin, 253
Steiner, D., 21–22
Steiner, J., xv, xvii, 7, 22, 30, 32, 55, 85, 137, 172, 248
symbol(-ism), xiv, xx, xxvi, 18, 32, 52, 69–70, 84, 88, 116, 121–127, 134, 147–148, 174, 216, 239, 251, 254, 256–257

Tizón, J., xviii
transference, xxviii, 17, 19–20, 53, 63, 71, 102, 118, 131, 147, 160, 162, 174–175, 190–191, 211, 214–215, 239, 243, 248, 251–252 *see also*: countertransference
  analytic, 71
  conflictive, 210
  delusional, 110
  determined, 251
  disassociated, 187, 252
  eroticised, 202
  infantile, 192
  interpretation, xxvi, 70, 121, 125, 159, 174, 179
  libidinal, 211
  maternal, 234
  plural, 212, 215, 252
  predominant, xxvi
  psychotic, 109, 118, 147–148, 168–169, 175–177, 200, 204, 208, 252, 256
    vertex, 195
  regressive, 191
  relationship, 109
transferential
  counter-, 148
    impact, 172
    risk, 186
  intensity, 256
  interpretations, 254, 256
  level, 252

process, 147
reactions, 175
vertex, 191, 215
Tuckett, D., xxviii

unconscious(ness), xxviii, 30, 32, 112, 139–140, 163, 188, 255 *see also*: conscious
  communication, 150, 256
  deep, xiv
  fantasy, 14, 56, 84, 135–136, 149, 185
  levels, 148, 243
  mind, xxi
  phantasy, xx
  repercussions, 150

violence, 8, 11, 40–42, 47, 62, 137, 171, 205, 219, 229–230, 238, 252, 257–258

Ward, I., xxvii
Williams, P., 161
Winnicott, D. W., 12–13, 16, 20
world
  delusional, xxvi, 38, 85, 137, 140–141, 143–144, 178, 187–188, 209, 214, 249–251
  external, 35, 127, 136, 251
  internal, xxiii, xxix, 38, 107, 109, 134, 143, 152–153, 177–178, 186, 201–202, 250, 256
  magical, 129
  new, 129
  outside, 58
  of pain, 57
  parallel, 138, 141
  perceptual, xv
  of pleasure, 57
  plural, 213
  psychotic, 142
  real, 128, 140–141
  separate, 35